Y0-ARW-760

The Green American Tradition

The Green American Tradition

ESSAYS AND POEMS FOR

SHERMAN PAUL

EDITED BY H. DANIEL PECK

Louisiana State University Press
Baton Rouge and London

98 97 96 95 94 93 92 91 90 89   5 4 3 2 1

Designer: Patricia Douglas Crowder
Typeface: Linotron 202 Trump Mediaeval
Typesetter: G & S Typesetters, Inc.
Printer: Thomson Shore, Inc.
Binder: John H. Dekker & Sons, Inc.

LIBRARY OF CONGRESS CATALOGING-IN-PUBLICATION DATA

The Green American tradition : essays and poems for Sherman Paul /
    edited by H. Daniel Peck.
        p.   cm.
    Bibliography: p.
    Includes index.
    ISBN 0-8071-1513-4 (alk. paper)
        1. American literature—History and criticism.   2. American
    poetry—20th century.   3. Paul, Sherman.   I. Paul, Sherman.
    II. Peck, H. Daniel.
    PS15.G74   1989
    810'.9—dc 19   88-27627
                                                             CIP

Published with the assistance of the University of Iowa and the Lucy Maynard
Salmon Fund of Vassar College.

Charles Olson, "On Stopping Looking Out" © 1987 by the University of
Connecticut. All rights reserved. From the Literary Archives, Homer Babbidge
Library, University of Connecticut, Storrs.

Robert Duncan, "The Effort" copyright by The Estate of Robert Duncan.

Grateful acknowledgment is made for permission to quote from the following: Mina
Loy, The Last Lunear Baedeker, ed. Roger L. Conover (Highlands, N.C., 1982); The
Complete Poems of Marianne Moore (New York, 1972); and Charles Olson, The
Maximus Poems, ed. George F. Butterick (Berkeley, 1983). New Directions granted
permission to reprint the following: Robert Duncan, "Often I Am Permitted to
Return to a Meadow," The Opening of the Field. Copyright © 1960 by Robert
Duncan; Robert Duncan, "Tribal Memories," Bending the Bow. Copyright © 1968
by Robert Duncan; and William Carlos Williams, "Love Song," "Primrose,"
"Riposte," Collected Poems, 1909–1939, Vol. I, Copyright 1938 by New Directions
Publishing Corporation. Quoted lines from The Poems of Hart Crane, edited by
Marc Simon, used with the permission of Liveright Publishing Corporation, © 1986
by Marc Simon.

Contents

The Green American Tradition

On Stopping Looking Out

Charles Olson

Juan de la Cosa, Cabeza de Vaca, David Ingram—me.
He walked with his eyes, he walked in his flayed skin, he walked
The blue on lighter blue of receding ranges,
water on water, the courses of buffalo,
and rivers, some snows, before there were so many men the trace
got obliterated. Now to restore
the double path, the world
and any man's mother, until
he can look into
himself, stare
at the fire, rouse himself
via himself, give out
what is in. What is
in?

Introduction

Charles Olson's "On Stopping Looking Out" was written for *The Maximus Poems* but ultimately not included in that large work. Published here for the first time, it names the key activities of exploration and renewal that characterize the life of scholarship honored by this book. Sherman Paul has admirably met the challenge issued by the poem's concluding lines, for his has always been—in the phrase that is the subtitle of his great work on Thoreau—an "inward exploration."

The spirit of Sherman Paul's work is immediately suggested by an overview of his achievements. His ground-breaking studies of Emerson and Thoreau, published in the 1950s, made secure his reputation as one of the leading scholars of his generation. At this point, he might have been expected to take up another subject belonging to mid-nineteenth-century America. Instead, he pursued the implications of Emerson's work—especially the vitally linked ideas of organic process and democratic culture—into the art and thought of the twentieth century. There followed in the 1960s and early 1970s a series of distinguished studies treating Louis Sullivan, Randolph Bourne, Edmund Wilson, William Carlos Williams, and Hart Crane. Later in the 1970s, Sherman Paul turned his attention to postmodernism with a book on Charles Olson, and in the past decade his work has focused on recent American poetry; two books and a monograph published in the 1980s treat the careers of seven poets whose contributions—written or selected by them especially for this volume, and published here for the first time—are gathered in Part IV.

Among Sherman Paul's many books, however, a retrospective work of 1976 most fully defines the range and depth of his commitments. *Repossessing and Renewing: Essays in the Green American Tradition* is an act of consolidation and self-definition. In it we find again Emerson, Thoreau, Sullivan, and Williams, now joined by others—such as Van Wyck Brooks—who had not received book-length treatment from the author but who are central to his understanding of American criticism and culture. *Repossessing and Renewing* is an acknowledgment that the lives and work of these figures constitute a living tradition, "the green American tradition." This phrase derives from Paul Rosenfeld, a music and cultural critic of the period around World War I who is himself a subject of *Repossessing and Renewing*. Here is the passage, from Rosenfeld's *By Way of Art* (1928), in which it appears:

Affirmation of man's whole nature, embrace of all the earth bound up with it . . . is the American principle. Presently not only in the idea of the American democracy, but in all vigorous American thought, it must come to us out of the air, the soil, the climate as well as institutionally, since it is so deeply ingrained in us from birth. If there is a green American tradition, it is this. The dreams of all our moral authorities from Emerson to Randolph Bourne have embodied it. The grandest of our expressions, Lincoln and Whitman's of yesterday, Stieglitz's of to-day, have projected it. . . . There has been no major American life uninspired of it.[1]

As Rosenfeld's ordering of moral authorities suggests, the green American tradition has its beginnings in Ralph Waldo Emerson, and Emerson's "angle of vision"—to extend the application of the title of Sherman Paul's first book—has determined its course ever since. To be more precise, the green tradition is a branch of Emersonian thought emphasizing organic process, vital expression, cultural and political democracy, and the cultivation of an indigenous art. The Emerson it draws upon is decidedly not the safe and pru-

1. Paul Rosenfeld, *By Way of Art: Criticisms of Music, Literature, Painting, Sculpture, and the Dance* (New York, 1928), 302–303.

dential figure who, by the later decades of the nineteenth century, had become the patron saint of the genteel critics, and who, after his death, was taken up by the New Humanists and the academy. Rather, the green tradition looks back to the young, anti-institutional thinker of *Nature* (1836), "The American Scholar" (1837), and the "Divinity School Address" (1838). This is the Emerson who had called for a full-scale revolution in thought, with implications for every area of American life.

Underlying all aspects of this revolution was a new attitude toward the past. Our lives, Emerson said in *Nature*, should be defined not by "tradition"—the burden of codified belief—but by an "original relation to the universe," the primary organic process of the self meeting the world. In calling for emancipation from tradition, Emerson was not, however, rejecting the past as such; rather, he was calling for a new, creative response to it. His theory of radical self-trust (what he called "self-reliance") put the individual person at the center of things, and led him in the essay "History," treated here by Richard Hutson, to argue that "the whole of history is in one man." Because of the potentially intimate "relation between the hours of our life and the centuries of time," the past exists for us as a vast resource, not as a monolithic authority.

This context explains the apparent historical irony of Emerson seeking to overthrow tradition, yet engendering one instead. For the green American tradition is characterized at every stage of its development by its search for—in Brooks's memorable phrase—a "usable past"; William Carlos Williams' *In the American Grain* and Charles Olson's *Call Me Ishmael* are but two key instances. In its creative appropriation of the past toward *present* thought and action, this tradition is distinctively and poignantly open. One of its central defining features is a continuous exfoliation into new forms and expressions. What Emerson said in his essay "Circles" (1841) of the life of individuals applies to the spirit of the green tradition: [I]t . . . tends outward with a vast force and to immense and innumerable expansions," and is continuously alert to "a greater possibility."

No one in Emerson's time lived more deliberately in anticipation of life's greater possibility than did Henry David Thoreau. *Walden*

(1854) is the chronicle of a two-year period during the 1840s when he had an especially fertile sense of expectancy. But over the course of the following decade, Thoreau developed a formal discipline for living in the nick of time. In his great Journal (1837–1861), the subject of my own essay, he found a form of writing that in its very procedures positioned the self at the forward edge of experience even as it gathered and redeemed the past through the art of memory.

Thoreau's Journal, which he had initiated at Emerson's urging, and *Walden* are distinctively, even idiosyncratically, American works; it is hard to imagine any other culture having produced them. And this too follows from Emerson's program, which called for cultural as well as spiritual self-reliance. In "The American Scholar" he expressed his impatience with Americans' dependence on "the courtly muses of Europe," and earlier in *Nature* he had asked his contemporaries to "demand our own works and laws and worship." Nowhere did this invocation have more importance or greater impact than in literature, and in "The Poet" (1844), Emerson showed how the literary artist might help to bring about American cultural independence.

The poet, according to Emerson's essay, could give voice and vision to America. Positioned "on the center," this "representative" figure stands "among partial men for the complete man." The ground for this claim lay in Emerson's belief that language has its origins in primary sensory experience; it is, he said, "fossil poetry," and when its metaphoric power is recovered and released by the poet, it can unite the self and the cosmos, and, by extension, the self and the community through the sharing of a common vision. As "liberating gods," poets were for Emerson possessed of "divine energy." Their creations are the result not of mere technical meter-making, but of "a meter-making argument." The strong transitive force of this phrase, and of the implications it carries, delivered a devastating blow to the polite verse ("poesy") of Emerson's time and laid the groundwork for a new American poetry of presence and voice. The performance poetry of avant-garde figures such as David Antin and Armand Schwerner, with its insistence on living speech, is but one example from our own time of the continuing influence of this liberating idea.

It was of course Walt Whitman who first answered Emerson's call for a poetry of living language and for the Bard who would instinctively know "the value of our incomparable materials." Accepting the cultural and moral responsibility that attended this role, he offered himself as the "reconciler" of America's mass diversity. In the 1855 Preface to *Leaves of Grass*, Whitman announced his intention of giving articulation to this "teeming nation of nations" and of thereby elevating democracy from its political to its higher cultural form. "The United States themselves," he said, "are essentially the greatest poem."

But there were others in Emerson's America who were not prepared or inclined to hear his call for democratic culture and a living language to express it. By the time *Nature* was published in 1836, our first great novelist James Fenimore Cooper was already at mid-career, and his work during this period (*Home as Found* [1838], for example) expresses a sense of doom regarding the future of the American experiment. The basis for this pessimism, however, can be found in one of his earliest works. In *The Pioneers* (1823), Cooper laments the destruction of the wilderness by the forces of an emerging society, and invests his hope in the orderly development of that society. The departure from Templeton of the Leatherstocking, who refuses to accept the terms of his altered environment, signals the writer's sense of historical inevitability and of the essential incompatibility of wilderness and civilization. But, as Thomas Schaub writes in his essay, the departure of the illiterate hunter also signals Cooper's exclusion of oral culture from his vision of American community. As a symbolic action, it represents an active prohibition of vital (and potentially subversive) speech that, in its capacity to unite word and idea, might keep the nation alive to its original revolutionary purposes.

It was just such vital speech, of course, that Emerson and his generation tried to recover, and speech was the characteristic mode of expression for all their great reforms. Although Emerson himself was ambivalent about direct involvement in reform movements (he was of greater service, he felt, in his study), he nevertheless found it within himself to speak out strongly for the cause, abolition, most urgently requiring his eloquence. Thoreau too, despite his reservations about reform and philanthropic movements (these deflected attention, he believed, from private moral reform), ascended the public platform out of his acute sense of the deep moral crisis of his time.

Emerson's and Thoreau's Concord neighbor Nathaniel Hawthorne was not similarly moved, however. He took a stance of imperious indifference to slavery, and in her essay Jean Fagan Yellin takes up one of the large unanswered questions about him: how this writer, so extraordinarily sensitive to the issue of psychological bondage, could have been so insensitive to the literal bondage of slaves. Hawthorne's failure to engage the greatest public issue of his time, except through an elaborate strategy of avoidance, is but one example of the way in which his deep-seated conservatism positions him against Emerson's party of Hope.

The great war that ended slavery brought with it industrialism on an unprecedented scale, and set the nation irreversibly on a course toward an urban future and a mass society, conditions that on their face seemed to make Emerson's thought irrelevant. By the late decades of the nineteenth century, Emerson himself had become a cultural icon, and many of his ideas, such as self-reliance, had lost the force of their original meanings. In this new America of the Gilded Age, Whitman acknowledged in *Democratic Vistas* (1871), the rich cultural democracy he and Emerson had foreseen had not yet been realized. "[I]ts fruition," he said, "lies altogether in the future"—a statement intended to keep his dream alive but also an admission of present failure.

At the turn of the century, however, Emersonian thought found a new context and new terms. The battle Emerson had waged for America's cultural independence from Europe in the 1830s was now fought again as the American West vied for cultural parity with the established, genteel culture of the East Coast. The focal point for this insurgence was Chicago, which, by 1900, had become the center for a remarkable display of creative activity in the arts and the social sciences. Among the most striking developments were the work of Thorstein Veblen in anthropology, Louis Sullivan in architecture, and John Dewey in education. They sought to overturn the empty formalisms of their disciplines and to replace them with principles true to living experience. Their respective plans and formulations cut through the artificially imposed, life-denying restraints of high Victorian culture. As Hugh Dawson shows in his essay, all these figures have at the center of their thought an essentially Emersonian, instinctual critique of culture whose closest analogue in our own time may be the work of such poets of the "primitive" as Jerome Rothenberg and Gary Snyder.

While Emerson's ideas found rich and direct expression in the work of Veblen, Sullivan, and Dewey in the early twentieth century, his legacy to women writers of this period was problematical. The degree to which his thought, as filtered through late Victorian culture, had become stultifying for women is suggested by the image of Edna Pontellier, in Kate Chopin's *The Awakening* (1899), growing sleepy while reading Emerson. In calling attention to this image, Virginia Kouidis reminds us that, from the time of Margaret Fuller's complex personal relationship with Emerson himself to the present day, women writers have not found easy admission into the green tradition; Rosenfeld's pantheon, it must be noted, is exclusively male. But, as Kouidis shows in her essay, several women writers in the early modernist period—novelist Dorothy Richardson and poets Mina Loy and Marianne Moore—turned Emerson's thought into a resource. They found in his subjectivism, which George Santayana had celebrated in his famous 1911 lecture "The Genteel Tradition in American Philosophy," a way of validating their private visions of experience and thus giving new meaning to self-reliance. In the later twentieth century, poets such as Lorine Niedecker and Denise Levertov have made important connections to the green tradition, and it remains the urgent business of criticism to place the distinctive contributions of these and other women writers.

Contemporaneously with the Chicago renaissance, another renaissance was being prepared for in New York by the great pioneering photographer Alfred Stieglitz. The early years of the century saw the inauguration of his celebrated quarterly *Camera Work* and the opening of his first gallery, "291," where he showed the work of American artists and encouraged a sense of community among them. In the same period, another community—linked intimately to the Stieglitz circle through mediating figures such as Rosenfeld—was forming among a group of cultural critics who, in 1916, launched their own short-lived but extraordinarily important little magazine.

The editorial proclamation of the *Seven Arts* (1916–1917), published in the first issue, begins: "It is our faith . . . that we are living in the first days of a renascent period, a time which means for America the coming of that national self-consciousness which is the beginning of greatness. In all such epochs the arts cease to be private matters; they become not only the expression of the national life but a means to its enhancement." These ringing words are highly reminiscent of Emerson's stirring call in the 1830s for American cultural independence. Like Emerson, the key figures of the Seven Arts movement—Brooks, Waldo Frank, James Oppenheim, and Randolph Bourne—were men of letters rather than academicians. Following Brooks, the intellectual leader of the group, they were critical of American society and its stark division between highbrow and lowbrow sensibilities. This division, they believed, conspired against art, which required a broad leavening culture in which to grow. But in their conviction that the American environment could be cultivated and made fertile for art, they differed from other contemporary critics such as the cynical H. L. Mencken and the expatriates T. S. Eliot and Ezra Pound. In the work of Sherwood Anderson, whom the *Seven Arts* helped make famous by publishing his stories, they found proof that great art could emerge from America's hinterlands.

World War I slowed the momentum of these insurgents. The *Seven Arts'* vigorous editorial opposition to America's entrance into the war, as well as its publication of Bourne's eloquent antiwar essays, exemplify the green tradition's vital intersection of art and politics and its vision of the moral responsibility of the writer. But this courageous position proved fatal to the magazine, which collapsed when its sponsor withdrew her support. Although its program remained alive in other publications, such as Frank's influential book *Our America* (1919), the group's confidence was shaken.

However, the greatest challenge to the Seven Arts program for an indigenous American art came not from the war itself but from the war's most famous literary expression, *The Waste Land* (1922). In his *Autobiography* (1951), William Carlos Williams would remember the effect of Eliot's poem on his generation: "These were the years just before the great catastrophe to our letters—the appearance of T. S. Eliot's *The Waste Land*. There was heat in us, a core and a drive that was gathering headway upon the theme of a rediscovery of a primary impetus, the elementary principle of all art, in the local conditions. Our work staggered to a halt for a moment under the blast of Eliot's genius which gave the poem back to the academics. We did not know how to answer him."[2]

In *Spring and All*, published the year after *The Waste Land*, Williams wrote of the difficulty of "cling[ing] firmly to the advance" in the period opening before him. The need urgently expressed in this work is for "contact," for a primary erotic relation to environment that, as Jeffrey Bartlett writes in his essay, is the very ground of Williams' poetry. A later work in the 1920s, *In the American Grain* (1925), is the poet's most systematic search for this ground; the test for all his figures from the American past is how intimately and authentically they had responded to the "local." As the extraordinary achievements of his later years show, Williams ultimately recovered his ground. His long and illustrious career is perhaps the green tradition's greatest example of its capacity to renew itself. But there is no doubt that in the 1920s, when the modernism of Eliot was ascendant, the tradition's ideals were severely challenged.

If Williams had been thrown off his stride by *The Waste Land*, Hart Crane found an impetus in Eliot's work. In fact, Crane learned from Eliot some of his most important (formal) lessons of modernism, at the same time absorbing through Frank the vision of the Seven Arts group. The result is the green tradition's greatest literary achievement in the period, *The Bridge* (1930), Crane's epic

2. William Carlos Williams, *The Autobiography of William Carlos Williams* (New York, 1951), 146.

poem fusing in its central image America's mythic past and its machine-age present. *The Bridge* gives Crane an exemplary role in the green tradition, but the fragmentary poems of his final years—considered in Edward Brunner's essay—show how difficult this role was to sustain. These poems reveal the writer's attempt to overcome the daunting complexity of his earlier work and to widen his audience—to become a public poet, like Whitman, of lofty moral themes. The utter failure of this attempt (most of the verse is uninspired and narrowly didactic) owes in part to Crane's deteriorating physical and emotional health. But more significantly, as Brunner shows, it was caused by the poet's failure of nerve and by the enormous inherent difficulty of reconciling the high culture of literary modernism with public taste.

No one in the period between the wars understood this difficulty better than did Edmund Wilson, who, working outside the academy, exemplified Emerson's American scholar in the ranging application of his intellect. As James Guimond writes in his essay, Wilson's two major works of fiction assess the green tradition's response to popular culture in the 1920s, 1930s, and 1940s. The two central women characters in *I Thought of Daisy* (1929) symbolized for him what Brooks identified as lowbrow and highbrow sensibilities, and the novel dramatizes the critic's struggle to mediate between the vitality of the former and the sophistication of the latter. By the early 1940s, when Wilson came to write the stories that constitute *Memoirs of Hecate County*, the terms of the issue had altered dramatically, as this book's devastating criticism of mass culture and rampant commercialism makes clear.

Memoirs of Hecate County was published in 1946, just as America was emerging from this century's second great war, and, as Wilson had anticipated, the period to follow issued an even greater (and graver) challenge to the green tradition than had the period between the wars. This was, in the phrase that is the title of a book by critic Isaac Rosenfeld, "an age of enormity." Considering the postwar situation in a 1949 essay from that book, Rosenfeld wrote: "Terror is today the main reality because it is the model reality. The concentration camp is the model educational system and the model form of government." Pointing to "an alienation from the world we saw coming," he defined a new condition of modern life in which "traditions are broken and culture is unavailable."[3]

Certainly one aspect of postwar enormity looming even more ominously for us now than for Rosenfeld in 1949 is the possibility of worldwide nuclear destruction—an event that would not only break traditions but would close them forever. In his essay, David Marc cites Rosenfeld's admonition that a "culture is dead when the experience of men has no place in it,"[4] and sees signs of life in the popular art of American television. Here, Marc argues, is an expression of a survival instinct, a saving response of humor, and a supple adaptability that make endurable life in a world never more than thirty minutes from oblivion. While television itself is one of the most pervasive (and culturally destructive, from Wilson's point of view) postwar enormities, the sources of its energy must concern the critic in the green tradition who, like Whitman, remains open to the creative possibilities of popular culture.

"But joy exists only in the minds of a few poets, though all men, unaware, may yearn for it": this is the way Isaac Rosenfeld concluded his despairing essay on postwar enormity, thus proposing a "ground . . . on which we may hope to make joy come alive."[5] The poets who made joy come alive in the years immediately following the war did so, as Rosenfeld suggests, against great odds. With cultural continuity broken and having no clear sense of immediate predecessors, several of them reached for inspiration back to the mid-nineteenth-century America of Whitman—the "old courage-teacher," as Allen Ginsberg called him in "A Supermarket in California" (1955). But new progenitors were soon to emerge, and none was more important than Charles Olson, whose six-foot, seven-inch frame dominated the scene at Black Mountain College in the early 1950s. Here Robert Creeley and Edward Dorn found their bearings and their direction toward a new postmodernist poetry, which Olson had called for in theoretical writings such as "Pro-

3. Isaac Rosenfeld, "The Meaning of Terror," *An Age of Enormity: Life and Writing in the Forties and Fifties*, ed. Theodore Solotaroff (Cleveland, 1962), 206, 208.
4. *Ibid.*, 206.
5. *Ibid.*, 209.

jective Verse" (1950). As Lisa Pater Faranda writes in her essay on
The Maximus Poems, Olson wished to consolidate the gains of
Williams and Pound toward the creation of a prosody measured by
"breath"—a prosody, that is, which would *enact* thought rather
than merely represent it.

The intensity of this generation's struggle to realize a new poetics is nowhere more vividly dramatized than in Robert Duncan's
long experimental poem of 1950 appropriately called "The Effort."
This work, whose text has long been thought lost and is published
here for the first time, rejects the characteristic modes of academic
verse in favor of a poetry defined by "presence," by the dance of
imagination, and by the immediate relation of self and world:

> I mean there are no symbols.
> There are signs.
> There are literal things
> in themselves.

There are no associations,
no "stream of consciousness"
>   but in the dance
>   the emergence of things:
>   the presence, literal
>   and exact to the mind.

That Duncan's "effort" of the 1950s was richly productive is evi-
denced by the collection of luminously beautiful poems he published at the end of that decade, *The Opening of the Field* (1960).
This book is considered in Bruce Wheaton's meditation on the specifically Emersonian role that Duncan gives to memory, a power as
redemptive in his work as it is in Thoreau's Journal.

While a vital new poetics was emerging in the 1950s, the dominant culture of this period was characterized by political reaction
and rigid conformity. Its primary human images were David Ries-
man's lonely crowd and William Whyte's organization man, with
their corresponding environments of the suburb and the corporation—conditions that sent Jack Kerouac's Beat generation on the
road, and underground. But in the late 1950s and early 1960s came
a new era and a striking new set of images. The civil rights move-

ment in the South and protests against the increasing American military presence in Vietnam brought to the surface and transformed the 1950s counterculture. The result was a revolution of thought, in politics and culture, as sweeping as had occurred in Emerson's time. Suddenly, institutional authority at all levels was under attack by the young, whose response to social and economic injustice was angry and sometimes—as in the Port Huron Statement of Students for a Democratic Society (1962)—penetrating.

A period of great promise and possibility, the 1960s were also a time of severe testing for the intellectual, who was now called, as Emerson had been, not only to the interior work of the mind but also to action. E. L. Doctorow's *The Book of Daniel* (1971) may be read as a record of this struggle. In his essay, John Callahan shows how the central character—caught up in a severe crisis of identity—overthrows traditional academic discourse in favor of the essentially oral, prophetic mode of storytelling. By recognizing his debt to the Yiddish and the black voices from his past, Daniel reestablishes an authentic relation to present experience. He learns anew, with the Columbia student uprising of 1968 as a background and an impetus to his thinking, the lessons of both "The American Scholar" and "The Poet": that "without [action] thought can never ripen into truth," and that only a living language can express that truth. The liberating effect of the Jewish oral tradition on Doctorow's narrator is, as Callahan suggests, closely analogous to the power of storytelling in black American culture. This points to a rich common ground shared by literature in the green and the black American traditions, and indicates the need for a fuller acknowledgment and affirmation of this important connection.

A majority of the essays included here treat figures about whom Sherman Paul has written full-length studies. They address his concerns with immediacy, as much so when they revise his positions as when they confirm or extend them. That these essays—all of which were written especially for this collection—follow closely the development of Sherman Paul's career is, in part, because the authors earned their doctoral degrees, under his direction, at steady intervals during the eighteen-year period between 1965 and 1983, and in some cases found their field of scholarly emphasis in one of his projects.

But the deeper reason for this correspondence is the intimate relation between Sherman Paul and the green American tradition. The epigraphs of the essays, taken from his writings, serve not only to show intellectual indebtedness but also to dramatize this relation. To a great extent the green tradition, which Sherman Paul has made it his life's work to recover and defend, is a *personal* legacy. That is to say, he himself may be considered its leading spokesman of the present day. Daniel Aaron took note of this in responding to *Repossessing and Renewing*: "He is the son of Emerson and Thoreau and Bourne and Wilson and Williams—a carrier of the torch." Aaron's final phrase implies the difficulty of defending the green tradition in a time such as ours, which is in many ways inhospitable to its presence and unreceptive to its lessons.

"I have tried to recover and hand over a tradition, brief and local as it is, and tell its story lest it be forgotten." These words, whose elegiac tone is unmistakable, were spoken by Sherman Paul in 1984 in the first annual Presidential Lecture at the University of Iowa (from which he received his bachelor of arts degree in 1941, and to which he returned to stay in 1967 after a long, distinguished career at the University of Illinois). Yet the title of his lecture is "The Onward Way." This is the prospective (Emersonian) emphasis that most truly characterizes Sherman Paul's life of scholarship, and the following essays were written, in part, as testimony that the green tradition has indeed been handed on. Analogously, the poems that appear here confirm the tradition's vitality and diversity in our time. But the book constituted by these essays and poems has another purpose as well: most important, it should be understood—in Olson's resonant phrase—as "Love made known,"[6] as an expression of profound gratitude and affection.

6. This phrase is the closing line of the *Maximus* poem that begins "[to get the rituals straight I have," treated in Lisa Pater Faranda's essay herein.

A Note on the Photographs

The four photographers whose works, listed below, appear in this
book are those about whom Sherman Paul has written in articles
and introductions. Except for his discussion of Alfred Stieglitz,
which appears in the Introduction to Paul Rosenfeld's *Port of
New York,* the relevant works are identifiable by title in the
bibliography.

"Reflections: Night—New York," 1896–97, Alfred Stieglitz,
  page 150
"Providence 1967," Harry Callahan, page 208
"Dog Bar Breakwater," September, 1976, Lynn Swigart, page 217
"Sherman Paul at Home in Iowa City," 1974, Lynn Swigart, page 328
"Midwest Landscape #53," 1962, Art Sinsabaugh, pages 328–29

    The jacket is illustrated by Harry Callahan's "Chicago ca. 1950,"
about which Sherman Paul has written: "Nothing vast or titanic
compromises Callahan's confidence in nature, represented best, perhaps, by his winter trees, which, like Williams', are 'wise' and 'stand
sleeping in the cold.'"
    Both Mr. Callahan and Lynn Swigart took a personal interest in
this project, and provided their works with generosity and enthusiasm. Art Sinsabaugh's daughters, Elisabeth and Katherine, gave

valuable encouragement. James Guimond, one of this volume's contributors and the author of a forthcoming study of American photography, played an indispensable role in helping select the photographs.

H. D. P.

Acknowledgments

Although Sherman Paul was unaware of this book's development until its surprise presentation to him in the fall of 1988, he may be considered its most important contributor. For he is the one who fostered the strong sense of intellectual community that became the project's primary impetus.

By itself, however, a sense of community does not make a book, and without the expert assistance of many people, this project could never have been brought to completion. First among them is Robert W. Lewis, editor of the *North Dakota Quarterly*, who made invaluable contributions of advice and information. His own tribute to Sherman Paul, the special spring, 1979, number of *NDQ*, served as an inspiration for this book; the reader is especially referred to William H. Rueckert's eloquent biographical essay in that issue.

Milton R. Stern read the entire manuscript with care and improved it with a number of key suggestions; to him as well I give special thanks. Beverly Jarrett, Associate Director and Executive Editor of the Louisiana State University Press, took an immediate interest in the project and gave it enthusiastic support. Barbara O'Neil Phillips, Assistant Managing Editor, skillfully guided the book through its final stages.

George F. Butterick and Robert Duncan did not live to see their contributions appear in this book. It was Mr. Butterick who, with characteristic generosity, selected and made available Charles Olson's "On Stopping Looking Out." Robert J. Bertholf assisted Mr. Duncan in locating the manuscript of "The Effort" and in providing it for the collection; for this, and for his learned note that accompanies the poem, I am grateful.

Nina Baym, Emory Elliott, Kim Merker, Robert F. Sayre, Richard Schimmelpfeng, Jack Stillinger, Albert E. Stone, and Frederick Woodard gave valuable assistance and encouragement. John Raeburn, Chairman of the University of Iowa English Department, played a key role in furnishing the materials of Sherman Paul's bibliography.

I am indebted to my Vassar colleague Frank Bergon for helping me think through the book's structure, and to my student Catherine Robbins for practical assistance with matters too numerous to mention. The Vassar College Research Committee gave the project generous support, including a grant for the procurement of photographs.

No one was of greater help to me in bringing this book to completion than Patricia B. Wallace, whose keen judgment I consulted throughout the course of its development. It was her wonderful suggestion—in the moment I first took up the project—that a volume honoring Sherman Paul should include contributions from the living poets about whom he has written.

H. D. P.

I / Emerson's Angle of Vision

RICHARD HUTSON

Two Gardens: Emerson's Philosophy
of History

His role, as he saw it, was not to reject totally, but, by
the alchemy of a fresh energizing mind, secure in
"principles," to adapt the usable content of his inheritance to the living needs of the present.
——*Emerson's Angle of Vision*

"Our age is retrospective." When Emerson opened his literary career with these words, he was not describing a condition of general
cultural passivity; rather, he was acknowledging a preoccupation of
the times. It would have been impossible for a sensitive intellectual of this era to ignore the prestige and popularity of historical
research and writing, which had given rise to a new and intense
historical consciousness.

Shortly after the publication of *Nature*, Emerson delivered a series of lectures, extending from December, 1836, to March, 1837,
entitled "The Philosophy of History." To a certain extent, he was
in these lectures conforming to fashion, responding to an audience
that wanted to hear something of the latest intellectual news.
Emerson had some ideas of his own on the subject, however, which
derived from his reading of the major thinkers of Germany, France,
and Great Britain—especially those thinking in the transcendentalist mode, all of whom were engaged in meditations on history
and historical consciousness. And, as he more fully assimilated the

ideas of these thinkers over the next few years and made them more distinctively his own, the materials of his "Philosophy of History" lectures matured into *Essays: First Series* (1841), which is his most important statement on the meaning of history.

The familiar twentieth-century criticism that Emerson's thought is ahistorical overlooks the intellectual context against which he felt obliged to formulate his own thoughts on history. In the last years of the eighteenth century, according to Michel Foucault, knowledge itself took "residence in a new space," marking a "profound breach" in the continuities of Western thinking; from that time to ours, "[h]istory has become the unavoidable element in our thought." We learn geology after an earthquake, Emerson noted. Analogously, major European thinkers, trying to come to grips with the profound social and political dislocations and discontinuities brought about by the democratic revolutions of the time, turned anxiously and excitedly to history. According to Goethe, "Anyone who has lived through the Revolution feels impelled towards history. He sees the past in the present, and contemplates it with fresh eyes which bring even the most distant objects into the picture."[1]

For Goethe or Burke or Hegel, the French Revolution was the primary event precipitating the Western world into history, and the resulting "*sense of history*," as Gustave Flaubert called it, was "completely new in our world." What was truly new and different about this era, according to Georg Lukacs, was the fact that "the French Revolution, the revolutionary wars and the rise and fall of Napoleon . . . for the first time made history a *mass experience*" as well as an international phenomenon.[2] In altering actual human social existence within the period of a single lifetime, the new realities of the late eighteenth century and early nineteenth century

---

1. Michel Foucault, *The Order of Things: An Archaeology of Knowledge of the Human Sciences* (New York, 1972), 217–19; Goethe quoted in A. Dwight Culler, *The Victorian Mirror of History* (New Haven, 1986), 5–6.

2. Flaubert quoted in Richard Terdiman, "Deconstructing Memory: On Representing the Past and Theorizing Culture in France Since the Revolution," *Diacritics*, XV (1985), 15; Georg Lukacs, *The Historical Novel*, trans. Hannah Mitchell and Stanley Mitchell (Lincoln, 1983), 23.

called everything into question, possibly even history (understood as sequential and progressive) itself. The cultural shock was profound.

Even in distant and provincial America, one could not avoid the implications of this change, even if a historical consciousness was much less urgent in a nation whose revolution had been more political than social. Although America did not produce a Burke or a Hegel, did not move toward a highly reflective philosophical or political meditation on history, its culture was nevertheless saturated at all levels with the idea of history. As George Callcott has written, "Never before or since has history occupied such a vital place in the thinking of the American people as during the first half of the nineteenth century."[3] Architecture, painting, theater, fiction, poetry, and oratory were filled with historical themes. Popular magazines, historical societies, state and local archives, genealogical societies, curricula in schools—all pointed to the new and unusual dominance of history as a major topic of interest. Americans, in their innocence and their cultural inferiority complex, seized upon history in an attempt to glorify themselves with what they understood to be signs of cultural maturity. For whatever reason, they were happy and eager to participate in the intellectual obsession of the time.

That *Essays: First Series* opens with "History" and closes with a meditation on the various arts *"as history"* suggests the degree to which the entire work may be understood as Emerson's philosophy of history and as his response to the philosophies of his European contemporaries. Whatever the focus of the intervening essays—justice, vocation, friendship and love, self-reliance—all of these serve to elaborate the book's central theme. In its form as much as in its content, the book provides a profound insight into the peculiar American uses of the past.

In the essay "History," Emerson begins by defining the work of history as an "innocent serenity": "Without hurry, without rest, the human spirit goes forth from the beginning to embody every

3. George Callcott, *History in the United States, 1800–1860: Its Practice and Purpose* (Baltimore, 1970), 25.

faculty, every thought, every emotion, which belongs to it in appropriate events."[4] History is the *event*, the ceaseless objectification of the human spirit, sublime in its integrity and impassivity. Looked at in this abstract way as an expression of spirit, it composes a benign intellectual spectacle. Moreover, Emerson takes maximum advantage of a certain vulnerability of history, namely, that it tends to be inaccessible to us except in textual form. "Books are the best type of the influence of the past," he says in "The American Scholar," where he also warns that there is a "right way" and a wrong way to read.[5] In "History" he uses the reading experience as evidence of the presence of the universal mind. For Emerson, echoing ideas from the eighteenth century, the fact of history suggests "the philosophical doctrine of the identity of all minds,"[6] but the reading of history illustrates the sovereignty and omnipresence of the universal human spirit in the reader. In the act of reading, a latent universality of the soul's experience betrays itself: "[I]nvoluntarily we always read as superior beings"; "[a]ll that Shakespeare says of the king, yonder slip of a boy that reads in the corner, feels to be true of himself" ("H," 4–5, 5). The behavior of reading points toward the doctrine of the sovereignty of the soul; such behavior cannot be explained unless we posit a latent universality in the individual mind that is activated in the reading experience. Once Emerson has established the possibility of the self's mastery over history, his task in the essay is to encourage the reader to acknowledge this mastery, to follow through with the implications of this insight rather than to sink back into deference before a text. The reader must, therefore, "transfer the point of view from which history is commonly read, from Rome and Athens and London to himself" ("H," 6).

Viewed more concretely, as an expression of local and provincial

4. "History," in *Essays: First Series*, ed. Joseph Slater, Alfred R. Ferguson, and Jean Ferguson Carr (Cambridge, Mass., 1979), 3, vol. II of *The Collected Works of Ralph Waldo Emerson*, 4 vols. to date. This essay will be cited parenthetically in the text with page number and will be identified by "H."

5. "The American Scholar," in *Nature, Addresses, and Lectures*, ed. Robert E. Spiller and Alfred R. Ferguson (Cambridge, Mass., 1971), 55, vol. I of *The Collected Works of Ralph Waldo Emerson*, 4 vols. to date.

6. *Ibid.*, 58.

pride, history has a much more limited value. In Emerson's own early venture into historical research and narrative, his two-hundred-year history of Concord given as "Historical Discourse in Concord" in September, 1835, he expresses a typical fear about America's historical shortcomings: "And yet, in the eternity of nature, how recent our antiquities appear! The imagination is impatient of a cycle so short." Taking their emphasis on history from English and European culture, Americans might well feel embarrassed because their remotest history could actually be traced to a specific and too recent date: "The town of Concord begins, this day, the third century of its history."[7] The prestige and authority of European history lay in the fact that its origins were lost in the sublimities of folklore and mythology distilled from the long history of ancient nations.

In its most straightforward sense, the American obsession with the past was an attempt to join the rest of civilization; but it was also an attempt to counter the "mocking British voices" that could invoke a much more weighty and lengthy history against the upstart nation. Washington Irving would achieve his literary success by massively supplementing the American with a British past and by affirming that America's past was simply Great Britain's. On the other hand, Tocqueville saw the United States as an anticipation of the Western world's future, the vanguard of history pulling the Europeans in behind it. "America," Hegel wrote in *The Philosophy of History,* is "the land of the future . . . a land of desire for all those who are weary of the historical lumber-room of old Europe."[8]

Despite the extraordinary attention paid to history in the mid-nineteenth century, Americans had good reason to construct, in R. W. B. Lewis' phrase, a "case against the past."[9] As Emerson's views suggest, the response to what Lewis called the "paradox" of

7. Ralph Waldo Emerson, "Historical Discourse in Concord," *Miscellanies* (Boston and New York, 1888), 3.
8. Robert Weisbuch, *Atlantic Double-Cross* (Chicago, 1986), 153; G. W. F. Hegel, *The Philosophy of History,* trans. J. Sibree (New York, 1956), 86.
9. R. W. B. Lewis, *The American Adam* (Chicago, 1955), Chap. 1. See also Fred Somkin, *Unquiet Eagle* (Ithaca, 1967), Chap. 2.

American attitudes toward history was to domesticate for an American audience some very abstract, specialized, and foreign philosophical reflections on this theme. Like his European and English contemporaries, Emerson groped for an enlightening perspective on the past, and ultimately he had no other pretension than to establish for himself, as clearly as he could, a ground from which to view history.

The point is that no matter where Emerson turned, history was the "unavoidable" in the thought of his time. And, in a quite specific way, it is the unacknowledged structure for all his thinking. Thus, even if Melville was right when he claimed, in *Mardi*, that "in these boisterous days, the lessons of history are almost discarded," the whole era in which Emerson and Melville lived was engaged in debate about the lessons history had for the present. The question for their time was what one was to do with history.

If history had, by the nineteenth century, taken on a new philosophical and popular authority, no one was quite certain what that authority was or how it might be put to use. European thinkers felt that they had to try to redeem the past, to reconstruct the present from the bottom up, to find a way either to eliminate what Hegel called the "monstrous slaughter" of human history or give direction to what Kant called the "folly and aimlessness" of past experience. In contrast, as Lawrence Buell has shown, the popular historical imagination in New England was used mainly as armament for local party warfare.[10] Whatever one's politics or mood or aspiration, history was called upon to explain, to prove, to argue, to defend, to praise, or to blame. This is to say that the American use of history in Emerson's time may look, from our perspective, rather naïve.

And it is also to remind us that Emerson's antihistorical remarks are always made in a cultural context. This context is defined, significantly, by the expectations of his New England Whig friends and acquaintances interested in empirical history and in the notion of history as "a great storehouse of lessons—for the most part, cau-

10. Lawrence Buell, *New England Literary Culture* (Cambridge, England, 1987), Chaps. 8 and 9.

tionary tales with grim endings."[11] On the other hand, Emerson himself characteristically tried to elevate American historical thinking beyond the level of party debate by applying what he called transcendental principles, or universals. Moving beyond political designation, he characterized the ideological debate of his time as the "opposition of Past and Future, of Memory and Hope, of the Understanding and the Reason"; these were, he said, "the two poles of nature" rather than the two political parties or any of the other historically identifiable political antagonisms of the time.[12] Thus Emerson's thought is notably relaxed about the direction and the politics of history. For him, polarity belongs to human nature in general. Even so, he does not attempt to conceal his preference for the party of Hope. In fact, he suggests that Memory and Hope cannot really be "mathematically" reciprocal terms, since he argued from Kant by way of Coleridge that memory is secondary to and conditioned by self-consciousness, by "insight," by the primordial affirmative dictates of the soul. There is, he says, "an emphasis in your memory" that is always "the soul's emphasis."[13] Accordingly, the Conservative of "the Times" invokes history as a "necessity not yet commanded," not yet required by the actual movement of events. Emerson is acutely aware that the prestige of history can be used as an ideological club to coerce thought and action prematurely, and thus could become a version of what he calls "force."

The ambiguity of Emerson's attitude toward history may be seen in his attempts to think about the present, "the Times." On the one hand, he says, "our age . . . builds the sepulchres of the fathers"; on the other hand, it commits itself to reform. The age is obsessed with the past, worshipping it even while wanting to ignore it. When Emerson writes, "Let us demand our own works and laws and worship,"[14] the apparent rejection of the past can be understood as the rejection of America's colonial status. By turning

11. Daniel Walker Howe, *The Political Culture of the American Whigs* (Chicago, 1979), 75.
12. "The Conservative," in *Nature, Addresses, and Lectures*, 184.
13. "Spiritual Laws," in *Essays: First Series*, 84, hereinafter cited parenthetically in the text with page number and identified by "SL."
14. *Nature*, in *Nature, Addresses, and Lectures*, 7.

against the past, he is often participating in the popular American attempt to achieve a cultural independence from Great Britain; in such a context he is not necessarily advising Americans to forget the heroic fathers or their own family genealogies.

In another context, however, Emerson's attack on history must be understood as a salutary response to what George Forgie has described as early-nineteenth-century Americans' need of encouragement to live their lives without feeling a depressing indebtedness to the founders of the new Republic. According to Forgie, many of Emerson's contemporaries identified themselves as the "post-heroic generation."[15] In the various transcendentalisms of the immediate past, in what Kant called his "Copernican revolution," Emerson found the principles that he thought would help his generation overcome the melancholy and debilitating comparison.

One of the most interesting things about Emerson's views of "the Times" is that they reveal an American analogue for the turmoil that sensitive Europeans saw as the consequence of the French Revolution and the formation of capitalist industrialism in England. Emerson sees his own period as profoundly unstable and revolutionary. As he looks out around him from his stable retreat in Concord, he characterizes his age as one committed to reform, to the purification and simplification of all aspects of social, political, and spiritual life. Americans are seething against any and all forms of restraint, against any kind of "usage which has not its roots in our own mind."[16] "The country is full of rebellion," and Emerson believes that this spirit of reform is different from anything that one can see in the past.[17] According to his view, the older sixteenth- and seventeenth-century church and political reformers "all respected something," such as "church or state, literature or history, domestic usages, the market town, the dinner table." But now all these objects of respect "and all things else" are "threatened by the new spirit" of reform in America. Emerson

15. Goerge Forgie, *Patricide in the House Divided* (New York, 1979), Chap. 1.
16. "Man the Reformer," in *Nature, Addresses, and Lectures*, 156.
17. "New England Reformers," in *Essays: Second Series*, ed. Joseph Slater, Alfred R. Ferguson, and Jean Ferguson Carr (Cambridge, Mass., 1983), 151, vol. III of *The Collected Works of Ralph Waldo Emerson*, 4 vols. to date. This essay will be cited parenthetically in the text with page number and will be identified by "NER."

claims that a vigorous skepticism toward "Christianity, the laws, commerce, schools, the farm, the laboratory, . . . kingdom, town, statute, rite, calling, man or woman" is bringing all issues under intense scrutiny.[18] He sees the world of institutions and ideas dissolving around him. But he understands this condition as good and natural. What Emerson sees going on in America is the work of "principles" as they assert their power to transform and purify the world according to the self-affirming power of "truth."

By 1841, Emerson had developed a fairly clear notion of what he means by "principles," and he interprets "the Times" from the perspective of these principles, as if the turmoil of the period were a providential expression of his own ideas. Twentieth-century historians have for some time characterized this era as the heyday of reform movements in the United States. "As early as 1815 Americans had begun to generate what would be the most fervent and diverse outburst of reform energy in American history," a "freedom's ferment" of religious, social, and political upheaval that "crested in the 1830s and 1840s," according to Ronald Walters.[19] Emerson can see "the Times" as verifying what he has always proclaimed, and, because of this, knowledge of principles coincides for him with knowledge of "the Times." Moreover, if "the Times are . . . the receptacle in which the Past leaves its history," history has bequeathed to his time the conditions for extraordinary human liberty and democracy. Despite the eternal presence of a "Conservative party," of "organized and accredited oracles" who call for conformity and conservatism, there now exists an opportunity to construct a world that is "real," a world that people do not have merely to "tolerate," but one they can "choose," "embrace and avow."[20]

Emerson can thus imagine a completely non-alienated and non-alienating political and social background to the Jacksonian era. That this world can succumb to various forms of alienation he is aware, and the essay form itself, as he practices it, is designed to overcome alienation by reminding his audience, through "illustra-

18. "Man the Reformer," 146.
19. Ronald Walters, *American Reformers, 1815–1860* (New York, 1978), ix.
20. "Introductory Lecture," in *Nature, Addresses, and Lectures,* 167, 170.

tion" rather than logic, of the conditions or "necessary foundation" of contemporary events. But such a position implies a social and political background supporting the kind of benign, liberal order that is possible only "when the government of force is at an end." "In this country," Emerson writes in "Politics," "we are very vain of our political institutions, which are singular in this, that they spring, within the memory of living men, from the character and condition of the people, which they still express with sufficient fidelity. . . . They are not better, but only fitter for us."[21]

For Emerson, Americans can "embrace and avow" the political framework of the country because it corresponds to their character, and this correspondence is based on memory as a power of nearness, as an intimacy between the expressive needs of character and the constitution of a political entity. When he vows, in "Self-Reliance," that he will have "no covenants but proximities," he seems to be advising everyone to throw off "this corpse of your memory."[22] But memory itself is, in "Politics," a proximity, a protection against alienation. Whether or not it is secondary, memory is so intimately bound up with principles that it necessarily does the work of "insight" and appropriation. Memory is completely integrated with and indistinguishable from consciousness.

If Emerson's principles are at one with consciousness, this consciousness is informed by a memory that notices and organizes features of his time from the vantage point of an identifiable historical perspective—specifically and inevitably the memory of the New England town. The Protestant heritage of New England, from which his own principles derive, he sees as spreading out, in his own time, into the various reform movements. They are "signs that the Church, or religious party, is falling from the Church nominal and is appearing" in the massive "spirit of protest" ("NER," 149). Protestantism in New England has utterly spilled over its former institutional divisions and has now established the possibility of a correspondence between principles and the ob-

21. "Politics," in *Essays: Second Series*, 128, 121.
22. "Self-Reliance," in *Essays: First Series*, 42, 33.

jective world, a complicity between Emerson's own principles
and events.

Emerson is not, then, afraid of the idea of revolution. Its prospect
in his own time is always exciting to him, but his sense of it is profoundly a version of Puritan conversion experience rather than an
extension of the preceding political or social revolutions in Europe
and America. Despite what he says about memory and political institutions elsewhere, implicit in his characterization of his "Times"
is the potentially contradictory premise that "politics" or the state
is not what he called a "proximity." Emerson often suggests that
the federal government had established a minimal and loose framework within which the soul would find nothing but encouragement for its expansion and enrichment. But he also notes that "our
society" is "encumbered by ponderous machinery" ("SL," 80) that
should be simplified or dismantled. In this way he interprets the
pervasive impulse for reform as a stripping away of what is unnecessary. But he also insists that the myriad reform movements have
gotten everything wrong. In fact, he reserves most of his criticism
for the reformers themselves rather than for the objects of their reform, and what he specifically attacks is the impulse to organize,
to enter into contracts. From Emerson's point of view, the attempt
to organize is always a compromise with the worldliness that the
reformers were trying to overcome.

Behind these particular criticisms of the reform movements,
there lies a vision of an ideal community similar to what Jonathan
Edwards observed about the Great Awakening: "[T]he town
seemed to be full of the presence of God"; "Our public assemblies
were then beautiful; the congregation was alive in God's service";
"There was now no discourse of anything but religion, and no appearance of any but spiritual mirth."[23] What Edwards represents
here is spontaneous social renewal, a spiritual enlivening that for
him seems to have no implications for social or institutional reor-
ganization. Whole villages underwent reformation without any secular aftereffects. In a conventional historical sense, nothing hap-

23. *The Basic Writings of Jonathan Edwards*, ed. Harold P. Simonson (New York,
1970), 101, 102.

pened at all. From an Emersonian perspective, however, what had occurred was the most important reformation of human life, an intense personal and social enlivening.

While something like this vision of community is at the back of Emerson's mind as a cultural memory, the social model that serves as the actual ground of his attack on various reform movements is what he calls "the affinities by which alone society should be formed" ("SL," 88). In "New England Reformers," he offers a model of community the paradox of whose definition is dissolved if we keep in mind that he is referring to the traditions of New England towns: "The union is only perfect when all the uniters are isolated. It is the union of friends who live in different streets or towns. . . . The union must be ideal in actual individualism" ("NER," 157). In contrast to this model, "our society"—the actual, diffuse social world of Emerson's time—is a "graduated, titled, richly appointed Empire, quite superfluous when Town-meetings are found to answer just as well" ("SL," 80). The simple natural and historical fact of the New England town provides the model from which the principle of economy as well as the even more important principle of self-government derive; it is from such a vantage point that we can, in Emerson's view, judge whether "the future will be worthy of the past" ("NER," 167).

Emerson's critique of reform and of America in general appears utopian because it seems to oppose all forms of organization, contracts, and associations. Despite his spiritual affirmations, his advice is either passivity or complete dissolution of the political or civil or religious institutions of his time—except for the one institution that he depends upon, the New England town. Of course, in his quest to achieve a plausible universalism, he seems to turn against the town: "The time of towns is tolled from the world by funereal chimes, but in nature the universal hours are counted by succeeding tribes of animals and plants, and by growth of joy on joy."[24] And in "History," Emerson says, "I am ashamed to see what a shallow village tale our so-called History is" ("H," 22). Thus in his appeal to find new terms for history and for historiography,

24. "The Poet," in *Essays: Second Series*, 23.

he enlarges his notion of a village tale to include the histories of "Rome, and Paris, and Constantinople." "Broader and deeper we must write our annals—from an ethical reformation, from an influx of the ever new, ever sanative conscience,—if we would trulier express our central and wide-related nature, instead of this old chronology of selfishness and pride to which we have too long lent our eyes" ("H," 23). It is, however, difficult to imagine how this new history could be written. Emerson wants to capture something of "the metaphysical annals of man"; he is in favor of "universal history," as Kant and others, including some Americans, called it. But the fact of the New England town is somewhere in the back of his mind, even as he insists upon keeping his distance from the village life of Concord.

Emerson does not quite acknowledge this cultural memory of the New England experience. Because he chose to move from Boston to Concord as an adult, he felt free to project upon Concord something of his conscious intentions, the strength of a desire and the whim to make of it what he wanted. Such a choice would be supported by his transcendentalist principles whereby consciousness and whim could generate society and history. He chose Concord; Concord or history had not chosen him. In his thoughts about the social, he can always abstract from the actual traditions and historical background of Concord. Indeed, when he leaves Boston for Concord, he writes, "Hail, to the quiet fields of my fathers," referring, of course, to his literal ancestors as well as to the fathers of New England.[25] He self-consciously moves into a heritage, into an archaic history, even as he refers to his new life in Concord as "this pleasing contrite wood-life which God allows me." The status of the New England town allows Emerson to believe that he has settled into nature rather than into New England's and his own past. He can even suggest that his retreat into nature is an imitation of high Romantic literary fashion: "[T]he current literature and poetry with perverse ingenuity draw us away from life to solitude and meditation" rather than into an activity that might pro-

25. Quoted in Ralph L. Rusk, *The Life of Ralph Waldo Emerson* (New York, 1949), 209.

mote the reform movements of the times.[26] In the context of
Romantic thinking, therefore, Emerson can rightly be accused of
obfuscating history and society by referring to them as "nature." In
Nature, the world itself is thought of as "a projection of God in the
unconscious." But as Pierre Bourdieu has observed, such an "unconscious" may enfold within it a "forgetting of history which history itself produces by incorporating the objective structures it
produces in the second natures of habitus." This orderly array of
social practices a member of a society carries out every day, without having to choose his or her behavior consciously, without having to be aware of following a set of social rules or of following the
dictates of a leader.[27]

To say that Emerson transmutes history into an unconsciousness
does not necessarily imply that his transcendentalism is conservative, a veiled defense of the vested interests of his time. It may well
be that in obfuscating history, Emerson implicitly recognizes the
demise of the importance of a seventeenth- and eighteenth-century
historical artifact—the town. To turn a cultural institution into
"nature" may express a desire for emancipation from preceding historical orders, a paradoxical detachment from society and the history of its traditions, and a joining with the remnants of those
orders.

Although Emerson acknowledges "the quiet fields of my fathers," the truth is that he lived in Concord as something of a
friendly alien. As Ralph Rusk notes, "After less than a year in his
rural retreat he dreamed of a choice social circle there. 'I will tell
you,' he wrote to Frederic Hedge, 'what society would please me;
that you should be the minister of Concord & George P.B. its school
master & Carlyle a resident whilst he lectured in Boston and Mrs
Ripley & Mr Alcott should be visitors.'"[28] In fact, his theory of
friendship as a peculiarly intense spiritual affinity between fellow
human beings is at once an acknowledgment of the town community and a supplement to that community because the actual town

26. "Self-Reliance," 34; "Introductory Lecture," 179.
27. Pierre Bourdieu, *Outline of a Theory of Practice*, trans. Richard Nice (Cambridge, England, 1977), 78.
28. Quoted in Rusk, *The Life of Ralph Waldo Emerson*, 232.

of Concord does not fulfill his vision of a consummate social life. Emerson has a need for solitude, but what he expresses even more insistently is a need for a particular kind of social life, both committed to the archaic community of "us country folk" and completely uncommitted to anything other than universal principles of individualism, to the sovereignty of consciousness. He accepts the village model of a community even as he implicitly rejects it in favor of a transcendental village of friends, believing that he can have the society he has chosen. But such a view implies a profoundly contradictory or ambiguous notion of social existence, at once a commitment to the organic communality of historical New England villages and a rejection of that same historical entity.

In the work of Hawthorne, we get a view of New England towns in a state of irreversible decline. With the ebbing of their economic power, these little towns had lost their actual autonomy and even that somewhat illusory historical autonomy to which they had been clinging since the American Revolution. By the 1820s, the development of capitalism and industrialism shifted power to the rising metropolitan centers, Boston and New York. Emerson never speaks of the historical autonomy of the New England towns, but he appropriates the phantasms of that communal and social autonomy to form a concept of the self-governing soul. He translates the dying innocence of the New England town into his notion of a self that is at once individual and representative. The social autonomy of the towns has been defeated by economic history and the emergence of a national politics. In an extraordinary labor of *aufhebung*, Emerson translates this communal autonomy into a representative self, freed from its actual historical background.[29] His concept of individualism is, in fact, impossible to understand or to realize without this complicated communal background, which he depends upon throughout his major works. Emerson's views on self-reliance and the autonomy of the individual powerfully invoke, if not a community, at least a community-effect, an implied commu-

29. Two important books on this topic of the American representative self are Sacvan Bercovitch, *The Puritan Origins of the American Self* (New Haven, 1975); and Mitchell Robert Breitwieser, *Cotton Mather and Benjamin Franklin: The Price of Representative Personality* (Cambridge, England, 1984).

nity that is no longer accessible except in the mythology of a universal or representative self. Moreover, the object of such a cultural work is now liberated into the new disciplinary society that we associate with the modern world. In Emerson's many allusions to "vocation," for instance, especially in "Self-Reliance" and in "Spiritual Laws," there is no way to determine whether he has in mind the orderly and ancient division of communal tasks in a New England village or whether he is predicting the constant ordering of roles that must fit together in a modern urban or bureaucratic field of anonymity. He captures in his thought both the nostalgia for an archaic and defeated social existence and an enthusiastic prophecy of modernity. The synthesis, as it were, is so powerful that it is impossible for Americans to escape it. Thus, Emerson's thought belongs both to the party of Memory *and* to the party of Hope, despite his many efforts to keep them apart.

The more we come to understand the form of the essay, the better we will be able to see how Emersonian transcendentalism as well as what we might call the Emersonian philosophy of history could only be expressed in such a genre. For the essay never had to be acknowledged as either historical or as a genre. It is an "open form," congenial for thrusts of thinking rather than systematic thought, experimentation rather than certainty. ("I simply experiment," Emerson says, "an endless seeker, with no Past at my back.")[30] Modern readers may feel that, in his essays, Emerson shows an unwarrantable confidence in their affirmations, but he explains the communal implications of his confidence and his absolutes: "If you meet a sectary or a hostile partisan, never recognize the dividing lines, but meet on what common ground remains. . . . Though your views are in straight antagonism to theirs, assume an identity of sentiment, assume that you are saying precisely that which all think, and in the flow of wit and love roll out your paradoxes in solid column, with not the infirmity of a doubt . . . assume a consent and it shall presently be granted."[31]

30. "Circles," in *Essays: First Series*, 188.
31. "Prudence," in *Essays: First Series*, 140–41.

Historically, the essay form was, as in Montaigne, an attempt to escape "the slightly dusty picture of classical Antiquity"; it is given to appropriating anything it wants from other genres and to escaping or overcoming or hiding the historical situation to which it alludes. According to Michel Beaujour, whatever else it does, the essay captures a "type of memory, both very archaic and very modern, by which the events of an individual life are eclipsed by the recollection of an entire culture."[32] Emerson claims that, for the representative self who is the protagonist of his major essays, "the crises of his life refer to national crises." Behind this note of the personal, however, he is stingy with the details of his personal crises or those of the nation. Yet, his essays are indeed a "recollection of an entire culture." And no matter how confident his affirmations appear, the essay as a form is well equipped to deflate its absolutes into the personal. It says, "This belongs to me and I have always said so." It is perhaps for this reason that Emerson says that "there is no doctrine of forms in our philosophy."[33] In other words, he does not separate the form of the essay from his "philosophy." They are one and the same.

Like transcendentalism itself, the essay carries within it a power to move beyond antagonism and polarity in a "deporting movement," an overcoming of struggle for the purposes of a serene innocence. It is the perfect instrument for the personal and the consensual, for affirmation and skepticism, for a historical consciousness that can either deny itself or affirm itself. It is the perfect instrument to express the profoundest ambiguity of America's and Emerson's attitude toward what he refers to as an "age of reflection." Like Emerson's thought itself, the essay engages in reflexivity, in a critique of the self-images of the age. But it also polices the impulse to reflection, sets aside a great number of things and topics that it wants to ignore or repress. The essay is a powerful constraint to reflection, since its generic task is to obscure the sources of its existence.

32. Montaigne and Beaujour quoted in Réda Bensmaia, *The Barthes Effect: The Essay as Reflective Text*, trans. Pat Fedkiew (Minneapolis, 1987), 97.
33. "The Poet," 3.

For what Emerson wants is to make use of the self's relations with the world *and* to stand in wonder before the world. We are always aware of these twin desires because of his powerful use of tacit reference (one version of which is his notion of polarity or compensation): "[W]hoever sees my garden, discovers that I must have some other garden."[34] When we read an essay by Emerson, we are obliged to see both the visible and the implied gardens of his thought, the fact and the phantasm, each giving the other its power, interweaving their products so that, in the end, we cannot be certain which we are perceiving because of the continuous play between statement and implication. Thought feeds off the unthought, off its background, but thus brings the background before us into a kind of presence.

We should not fault Emerson for not thinking radically enough. There is no need for him to acknowledge fully the traditions of philosophy and theology and social praxis from which he builds his own reflections, like a rag-and-bone man, any more than he needs to acknowledge the paradoxes and contradictions within those traditions. Emerson is perhaps the best spokesman we will ever have for both the distortions and the truths of historical continuity in America; indeed, the image of his two gardens belongs to American thought itself. For example, his cosmopolitan and deporting gestures before history extend into the twentieth century in poets and thinkers such as T. S. Eliot and Ezra Pound, whereas his imagined community of the New England town anticipates the cultivation of the local in William Carlos Williams and Charles Olson. The power of Emerson's thought lies in its inextricable weave of nostalgia, critique, and foresight. This is to say that his thought is our memory, our palimpsest. He is our great sublimated puritan remembrancer whose thought transformed history and thus preserved history for us as a commitment to modernity. Once the past has been so carefully and thoroughly woven, in Goethe's words, "into the fabric of our inmost self," there will no longer be a "past that one is allowed to long for."[35]

34. "Prudence," 131.
35. Goethe quoted in Terdiman, "Deconstructing Memory," 14.

H. DANIEL PECK

Killing Time / Keeping Time:
Thoreau's Journal and the Art of Memory

The *Journal* was thus a kind of memory, in which
thoughts were hived against the time when, as Emerson said, these golden boughs joined hands.
     —"A Note on the Composition of *Walden*"

On January 8, 1842, the day his brother John began to experience
the first symptoms of the virulent infection that would kill him
three days later, Henry Thoreau was thinking of time. In his Journal, he asks meditatively: "Of what manner of stuff is the web of
time wove—when these consecutive sounds called a strain of music can be wafted down through the centuries from Homer to me—
And Homer have been conversant with that same unfathomable
mystery and charm, which so newly tingles my ears.— These single
strains—these melodious cadences which plainly proceed out of a
very deep meaning—and a sustained soul are the interjections of
God."[1] The sense of mystery expressed here regarding time's conti-

    1. *Journal 1: 1837–1844*, ed. Elizabeth Hall Witherell *et al.* (Princeton, 1981),
361–62. All subsequent citations of this work, appearing parenthetically in the text,
will be identified by *P*, I, and page number. This edition of the Journal presently
runs to two volumes, the second of which comes forward to the spring of 1848.
Edited typescripts of Journal entries from this date until mid-February, 1854, have
been prepared by The Writings of Henry D. Thoreau, and the project's editor-in-
chief, Elizabeth Hall Witherell, has graciously allowed me to quote from these typescripts in cases where a passage falls within this period. For the convenience of the

nuity (its "music"), and the intimacy thus afforded between Thoreau and voices of the ancient past, are familiar; his Journal shows repeated expression of these sentiments from the time he began to keep it four years earlier in the autumn of 1837.[2]

Thoreau's Journal falls silent in the weeks immediately following John's death, and when we finally witness another extended meditation on the theme of time, it is clear that something profound has happened. On March 26, two and a half months after the most deeply felt loss Thoreau was to suffer, we find this:

> The wise will not be imposed on by wisdom— You can tell—but what do you know?
> I thank God that the cheapness which appears in time and the world— the trivialness of the whole scheme of things—is in my own cheap and trivial moment.
> I am time and the world.
> I assert no independence.
> In me are summer and winter—village life and commercial routine— Pestilence and famine and refreshing breezes—joy and sadness—life & death. How near is yesterday— How far to-morrow! I have seen nails which were driven before I was born. Why do they look old and rusty?—
> Why does not God make some mistake to show to us that time is a delusion. Why did I invent Time but to destroy it.
> Did you ever remember the moment when you was not mean?
> Is it not a satire—to say that life is organic?—
> Where is my heart gone—they say men cannot part with it and live.
> Are setting hens troubled with ennui   Nature is very kind—does she let them reflect? These long march days setting on and on in the crevice of a hayloft with no active employment—
> Do setting hens sleep? (P, I, 392)

There is much here—especially the almost suicidal trivialization of the self—to suggest the acute Oedipal guilt that psychoanalytic critics have posited as Thoreau's dominant response to his broth-

---

reader, I have included in parentheses following such quotations the location of the comparable passage in the 1906 Riverside edition (*The Writings of Henry David Thoreau: Journal*, ed. Bradford Torrey), cited as *R*. For all quotations after mid-February, 1854, my source is the Riverside edition.

2. An example is a passage written August 22, 1838, less than a year after Thoreau had begun his Journal: "How thrilling a noble sentiment in the oldest books— in Homer The Zendavesta—or Confucius!— It is a strain of music wafted down to us on the breeze of time, through the aisles of innumerable ages. By its very nobleness it is made near and audible to us" (P, I, 52).

er's death.[3] But I want to focus on the passage's figuration of time, so markedly different from that in the earlier entry. In both instances, the essential form is interrogative. But where the questions in the January 8 passage work toward a sense of appreciative wonder at time's continuity, here there is nothing of either appreciation or wonder. These responses have been replaced by confusion and anger, and the God characterized before by propitious "interjections" into the stream of time has been replaced by a deity who refuses to disclose the true nature of the temporal order. This covert God, as well as the passage's tense despair and its riddling, enigmatic forms of expression ("You can tell—but what do you know?"), may remind us more of Emily Dickinson than of the buoyant author of *Walden*. The questions—insistent, desperate, and deeply cynical—challenge all Thoreau's prior assumptions about natural process: "Is it not a satire—to say that life is organic?"

Yet while angry and assertive, these questions are not solely rhetorical. When Thoreau asks, "Why does not God make some mistake to show to us that time is a delusion," he is expressing his deepest wish that time, as the deliverer of his brother's death, should cease to have reality for him; he is asking that he should no longer have to live in time, to endure the experience of time. The strategy he has employed toward this end is to have killed time by containing it, by taking the entire temporal order—"summer and winter"—within himself.

But the manner of Thoreau's question also reveals his perplexity at the fact that, despite his willed sense of its unreality, time continues to beat out its inexorable rhythms, as if nothing had happened. We know that this same sense of perplexity had preoccupied him for at least a month previous to the writing of this passage, because on February 21 he had set down in his Journal a sentence whose conclusion is missing but whose meaning is unmistakable: "I feel as if years had been crowded into the last month [the period since John's death]—and yet the regularity of what we call time has been so far preserved as that I . . . " (*P*, I, 365). For all his desire to live entirely within his "own cheap and trivial moment," to retreat

3. See especially Richard Lebeaux, *Young Man Thoreau* (Amherst, 1977), 167–204; and Lebeaux, *Thoreau's Seasons* (Amherst, 1984), 4–6.

into a realm of pure consciousness, Thoreau could not ignore the
sound of the world. This inability is, of course, a mark of his essential psychic health, closely related to the palpable sense of nature
that gives a work such as *Walden* so much of its power.

But here Thoreau's awareness of that sound establishes a severely arhythmical relation between the time of consciousness and
the world's time, and this in turn results in a profound sense of dislocation and isolation. As the question "Why did I invent Time but
to destroy it" reveals, he is anything but comfortable in his self-
determined imperial role, which protects him from the independent force of time but does so at a terrible cost. The passage reveals
Thoreau's awareness that he could not kill time without killing the
body of the world and the sound of its heartbeat, as measured, for
example, by the life-sustaining song of the cricket, which pervades
his Journal early and late,[4] or the celebrated sounds that are the
title of Chapter Four of *Walden*.

By killing time, Thoreau has killed the vehicle of temporality in
which the world and the self have their being and their relation; in
this sense, he has committed suicide, as, indeed, at some level he
had intended to—paradoxically alienating himself from the very
world he has "contained." For this most grounded of writers, a man
who depended utterly on the variety and otherness of the world to
feed his imagination, here was an untenable position; the impossible alternatives it implies are suggested by the famous phrase
from *Walden*: "As if you could kill time without injuring eternity." The passage, in other words, shows Thoreau trapped deeply
within a solipsism of his own making, resulting in a condition of
severe psychological impasse.

The Journal passage of March 26, 1842, can thus be understood
(and, in fact, is easily recognized as) a classic case of compensatory
overempowerment, prompted by a crisis that has put the writer's
relation to time and the world in doubt. But this overempowerment
has a philosophical as well as a psychological dimension, for if we

4. In a passage titled "Crickets" from the early Journal (August 29, 1838), for example, Thoreau wonders if the sound of the crickets is "not earth herself chanting
for all time" (*P*, I, 54).

were to detach phrases such as "I am time and the world" and "In me are summer and winter" from their context, they would remind us of nothing so much as ideas expressed in Emerson's early essays, especially the essay "History" (1841). This work, published less than a year before John Thoreau's death, set forth the revolutionary proposition—derived in part from European Romanticism—that "the whole of history is in one man,"[5] and, like *Nature* (1836) before it, announced and celebrated the primacy of individual consciousness over the entire temporal order.

It is possible that the sentence in Thoreau's Journal passage, "I have seen nails which were driven before I was born," is an unconscious echoing of the following sentence in "History": "I have seen the first monks and anchorets without crossing seas or centuries."[6] But Emerson's claim to a visionary perception of the past is an unambiguously celebratory claim for the empowerment of consciousness and part of his larger program for self-reliance. Thoreau's claim to have seen nails driven before he was born, on the other hand, is immediately qualified by the troubled question, "Why do they look old and rusty?" The past, which ought to have rendered itself freshly to his eyes, is even in the instant of its perception found tarnished, since *everything* within the field of Thoreau's vision—past and present—is tarnished. The very cosmos is tarnished for him.

In fact, the way in which the question "Why do they look old and rusty?" undercuts the previous sentence's claim for visionary reach is characteristic of the entire passage, with its clearly established pattern of assertion and withdrawal ("I am time and the world. I assert no independence"). This is the rhythm of radical empowerment and the (necessary) reflexlike counterresponse of self-negation: I am everything, I am nothing. For this disciple of Emerson, at least in this moment of his intense despair, there can be no great surge of Emersonian empowerment without immediate

5. "History," in *Essays: First Series*, ed. Joseph Slater, Alfred R. Ferguson, and Jean Ferguson Carr (Cambridge, Mass., 1979), 3, vol. II of *The Collected Works of Ralph Waldo Emerson*, 4 vols. to date.

6. *Ibid.*, 16.

disempowerment and without a virtual swamping of the self in its self-created isolation. The passage can be read, then, as a short-circuiting of the Emersonian idea of the self's centrality to time and space. The speaker's killing of time is a gesture as pathological in its self-destructiveness as is the smashing of the quadrant by Ahab—another Emersonian figure who, in destroying the instrument that locates his temporal and spatial "position," takes self-reliance to its most extreme, transcendental limits.

Thoreau, of course, is no Ahab, and the comparison underscores the aberrational character of the Journal passage, whether it is viewed in a psychological or a philosophical (Emersonian) context; the intensity of response belongs to the experience of mourning. Yet while the passage's extremity, even hysteria, is unlike Thoreau, the basic tendency it expresses is not. Frederick Garber has described the characteristically undulating motion of Thoreau's redemptive imagination: expansion outward to bring all of nature within the embracing reach of consciousness, followed by periodic withdrawal.[7] Understood in this way, the response dramatized by the passage can be located at the extreme end (the place where grief had taken him) of his imagination's polar movement, and seen as a severely exaggerated expression of one of his most characteristic tendencies.

It is also characteristic of Thoreau to have understood the crisis of his brother's death as a breach in the temporal order and to have measured his grief according to his alienation from that order. As the initial passage we examined suggests, this writer—from the earliest stages of his intellectual life—was deeply committed to establishing a *personal* relation to time and was habitually given to contemplating its pleasing mystery. Sudden, inexplicable death broke this relation and shook Thoreau's faith in the benign continuity of time's progression, which was the very thing that made possible an intimate relation to the past. Thus his figuration of time as a continuum on which the self might ride without hazard had been severely challenged, in something of the same way that

7. Frederick Garber, *Thoreau's Redemptive Imagination* (New York, 1977).

his relation to nature was later challenged by his unnerving realization—on Mount Katahdin—of its frightening otherness.[8]

The Journal entry of March 26, 1842, can thus be seen to focus Thoreau's essential problem of time: how to contain its unpredictable and wayward fluctuations within the safe perimeter of consciousness, yet also to honor the independent rhythm of temporality in which the self has its earthly being—how, in short, to keep time without killing it.

The most immediate effect of the crisis the passage records was to give Thoreau's general and long-standing concern with time a decidedly elegiac focus, and to cast time—especially its manifestation in the currents of history—as the foe from whom he would have to redeem his losses. His brother's death had alerted him to the possibility of *permanent* loss, to the possibility that the living world of love and relation that constitutes the present could suddenly vanish without a trace. We know that Thoreau's first book, *A Week on the Concord and Merrimack Rivers* (1849), which recounted a voyage he and his brother had made in 1839, was written as an elegy to John, and that part of its purpose was to recover what earlier had seemed irrecoverable. The long gestation of this book was certainly Thoreau's mourning work of the 1840s, and it is possible that the Journal passage's mysterious hens "setting on and on" signal the writer's incipient awareness, even in the immediate aftermath of his tragedy, that such gestation would be necessary— that he would have to kill time in this other, potentially more fruitful, sense.

The writing of *A Week* helped Thoreau, as I have observed elsewhere, to understand that, paradoxically, an immersion in the flow of time was necessary to overcome time, and that he would have to confront and experience the destructive force of history in order to recover from it his own and his region's lost past.[9] The problem of

---

8. Thoreau, *The Maine Woods*, ed. Joseph J. Moldenhauer (Princeton, 1974), 70–71. The best treatment of this experience is Garber, *Thoreau's Redemptive Imagination*, 66–128.

9. H. Daniel Peck, "'Further Down the Stream of Time': Memory and Perspective in Thoreau's *A Week on the Concord and Merrimack Rivers*," *Thoreau Quarterly*, XVI, nos. 3–4 (Summer/Fall, 1984), 93–118.

A Week, however, as a comprehensive response to the issue of time that his brother's death had focused for him was that even though it was, as he called it, an "unroofed book" (*R*, II, 275)—one day's voyaging adventure opening provisionally on the next—it was essentially an elegiac and retrospective response to experience. The fragments recovered and synthesized belonged largely to the past. Built upon a journey with a beginning and an end, its linear form called for—and got, in its lyrical closing chapter—resolution and closure. In view of the longer-term requisites of Thoreau's life and career, this was both the achievement and the limitation of *A Week*.

For all its rivering upon the stream of time, *A Week* could not open itself to the living instant of the present, the nick of time. While it bore lessons for the conduct of life, it could not provide an overarching context in which the future could be confidently anticipated. Thoreau needed a book that could commemorate the past as faithfully as *A Week* had, but could also in the very act of composition replicate the continuous issuance (or what Whitman called "efflux") of time into the world, and could, through the comprehensiveness of its perspective, draw the design of the future. Such a book would be even more unroofed than *A Week*, and would have no beginning and no end.

Thoreau's Journal is a lifework, in the sense that it ultimately became his central literary concern, but also in the literal sense that it belonged to his life. It is as much a part of that life as are the writer's daily walks, to which it is closely related.[10] When the life begins to fail under the debilitating effects of tuberculosis, the Journal becomes intermittent and finally falls silent, but it never really ends. In fact, if the reports of Thoreau's serene acceptance of death in his final days are true, the life itself ended with a far greater sense of closure than does the Journal. Its final entry, like all the thousands that precede it, stands there expectant, awaiting another.[11]

10. See William Rossi, "The Journal, Self-Culture, and the Genesis of 'Walking,'" *ibid.*, 138–55.

11. Thoreau died on May 6, 1862. For brief accounts of his last days, see Walter Harding, *The Days of Henry Thoreau* (New York, 1965), 464–66; and Robert D.

If we are unable to locate an entry that marks the Journal's formal close, we have no trouble finding the one that marks its inauguration. It was written on October 22, 1837, shortly after Thoreau's graduation from Harvard, and begins: "'What are you doing now?' he asked, 'Do you keep a journal?'—So I make my first entry to-day" (P, I, 5). The unnamed "he" is almost certainly Emerson, and the pedagogical force of the question is unmistakable. By 1837, Emerson had been keeping his own journal for seventeen years and, convinced of its inestimable value to his own growth, had encouraged others in his circle to do so as well. This private discipline of mind and spirit had a significant public and collective aspect as well, since it was the practice of these Emersonians to share their journal writing with one another and even sometimes to publish excerpts in the *Dial*. So much a part of the regimen of the Transcendentalists' way of life did journal keeping eventually become that at least one of Emerson's followers forced the discipline on his unwilling children.[12]

Thoreau did not need to be forced; he responded to Emerson's call with the fervor of a disciple, eagerly taking up the literary instrument that, the Transcendentalists believed, was best suited for capturing the inspiration of one's genius in the moment of its inception. The point, of course, is that in initiating a journal, he was joining a going concern, jumping aboard the express train of radical thought in America in the 1830s, and adopting one of its requisite practices. This is the sense in which Thoreau's Journal may be said to have no beginning. The telling connective "So" ("So I make my first entry to-day") suggests not only the student's obedience to his teacher's call but also the almost automatic, gestural quality of his action.

Given this context, Thoreau's Journal in its first weeks and months is exactly what we would anticipate: a highly self-conscious

---

Richardson, Jr., *Henry Thoreau: A Life of the Mind* (Berkeley, 1986), 388–89. The Journal's final entry, made on November 3, 1861, closes with a description of the railroad causeway following a violent storm (R, XIV, 346).

12. That was Bronson Alcott, as noted by Lawrence Buell, "Transcendentalism's Literature of the Portfolio" (Paper delivered at Modern Language Association meeting, December 27, 1986, New York City).

and studentlike practice board of ideas. Initially, these ideas are grouped according to topics designated by headings, such as "Solitude," "Beauty," "Truth," and "Harmony." By 1840, the headings have dropped away and the entries have become more flowing, interrelated, and organic—their evolving form reflecting the originality and sophistication that increase steadily through the new decade.[13] The volume called Long Book, which Thoreau kept from the fall of 1842 to March, 1846 (roughly, from the time of his brother's death to the period of the Walden experiment), as well as the several volumes he kept at the Pond between 1845 and 1847, richly anticipate both *A Week* and *Walden*. Numerous passages from these works appear well formed in their earlier Journal versions.

But for all the increasing sophistication of its entries, the Journal of the 1840s—considered as a whole—lacks the sense of a coherent literary undertaking, that is, the sense of an integral, self-contained set of purposes transcending the document's use as a source book and workshop for ideas. One obvious indication of this is its physically fragmentary nature: Thoreau cannibalized his Journal in this period for his other writings, freely pulling extracts from it for use in lectures and essays and in drafts of *A Week* and *Walden*.

However, as modern scholarship has discovered, he altered this practice in 1850 and began to preserve his Journal entries in full, usually by copying out the material he wished to employ elsewhere.[14] This discovery has large implications, the most important of which is its confirmation of what Perry Miller recognized many years ago as a significant departure. Miller noticed that in the early 1850s the Journal becomes "a deliberately constructed work of art."[15] There is no doubt that the entries written in this period have a far more consistently formal, elegant, and coherent aspect

13. What we have of Thoreau's earliest Journal volumes—those he kept from 1837 through mid-1842—are versions the author transcribed from their (largely) missing originals. See Robert Sattelmeyer's "Historical Introduction," *P*, I, 601.

14. See Rossi, "The Journal," 141; and William Howarth, "Successor to *Walden*? Thoreau's Moonlight—An Intended Course of Lectures," *Proof* 2 (1972), 92–93.

15. Perry Miller, *Consciousness in Concord: The Text of Thoreau's Hitherto 'Lost Journal' (1840–1841) Together with Notes and a Commentary* (New York, 1958), 4.

than do those that appear earlier. By 1851, Thoreau is writing not only *in* his Journal but *for* it as well.

Miller had a ready explanation for this striking development. It owed, he said, to the writer's disappointment at the commercial and critical failure of his first book, *A Week on the Concord and Merrimack Rivers.* Because of this public failure, Miller argued, Thoreau turned his attention to the making of a private book, his Journal. Its success would always be measured by his own standards rather than by those of the literary marketplace. As ballast for this theory of compensation, Miller cited a Journal passage of January 27, 1852, in which Thoreau speculates that "thoughts written down thus in a journal might be printed in the same form with greater advantage—than if the related ones were brought together into separate essays" (*R*, III, 239). Miller found here evidence that Thoreau "was crying 'sour grapes' about something he desperately wanted [public acclaim as the author of books and essays] but could not get. . . . [T]he tone to notice is the alacrity with which he was accommodating himself to defeat."[16]

This severe judgment, obviously proceeding from Miller's characteristic animus toward Thoreau, has been surprisingly influential,[17] and it needs revision. That Thoreau was disappointed in the public failure of his first book is certain. But to say that this disappointment alone accounts for the maturation of his Journal ignores the imperatives of form and development within the work itself. The most misleading aspect of Miller's formulation is the exclusive emphasis on the Journal's emergence as "a work of art." To consider this document's developing coherence solely in terms of the writer's formal objectives is to misinterpret the way in which Thoreau understood the evolution of art from thought and experience. Form, for him, is not an end in itself, but is the result of an organic process of discovery—of self and world. This is not to deny

16. *Ibid.*, 31.
17. For example, the findings of Sharon Cameron's *Writing Nature* (New York, 1985), for all the considerable light they shed on the Journal's significance, are skewed by Cameron's general acceptance of Miller's compensation theory. The result, I think, is an exaggeration of the formal differences between *Walden* and the Journal, and a neglect of the Journal's later volumes.

that Thoreau wanted to be a writer, which he clearly, and sometimes desperately, did. But he conceived of this vocation as a full
spiritual calling that required something much more than attention to craft as such.[18] Before Thoreau could begin to entertain the
formal possibilities of his Journal, it was necessary to reconsider its
most fundamental human purpose.

We find evidence of such a reconsideration in a passage written during January or early February, 1851, a year before the passage cited by Miller: "I would fain keep a journal which should
contain those thoughts & impressions which I am most liable
to forget that I have had   Which would have, in one sense the
greatest remoteness—in another the greatest nearness, to me" (R,
II, 143). The second sentence rehearses the writer's familiar penchant for abstracting experience into its most essential aspect. But
the initial sentence posits a specifically commemorative purpose
for the Journal and asserts this as a new imperative. To have suddenly asked himself for such a journal—a repository of valued
thought and experience, a kind of surrogate memory—fourteen
years after he had begun to keep a journal seems an unlikely development, since this document had always implicitly served him in
this way. Yet what is happening here is a *re*discovery, a deepening
of awareness, a coming into fuller knowledge of what is already
known, with a fresh understanding of the implications of prior
practice.

The preservation of experience endangered by loss had been, of
course, a central theme of *A Week*, and it seems to me likely that
Thoreau's sharpened sense of his Journal's commemorative purpose—reflected in many of the entries during this period—is a direct outgrowth of what he had learned in thinking through the
development of that work.[19] This, rather than disappointment in
commercial failure, is the most important legacy of *A Week* to the

18. The definitive treatment of Thoreau's spiritual vocation is Sherman Paul,
The Shores of America: Thoreau's Inward Exploration (Urbana, 1958).
19. For example, there is widely expressed in the Journal of the early 1850s a
strong, Wordsworthian desire to repossess childhood experience. A passage of
July 16, 1851, reads: "In youth before I lost any of my senses—I can remember
that I was all alive—and inhabited my body with inexpressible satisfaction" (R, II,
306).

mature Journal, and establishes an authentically generative relation between what may be considered Thoreau's first and second "books." It may also be true that the formal elegance of the writer's post-1850 Journal owes, in part, to the way in which the composition of *A Week* taught him how the "day" might be used creatively as a synthetic unit of thought. Furthermore, the Journal's increased formality and coherence in this period belong to the care that Thoreau was now giving to the act of commemoration.

In the years after the publication of *Walden* (1854), Thoreau's insight that his Journal could preserve for him what otherwise would be lost to the attritions of time and experience is fully consolidated, as the deliberate tone of a passage from February 5, 1855, suggests: "In a journal it is important in a few words to describe the weather, or character of the day, as it affects our feelings. That which was so important at the time cannot be unimportant to remember" (*R*, VII, 171). But, as I have indicated, Thoreau already was moving toward this insight in the earliest days of 1851, and the immediately subsequent weeks and months reveal a steadily deepening understanding of the Journal's commemorative purpose. Although the following passage from an entry of August 19, 1851, does not specifically refer to the Journal, it nevertheless makes clear in its obvious excitement of discovery the importance of a new emphasis: "What if a man were earnestly & wisely to set about recollecting & preserving the thoughts which he has had! How many perchance are now irrecoverable!— Calling in his neighbors to aid him" (*R*, II, 406).

What Thoreau is implicitly describing here is a book of memory, and a passage written in the following year reveals the Journal's newly enlarged purpose: "A Journal.—a book that shall *contain* a record of *all* your joy—your extacy" (July 13, 1852; *R*, IV, 223, emphasis added). I mean to stress here the Journal's special capacity for comprehensiveness. Other kinds of books (such as *A Week*) tell only the "story" of a life, which is to say, a retrospective and necessarily selective rendering. But a journal renders the life as lived, comprehensively; it "contain[s] a record" not only of "all your joy" but also of apparently incidental experiences or perceptions whose hidden significance might later emerge as part of a larger pattern or, conversely, as an important departure from the normal round. One never could know precisely what is important to remember in the moment; only time would tell.

To read one's journal would be both to reexperience the discrete moments of time past—thus commemorating them—and to tally those moments against the present as a way of measuring change. A passage from a September 12, 1851, entry shows Thoreau reading his Journal specifically for the purpose of comparing past and present. The results surprise him: "I can hardly believe that there is so great a diffirence between one year & another as my journal shows. The 11th of this month last year the river was as high as it commonly is in the spring—over the causeway on the Corner Road. It is now quite low. Last year Oct 9th the huckleberries were fresh & abundant on Conantum— They are now already dried up" (R, II, 498). Although the particular change—the level of the river—revealed by the Journal in this case does not in itself have great importance, the incremental force of hundreds of such observations is to show Thoreau the very *nature* of change, its largest rhythms and patterns. Most important, such knowledge of change reveals what in nature is *un*changing, and the climactic moment in *Walden*, when Thoreau recognizes the Pond's utter permanence ("all the change is in me"), owes its authenticity precisely to the double vision of experience the Journal affords. That moment is earned by the Journal.

Later in the 1850s and early 1860s, Thoreau's comparison of natural phenomena from different seasons and years would become far more systematic and ranging than at this relatively early point, though even in this period he was preparing for this, making indexes to his Journal volumes. It is clear that by the fall of 1851 the Journal is already what Gaston Bachelard would call a material memory, a book deliberately conceived to "keep" time by enlarging the temporal view of reality through the process of cross-reference.[20] Increasingly, this process becomes Thoreau's major strategy for translating facts into truths—the imperative first publicly expressed

20. See Gaston Bachelard, *The Poetics of Reverie: Childhood, Language, and the Cosmos*, trans. Daniel Russell (Boston, 1969), and other of Bachelard's works.

in his early essay "Natural History of Massachusetts" (1842).[21]
Facts would, that is, gain spiritual significance through their gradually revealed placement along the span of time. The disciplined recording of alert observation would provide an invaluable record of facts that, when later remembered (which is to say, reconfigured) in relation to other facts, might reveal the direction and nature of change. When the past was viewed in this way, and *viewing* is indeed the right word, it might become possible literally to "see" time, and to see it whole—as a full matrix of past, present, and even future.

In other words, at the same time in the early 1850s that Thoreau is discovering he might keep time through the power of commemoration, he is also discovering that he might keep time in still another, closely related sense: by spatializing the temporal process. At a key moment in the spring of 1852 this conception breaks through into overt awareness. The momentousness of the breakthrough is signaled by the initial phrase in this Journal passage: "For the first time I perceive this spring that the year is a circle— I see distinctly the spring arc thus far. It is drawn with a firm line" (April 18, 1852; *R*, III, 438).

Like Thoreau's insight regarding his Journal's potential for commemorating experience, this discovery must be understood as a deepening of an already perceived truth. By 1852, he had for many years been an acute and faithful observer of seasonal change and had already written several drafts of *Walden*, a book that from the outset was structured according to the seasons. That he should at this late date have reacted profoundly to his perception of an age-old truth, the cyclical nature of seasonal change, may be difficult to comprehend.

Yet this was, I believe, an entirely authentic discovery for Thoreau—indeed, the most important and determinative in his imaginative life. To understand its full importance, we need to give strong emphasis to the word *see* in the passage's second sentence: "I *see* distinctly the spring arc thus far." What Thoreau announces here is

21. This idea was first expressed in Thoreau's Journal in an entry made on December 16, 1837: "The fact will one day flower out into a truth" (*P*, I, 19).

that he has, for the first time, apprehended the temporal flow of nature's change in clearly spatial terms; he has set temporality on a plane, an "arc," along whose rim rides the flow of time. In this way, time is "contained," given a boundary, one that coincides with consciousness itself. The "line" that describes the circle, "drawn" by the divine artist from whom all time flows, is "firm." Unlike the porous, multiple figures of Emerson's essay "Circles" (1841), expanding ever outward "wheel without wheel,"[22] Thoreau's circle is unitary. Like Walden Pond, it characteristically looks inward from its perimeter toward its own deep and complex interior. Emerson's "breakthrough into spaciousness," described by David Porter, has a distinctly different character from Thoreau's equally dramatic breakthrough.[23]

From the moment Thoreau apprehends the "circle" of time, he remains steadily faithful to its implications. The intensity of his commitment to this design may remind us of William Butler Yeats's commitment to the "great wheel" in A Vision (1937), which, like Thoreau's own wheel of the turning seasons, answered the poet's deepest need for an ordering structure of reality.

The impact of Thoreau's discovery in 1852 is everywhere evident in his later writings. Most obviously, it informs Walden, whose spatial purity and sense of timelessness contrast so markedly with A Week's deliberate engagement with time. But the most profound effect is in the Journal, where Thoreau's daily observations reveal an increasingly sure sense of nature's spatial and temporal coherence. The ease with which he begins to travel imaginatively around the circle of time is suggested by an entry of March 4, 1854, where the fragrance of a plant "carries me back or forward to an incredible season" (R, VI, 149). Analogously, the Journal of the early 1850s exhibits more and more frequently a syntactical conflation of past and future, such as Thoreau's reference to "days which remind me of the Indian summer that is to come" (September 21, 1854; R, VII, 47). In many entries during this period, we find the writer virtually identifying phenomena of past and future, as in phrases such as

22. "Circles," in Essays: First Series, 180.
23. David Porter, Emerson and Literary Change (Cambridge, Mass., 1978), 134–59.

"that reminiscence or prophesying of spring" (February 11, 1853; R, IV, 492). When time is conceptualized as a circle, memory and anticipation come together as a single timeless dimension of experience.

Thoreau's articulation of his spatial vision of reality culminates in a set of charts, sometimes known as the "Kalendar," which he developed near the end of his life (between 1860 and 1862). These charts, each of which treats a single month of the year, are nothing less than an attempt to lay all of nature's phenomena out on a flat plane, an attempt, that is, literally to graph their temporality—to make a comprehensive picture of time.[24] Each chart lists vertically down its left margin a long and varied set of natural phenomena (such as the occurrence of frost, or the level of the river); across the top of the page we find the headings 1852, 1853, and so on through 1860 or, in some cases, 1861. The lines Thoreau drew to coordinate the vertical (phenomenal) and horizontal (chronological) dimensions form a grid, the spaces of which the writer filled in with his particular observations from the Journal of these years—working from lists he had made earlier by culling the Journal. The act of transferring these observations from his Journal, where they are necessarily embedded in a temporal context, in the very flux of time, to the charts, where they stand utterly flat on the page as a derived spatial abstraction, replicates the essential impulse of the mature Journal. Whatever specific purposes Thoreau had in mind in creating these documents, and however one judges their philosophical or scientific efficacy, they must be seen as the ultimate extension of the Journal itself, a realization of where it had been going at least since 1852.[25]

Frances Yates, in *The Art of Memory*, describes the way in which orators of antiquity converted the materials of memory into spatial

24. These unpublished documents are in the Pierpont Morgan Library, New York City. The project is apparently incomplete, with charts missing for some months. In view of the magnitude of what Thoreau was attempting, this incompleteness is not surprising, even when we take into account his failing health during his last years.

25. The specific form of the charts derives from eighteenth- and early-nineteenth-century models—Gilbert White's *Garden Kalendar* (1751–68), for example—whose observations of phenomena had been recorded in this way. For a discussion of the

(architectural) form. This process, of course, was but an exercise enabling them to master vast amounts of information.[26] But, as Yates shows, a deepening of the relation of memory to spatial imagery occurred in the medieval art of Ramón Lull and other thinkers of the Middle Ages, where "memory serves to visualize a cosmological and philosophical system, a spatial pattern, whose relational aspects are explored by the searching mind." These words summarizing Yates's argument belong to Rudolf Arnheim, who broadens her discussion from its context in medieval cosmology to a fundamental human need. "Man is given," he says, "the task of coping with mortality—not only his own but also that of all other constituents of his world," and to this task he brings the art of memory, which is nothing less than a "translation of time into space," a way of overcoming "the mortality of the present moment."[27]

The essential set of truths that Thoreau grasped in the early 1850s was that his Journal might enact for him an art of memory in just this sense: specifically, that it could faithfully record and preserve his most valued perceptions, *and* that it might help him organize these perceptions into a unified vision of life:

It is surprising how any reminiscence of a different season of the year affects us— When I meet with any such in my journal it affects me as poetry and I appreciate that other season and that particular phenomenon more than at the time.— The world so seen is all one spring & full of beauty.— You only need to make a faithful record of an average summer day's experience & summer mood—& read it in the winter—& it will carry you back to more than that Summer day alone could show—only the rarest flavor— the purest melody—of the season thus comes down to us (R, V, 454)

This Journal passage was written on October 26, 1853, less than a year before the publication of *Walden*, and it anticipates the way in which *Walden* is a distillation of remembered experience—another

ecological visions of White and Thoreau, see Donald Worster, *Nature's Economy: A History of Ecological Ideas* (Cambridge, England, 1977), 2–111. For Thoreau's interest in phenology (the study of seasonal change) as expressed in the late Journal and other of his late writings, see William Howarth, *The Book of Concord: Thoreau's Life as a Writer* (New York, 1982), 162–89.

26. Frances Yates, *The Art of Memory* (Chicago, 1966), esp. 1–198.

27. Rudolf Arnheim, "Space as an Image of Time," in Karl Kroeber and William Walling (eds.), *Images of Romanticism: Verbal and Visual Affinities* (New Haven, 1978), 1, 3.

book of memory, in this sense. But the passage itself is also such a distillation. It begins with Thoreau's delighted surprise at what his Journal can do for him, though quickly affirming his absolute confidence in it ("You only need to make a faithful record"). Reflecting upon its capacity to preserve a newborn summer's day, he implicitly shows how the Journal—always positioned at the forward edge of experience—captures what in *Walden* he called "the bloom of the present moment." But his purpose here is to explain how that moment, now reexperienced later through reading the Journal, becomes "poetry" through the act of commemoration, through the mediating, enhancing effects of memory itself—thus suggesting that for him art is intimately related to memory, in some sense *is* memory.[28] The vision earned through this process is one of pure spatial coherence ("The world so seen is all one spring"), another anticipation of *Walden*. In all these ways, this Journal passage of 1853 shows us how Thoreau discovered, within a book he was already writing, his book of memory.

28. *Cf.* Emerson, in his essay "Memory": "The memory has a fine art of sifting out the pain and keeping all the joy" (*Natural History of Intellect and Other Papers* [Cambridge, Mass., 1904], 104). For the importance of recollection in Thoreau's work, see Paul, *The Shores of America*, 192–93; and Alfred Kazin, *An American Procession* (New York, 1984), 70–71.

THOMAS HILL SCHAUB

"Cut in Plain Marble": The Language of the Tomb in *The Pioneers*

Ever since Emerson, whose lectures on all accounts
are his *poetry*, American poetry has tried to get beyond fixity and determinism, to destroy arbitrary
boundaries, in order to release the energy and impulse
of creation and restore the self's place *in* the world.
                    —*In Search of the Primitive*

In the last scene of *The Pioneers* (1823), the inheritors of Templeton—Oliver Effingham and Elizabeth Temple—enter the cemetery
of Major Effingham and Chingachgook, laid side by side, and find
there Natty Bumppo trying unsuccessfully to read the words chiseled on the two headstones. Thinking himself alone, Natty says
aloud, "'Well, well—I'm bold to say it's all right! There's something I suppose is reading; but I can't make anything of it.'"[1] Those
who can read the words on the headstones shortly arrive and convey to Natty the message inscribed upon them. To Natty's delight,
even the name "Bumppo" appears lettered on Major Effingham's
tombstone, so Natty too is already a figure of the remembered past,
though still present.

Typically, this final scene, which ends with Natty's departure for

---

1. James Fenimore Cooper, *The Pioneers*, ed. James Franklin Beard (Albany,
1980), 450. All subsequent page references are to this edition and are included parenthetically in the text.

the West, is understood to dramatize the uneasy resolution of the generational and property conflicts that are the ostensible themes of *The Pioneers*, but it is worth noting that Cooper has staged his novel's resolution in terms of a confrontation between a living speech and a cryptic writing. In this confrontation, Natty, we may say, is the figure of voice, a speaker of the wilderness, while the inheritors of Templeton—those who have erected the tombstones— are figures of writing, for this cemetery is a place of writing and literacy. It is the place where the spirit is converted to the letter, where the living wilderness becomes a grave site, and the inhabitants of that world die into the world of written memory, the world of inscriptions, epitaphs, history, and literature.

By placing the illiterate but eloquent woodsman directly before the stubborn silence of the written memorials, Cooper reproduces the legal and moral conflicts of his novel as a divorce between meanings and the words we use to preserve their memory. Our sense of Cooper's ambivalences is considerably deepened when we realize that he cannot help allegorizing the future of Templeton as a kind of funeral parlor in which the living are precisely those who are left behind when the voice of spirit departs. What is striking is that Cooper makes this choice, even in his imaginative repossession of the world he had lost.

The scene appears to be, in small, an enactment of the entire novel as an effort to set the record straight. Once Natty hears the epitaphs read aloud, he is quick to say that one of them is not "all right," for he hears in Oliver's voice that Chingachgook has been misspelled: "'The name should be set down right,'" he insists, "'for an Indian's name has always some meaning in it.'" Oliver promises to "'see it altered'" (452). Between the two of them, Natty and Oliver manage to adjust the words to meanings, so their literal form expresses the pressures of the spiritual essence they are meant to identify and commemorate.

This would appear to be an essential act of advancing civilization. Unless it remembers correctly what it dispossesses, society loses all claim to represent the spirit, becoming merely the dead letter signifying the absence of meaning rather than its continuity. This possibility worried many of Cooper's contemporaries. In one of his journal entries for 1838, Emerson wrote, "This country has not fulfilled what seemed the reasonable expectation of mankind." Similarly, we should understand Thoreau's spiritual desire to "speak somewhere *without* bounds" and "to lay the foundation of a true expression" as a political exhortation to rewrite America. He knew that the "truth" of language, like the promise of the American experiment, "is instantly *translated*; its literal monument alone remains."[2] In contrast, *The Pioneers*, as James Beard has noted, is "an imaginative repossession of [Cooper's] heritage" (xxxi–xxxii), but instead of repossessing an original promise for the nation, the novel seems dedicated to securing what was left. Although Cooper became progressively disillusioned with American democracy, we can see even in this first novel of the Leather-stocking series that he has already decided that the only thing left to fight over is the "literal monument."[3]

There are many elements in *The Pioneers*, mostly gathered about the figure of Natty Bumppo, that suggest Cooper intended to ensure that the literal monument would be vested with what Thoreau called "the volatile truth" of its origin. Certainly this final scene suggests that without Natty's mediation, there can be no guarantee that civilization's literal forms bear any relation to the spiritual "meaning" they displace. Natty's disappearance into the forest thus has this further significance, that it is the disappearance of meaning itself (or the conditions of meaning)—the loss of that which makes words good, of reference and origin, as if writing, in displacing the voice of the wilderness, had gone off the gold standard.

Furthermore, Cooper's treatment of Natty appears to confirm the characteristic privileging of speech over writing: of inspired oratory

2. Stephen E. Whicher (ed.), *Selections from Ralph Waldo Emerson* (Boston, 1957), 90; Thoreau, "Conclusion," *Walden*, ed. Sherman Paul (Boston, 1960), 221.

3. It has been customary, since D. H. Lawrence's *Studies in Classic American Literature* (1923), to assess Cooper's historical vision from the standpoint of the Leather-stocking series considered as a whole. From that vantage, Cooper's tendency to imagine a past appears to grow increasingly less "realistic" as his sense of American society becomes more bitter and pessimistic. For my purposes, the novel is best treated alone, since part of my interest lies in noting how early Cooper was disposed toward rejecting America's more idealistic possibilities. *The Pioneers* came very early indeed, being the first in the Leather-stocking series, and only the third of thirty-two novels Cooper wrote between 1820 and 1850.

over written discourse, of communion over reading, of the direct over the indirect, of the immediate over the mediated. Natty's "immediacy," of course, is predicated upon his virtual identity with the wilderness. As Wayne Franklin has argued persuasively, Natty's "voice is lyric rather than social, the articulation of a silence brooding in the landscape." Unlike the settlers, Natty "does not live in this world [the landscape] so much as he expresses it." Natty brags to Oliver " 'I never read a book in my life,' " but he can read in the landscape the sign of its Creator: " '[N]one know how often the hand of God is seen in the wilderness, but them that rove it for a man's life' " (293–94). Later in the novel, during the courtroom scene, Natty says that in the wilderness " 'he could always look into the windows of heaven' " (370). Natty's reading, that is, is a kind of vision, an unmediated transparency. What he cannot read are the opaque signs of the letter and the literal civilization that is writing itself across the New World landscape. Because Natty's voice is everywhere associated with the expression of the truth and spirit that lie within the natural world, his is an organic speech whose forms are the expression of meanings. The natural world, as Joel Porte has noted of *The Pathfinder*, "becomes a paradigm for authentic utterance of any sort, but especially for poetry—true speech."[4] " 'How is it, John?' " Natty asks Chingachgook, " 'do I speak the true word?' " (290). The novel's answer is an unhesitating yes.

This brief reminder of what must be, for most readers, an accepted fact of Natty's portrayal serves to underline the paradox that the plot of *The Pioneers* eventually finds no comfortable space for Natty's voice, except the space of writing. Of course it is a feature of novelistic representation that speech can never appear except in writing, but this tautology should not obscure the peculiar (and schematic) emphasis Cooper's final scene places upon both the expulsion of Natty and the transformation of his voice into the world of written memory—even within the novel. Seen as such, this writing *within* writing alters our understanding of Cooper's inner conflict between civil order and wilderness freedom, about which

4. Wayne Franklin, *The New World of James Fenimore Cooper* (Chicago, 1982), 90, 88; Joel Porte, *The Romance in America* (Middletown, Conn., 1969), 32.

nearly all critics after Smith have written. This focus helps reveal the vested interests that conflict involves, which in turn helps explain why there is no room for the voice of nature in the temple of civilization.[5]

In fact, one may argue that the very qualities that privilege speech over writing are those Cooper finds most subversive. Attributing them to Natty was not only a genuine means of celebrating life in the wilderness but also, less obviously, a means of excluding Natty from the world to which Cooper ultimately owed his allegiance. After all, Natty is but the means by which Cooper himself adjusts forms to meanings. The writing of *The Pioneers* redeems the spirit entombed within the novel, and, further, Cooper seems to suggest that without the novel the spirit would not exist at all. Again, in an important sense all narrative is redemptive, but here he is not just recovering his boyhood in Cooperstown. The interesting and paradoxical fact about Cooper's memory is that he chooses to instantiate there a spiritual voice that he must then silence in order to fully recover and inherit that memory as a continuity with his past. Natty's privileged role as nature's spokesman is then a kind of false redemption, being a fiction that has no place in the world of fact.

Correspondingly, Cooper must walk a fine line between his treatment of nature as the origin of those virtues upon which a just society is founded and his treatment of nature as a source of those qualities that threaten the community's durability. Thus, speaking is at once associated with the "true word" and with those inner feelings and passions that must be held in abeyance for the good of

5. See Henry Nash Smith, *Virgin Land* (Cambridge, Mass., 1950), 59–70, where Smith argues that the conflict of *The Pioneers* pits "old forest freedom" against "the new needs of a community." In *Regeneration Through Violence* (Middletown, Conn., 1973), Richard Slotkin reads the novel as a conflict between "the Indian world and the white" (485). In his critical biography of Cooper, *Fenimore Cooper: A Study of His Life and Imagination* (Princeton, 1978), Stephen Railton views the conflict between "the values of civilization and the freedom of the wilderness" as a reflection of an inner battle with his father, William (75–113). Eric J. Sundquist, in *Home As Found* (Baltimore, 1979), argues that "at stake in the first Templeton book is Natty's refusal to abide by the letter of the law" (27). John P. McWilliams, Jr., in *Political Justice in a Republic* (Berkeley, 1972), reads the novel as a reflection of Cooper's political thought, "torn between the individual's right to freedom and the community's need for order" (101).

the community. In this way the most visible dualism of the novel, between Natty's wilderness and Judge Temple's settlement, is transformed into the opposition between passion and rationality. Passion is shown to exist wherever there is animal blood: in the eyes of the panther; in the hearts of Natty and Chingachgook, unlawfully pursuing the buck; in Oliver, too, who is "inflamed beyond prudence at the sight" of the buck; and in both Judge Temple and his daughter, who show similar unrestrained enthusiasm for the slaughter of pigeons. By existing in both wilderness and civilization, passion erodes the opposition between them; but rationality is firmly rooted in civilization and its forms. About the hierarchy of reason over passion, Cooper had no ambivalence, as the countless passages describing the "ascendency" of reason over the feelings attest.[6]

The connection between these two pairs of opposing qualities—between speech/writing and passion/reason—is most explicitly presented in the reactions of the townspeople to Minister Grant's sermon. In Hiram Doolittle's opinion, Grant's sermon was a "'tonguey thing'" (a compliment, in Hiram's idiom), though there were parts he would have changed. Still, "'as it was written discourse,'" Doolittle concedes, "'it is not so easily altered, as where a minister preaches without note'" (158). Appropriately, Doolittle voices his criticism in the tavern of the Bold Dragoon, the scene of passion and intemperance, which follows immediately upon the church service. The last words of the previous chapter, in fact, anticipate this intemperance: "'[T]here is such a thing,'" Minister Grant tells his daughter, "'as the idolatry of our passions'" (144).

The landlady of the tavern, Mrs. Hollister, agrees with Hiram and brings out the argument's subversive implications more forcefully: "'[H]ow can a man stand up and be praching his word, when all that he is saying is written down, and he is as much tied to it as iver a thaving dragoon was to the pickets?'" (158). For Hiram and Mrs. Hollister, the written word is a formal convention separating the reader and the listener from the realm of meaning and spirit.

6. For a discussion of the role of human passion in the novel, see Thomas Philbrick, "Cooper's *The Pioneers*: Origins and Structure," *PMLA*, LXXIX (December, 1964), 579–93.

For them, "praching" one's "word" ought to mean a more evangelical, inspired, and untutored speech, in which the Word and the word, meaning and name, are united.

Judge Temple responds to these criticisms of his minister by peremptorily "waving his hand for silence" and calling a halt to this incipient rebellion against the minister's authority: "'[T]here is enough said; as Mr. Grant told us, there are different sentiments on such subjects, and in my opinion he spoke most sensibly'" (158), whereupon the judge abruptly changes the subject. In the midst of the tavern conversation, "sensibly" is meant to resonate with the Augustan connotations of rationality and temperance, and it has as its foils not only the drinking and uninhibited behavior that follow but also—implicitly, since the objections have been silenced—the passionate, evangelical preaching of those who speak without or outside "written discourse." As Richard Slotkin has pointed out of this tavern chapter, one of the foils for the action that follows is the judge's news of further bloody excesses by the French Jacobins—a reminder of the precarious instability of Templeton itself and the need for legal forms that assure stability.[7]

Although Cooper's portrait of Minister Grant is in part patterned after his father's "efforts to establish an Episcopal church upon a community of nonconformists,"[8] Cooper appears to have designed the minister's church service as another instance of the "composite order" that characterizes all aspects of the new settlement. During his sermon Minister Grant makes reference to the distinction between a "service of forms" and a service more "evangelical," and Cooper tells us that Mr. Grant knew that the forms would be uncomfortable and disturbing to many of his congregation, "mostly a primitive people in their habits," many of whom would view "the introduction of any such temporal assistance as form, into their

7. Slotkin, *Regeneration Through Violence*, 486–88. "In spite of his Quaker heritage," Robert Spiller notes, Cooper's father "apparently early adopted the view of the New York aristocracy that there might be ways of getting into heaven other than that of the Church of England, but that no gentleman would choose any of them: 'The Episcopal mode of worship,' as Robert Troup once wrote to Rufus King, 'so friendly to the government, so hostile to Jacobinism'" (*Fenimore Cooper: Critic of His Times* [New York, 1931], 30).

8. Leon Howard, "Introduction," to *The Pioneers* (New York, 1965), xi.

spiritual worship, not only with jealousy, but frequently with disgust" (126). In fact, Mr. Grant is something of a utilitarian, a "sensible" man, who had "been known to preach a most evangelical sermon, in the winning manner of native eloquence, without the aid of a cambric handkerchief!" In his first sermon before the people of Templeton, however, he "endeavored to steer a middle course" (126–27), though giving to his presentation enough of the Anglican formality that it raises the hackles of Doolittle and Mrs. Hollister. This provides the occasion for the issue of authority underlying Cooper's representation of speech and writing, passion and reason.

Cooper is here alluding to a conflict in preaching styles that was most fervent and divisive during the Great Awakening in the 1740s, some fifty years prior to the time period in which the action of *The Pioneers* takes place. According to two accounts of this conflict, Harry Stout's *The New England Soul* and Alan Heimert's *Religion and the American Mind*, the central issue revolved around whether ministers ought to appeal, as Jonathan Edwards put it, to the "head" or the "heart." To accomplish this, "only the spoken word," more and more people came to believe, had a "proper 'tendency' to impress truth on men's 'hearts and affections.'"[9] Certainly this is the conviction shared by Hiram Doolittle and Mrs. Hollister.

Listening to written sermons often led an audience to suspect that the minister himself was without the Spirit. The question Mrs. Hollister asks is precisely the question that evangelicals used to inculcate doubt in the congregations of established ministers during the Great Awakening and after. The entrenched hierarchy of the ministers—many of whom read sermons "verbatim in the manner of a prepared essay"[10]—naturally rebelled against these insinuations, and the terms of the ensuing debate played out the logical extensions of the opposition between the head and the heart: one either addressed the "understanding" or the "affections"; one achieved faith either by "reason" or by "enthusiasm."

9. Alan Heimert, *Religion and the American Mind: From the Great Awakening to the Revolution* (Cambridge, Mass., 1966), 223, 228.
10. Harry S. Stout, *The New England Soul: Preaching and Religious Culture in Colonial New England* (New York, 1986), 192.

This conflict also divided along distinctions of class and authority. Stout recounts that the Great Awakening differed from earlier revivals in that "it often became a revival *against* their established churches." Itinerant preachers such as George Whitefield and Gilbert Tennent, who possessed unusual oratorical skills but no local allegiances, "ignited smoldering social tensions by calling into question the authority of local ministers and, in the process, challenging their monopoly on the Word." The democratic challenge they posed lay precisely in the means of receiving the Spirit, whether through rational understanding or through the conviction of the heart: "[I]f the source of true enthusiasm came from without—as Edwards insisted it did—then *anyone* was a potential candidate for remaking, and distinctions of learning or breeding lost their significance."[11]

The further relevance of Heimert's study to this reading of *The Pioneers* lies in his assertion—the polemical thesis of his book— that it was the Calvinist evangelical movement of the Great Awakening that established the momentum and conditions, the willingness of the people to revolt against England, rather than the established Liberal clergy or the influence of Enlightenment thought: "It would appear," he writes in the introduction, "that the uprising of the 1770's was not so much the result of reasoned thought as an emotional outburst similar to a religious revival." In this respect, Cooper helps substantiate Heimert's controversial thesis, for though he is writing *The Pioneers* some fifty years after the American Revolution, he too associates—his valuation is the reverse of Heimert's—the act of revolution with the unstable (and destabilizing) elements of religious "fanaticism." In the chapter of *The American Democrat* (1838) titled "On Religion," Cooper criticizes those forces of revolution that continue to exert cultural power despite their success in having created a new nation: "The causes which led to the establishment of the principal American colonies, have left a deep impression on the character of the nation. . . . Fanaticism was the fault of the age, at the time our ancestors took possession of the country, and its exaggerations have

11. *Ibid.*, 197, 207.

entailed on their descendents many opinions that are, at the best, of a very equivocal usefulness."[12]

The ostensible purpose of these few pages on religion is to inveigh against the tendency of the population to "split straws on doctrine" and to urge the citizenry to abide by "the great essentials of the Christian character." But chief among these "essentials" is humility—"religion's first lesson," he writes. Thus the fundamental motive of this section is to pacify those unhappy with their "temporal condition" by reminding them that eventually all men go to a "state of being" that "will render the trifling disparities and the greatest advantages of this life, matters of insignificance." Religion ought to be a curb on the inherent danger of democratic rhetoric, that by declaring all men equal it leads them to seek equality not in name only, but in station, in property, in all the goods of this world. In this context, the true danger of "sectarianism" is the threat it poses to the established equanimity of the social and political state. "Equality of condition," Cooper writes in an earlier chapter, is "incompatible with civilization, and is found only to exist in those communities that are but slightly removed from the savage state."[13]

That Cooper had in mind, as early as *The Pioneers*, such thoughts about the relationship of religious fanaticism and challenges to political authority is evident from the fact that those characters who find Minister Grant's sermon lacking in the power of the spoken word are shown to be in need of regulation and reform: the avaricious Hiram Doolittle (and his confederate, Jotham Riddel), the landlady of the drinking house, and Remarkable Pettibone, the "petty" housekeeper who resents submitting to the authority of Judge Temple's daughter Elizabeth. Especially in the confrontations between Remarkable and Elizabeth do we see that the quarrel with Minister Grant's written discourse involves both authority and class: "The idea of being governed," Cooper writes of Remarkable, "or of being compelled to pay the deference of servitude, was absolutely intolerable." Thinking to bring this matter up with Eliza-

<hr/>

12. Heimert, *Religion and the American Mind*, 21; James Fenimore Cooper, *The American Democrat* (New York, 1956), 186.

13. Cooper, *The American Democrat*, 186, 185, 40.

beth, Remarkable chooses "a subject that was apt to level all human distinctions, and in which she might display her own abilities." This subject is the minister's sermon, and she makes the same criticism of it that Hiram and Mrs. Hollister offered earlier: "'It was quite a wordy sarmont that Parson Grant give us tonight,' said Remarkable.—'Them church ministers be commonly smart sermonizers; but they write down their ideas, which is a great privilege. I don't think that by nater they are as tonguey speakers for an off-hand discourse'" (169–70). Elizabeth emerges the victor from this exchange, for Remarkable is unwilling to rebel openly and ends up flattering the very practice she set out to question. Elizabeth is quick to use this against her and close the discussion with a renewed assertion of her authority: "'You have found an excellence in the church liturgy, that has hitherto escaped me,' said Miss Temple. 'I will thank you to inquire whether the fire in my room burns: I feel fatigued with my day's journey, and will retire'" (170).

Clearly, all of this is meant to be an amusing anecdote at Remarkable's expense. Cooper seems to be quite at home having fun with the servants and their lovable "resentment," but resentment and humility constitute another of the novel's key oppositions. Both terms were central to Cooper's understanding of American democracy and its inherent dangers. Remarkable's rebelliousness is a version of that unwillingness to accept a subordinate station that Cooper thought was the natural consequence of the Republic's rhetoric: "The terms liberty, equality, right and justice, used in a political sense, are merely terms of convention, and of comparative excellence, there being no such thing, in practice, as either of these qualities being carried out purely, according to the abstract notions of theories."[14]

Here social stability has a vested interest in accepting (and maintaining) a distinction between names and things, theory and practice. In such a context, any figure—Natty Bumppo, for example—in whom name and thing, word and meaning, are united in a way of life is a direct threat to the social status quo. In Cooper's mind

14. *Ibid.*, 188.

the dangers of "theory" were allied with the evangelical power of those who are "tonguey" by "nater" (as Remarkable puts it), and thus with nature itself as a source of ideals or "names" that in "practice" could prove to be more subversive than salutary. The effort to wrench "practice" into conformity with "theory" only results in the simplifications of ideology and the discontents of "fanaticism." This is Cooper's message throughout *The American Democrat*: "[S]ociety is always a loser by mistaking names for things. Life is a fact, and it is seldom any good arises from a misapprehension of the real circumstances under which we exist."[15]

"The real circumstances under which we exist," of course, are always a negotiable reality; for Cooper, however, the passions and affections of men and women were the least reliable guides to that reality. Nowhere is this tightly knit complex of oppositions more evident than in the scene of Natty's trial and defeat before the law. Throughout the exchanges of the trial, the force of feeling, which has its expression in outbursts that are unacknowledged by the rules of evidence, contends with the silence of the written law: "[T]he feelings of the old hunter were awakened," and Judge Temple is "strongly affected by the simplicity of the prisoner" (365–66); Billy Kirby and Natty engage each other "with a freedom and familiarity that utterly disregarded the presence of the court," and the judge, asserting his authority, says, "'This is an improper place for such dialogues'" (367). When Judge Temple pronounces the sentence following the jury's guilty verdict, Natty appeals to the personal debt the judge owes him—for saving Elizabeth from the panther—but Marmaduke insists that his "private feelings" must be subordinated to the law. Perhaps this is the place to recall that when Major Effingham saved the life of Chingachgook, the Delawares gave to the major the very land over which Judge Temple now imposes his law. In the world before writing, a man is as good as his word: "'[W]hat the Delawares give, lasts as long as the waters run,'" says Mohegan (291). When popular opinion threatens to overturn his sentencing, the judge calls an abrupt halt to the proceed-

15. *Ibid.*, 118.

ings: "'There must be an end to this,' said the Judge, struggling to overcome his feelings. 'Constable, lead the prisoner to the stocks. Mr. Clerk, what stands next on the calendar?'" (370–72).

Here the spoken expression of nature and passionate feeling are circumscribed by the law, whose signs are the inflexible stocks and imprisoning walls of the jail, but the jailing of Natty is only the prelude to the final circumscription, which takes place in the cemetery in the closing scene. The cemetery itself represents the final victory of writing over speech, though as in the case of Natty's jail, which proves vulnerable to escape, Cooper has constructed the final scene of *The Pioneers* as a resurrection that does not violate the necessary circumscriptions of the law or the facts of life so much as it transcends them.

Cooper anticipated this scene in the novel's first paragraph, where he provides a schematic and prophetic summary of social advance, of which the subsequent action is to be a particular instance: "[T]he expedients of the pioneers who first broke ground in the settlement of this country, are succeeded by the permanent improvements of the yeoman, who intends to leave his remains to moulder under the sod which he tills, or, perhaps, of the son, who, born in the land, piously wishes to linger around the grave of his father" (16). Already we see Cooper plotting to enlist the rebellious energies of the hunter in the program of the farmer, by expelling him as a "pioneer." In the final scene, Cooper uses Natty to fulfill the novel's prophecy and to give his idea of the "natural course" of westward movement the imprimatur of the dispossessed: "'You've come to see the graves, children, have ye,'" says Natty to Elizabeth and Oliver when he notices their presence. "'[W]ell, well, they're wholesome sights to young as well as old'" (450). To a degree Natty even envies his dead friends their existence in writing, and wonders "'who will there be to put me in the 'arth, when my time comes!'" (450). He is excited, then, when he hears from Oliver that his own name has been engraved in stone as part of Major Effingham's epitaph: "'And did ye say it, lad? have ye got then the old man's name cut in the stone, by the side of his master's.'" Overcome with emotion, Oliver manages to stammer, "'It is there cut in plain marble; but it should have been written in letters of gold!'" (451).

Unbeknownst to Natty, of course, Cooper's descriptions of him in this scene suggest that he is already dead, for when Elizabeth and Oliver enter the graveyard, they see "the hunter himself . . . stretched on the earth, before a head-stone of white marble" (450). While it may be objected that Natty is in this position to inspect the inscriptions ("pushing aside with his fingers the long grass that had already sprung up from the luxuriant soil around its base"), the wording here and elsewhere in this passage unmistakably suggests that Natty is undergoing death and transfiguration.[16] After listening to Oliver read the inscriptions aloud, Natty—this is the wording in the text—Natty "raised himself from the tomb" (452) and, turning to take his leave, he "stooped to lift a large pack from behind the tomb, which he placed deliberately on his shoulders." Indeed, Cooper describes Natty's departure from the immediate site of the graves as a kind of supernatural vanishing: " 'He is gone!' cried Effingham" (453).

We understand that Natty, like the natural world for which he speaks, is in his autumnal season, but Cooper wants to align his hunter with the cycles of nature *and* to imbue him with the immortality of the god who created nature. These repeated references to the tomb are a conscious evocation of the Resurrection, in which Natty is an image of the sacrificed god who redeems and condones the progress of the nation across the virgin land. In exploiting the Christian myth, Cooper equates Manifest Destiny with history itself, the natural though fallen advance of human time as it unrolls within the Christian promise of redemption. At the same time, by resurrecting Natty in this manner, Cooper differentiates him from Judge Temple in such a way that the conflict between them disappears, since what had been a conflict in this world between the wilderness and the settler, between the illiterate voice and the written word, is now translated into the traditional and irremediable conflict of tragedy, between the world of the gods and the world of men. The only safe place, Cooper seems to feel, for the

16. In this suggestion we see an anticipation of the actual death and resurrection of the character rendered by Cooper in the two later novels, *The Prairie* (1827)—in which Natty dies—and *The Pathfinder* (1841), in which Cooper revives his hero as a young man.

spiritual values inspired by the wilderness is beyond the boundaries of the social world whose political rhetoric is informed by those values.[17] Thus when the forest once again envelops Natty, he is tucked or folded into a pre-narrative world where he may survive as myth, without having any political consequences.

All resurrections require a sacrificial death that precedes them, but this somewhat subliminal effort to *translate* Natty's life is troubled by the pervasive accents of a literal and irrevocable death. The overt message of the final sentence of the book is that Natty is heading into the forest to lead the westward movement of the nation into the future, preparing the way for civilization: "He had gone far towards the setting sun,—the foremost in that band of Pioneers, who are opening the way for the march of the nation across the continent" (456). But even here, the upbeat newsreel-like vigor of "the foremost in that band" has to contend with the image of an exhausted man in the evening of his life ("He had gone far towards the setting sun").[18] Clearly Cooper means to emphasize the imminence of Natty's death, for Natty has just been communing with the dead, and his dogs, in the prior paragraph, are "scenting around the graves and the silent pair [Oliver and Elizabeth], as if conscious of their own destination" (456). There are two "destinations" implied here: one is the West of the American future and the other is the death of the American past required by that future. The uneasiness with which these two are yoked together is then reproduced in the awkwardness of the novel's final sentence.

This antinomy has been implicit in the setting of the last scene, for Cooper has located the cemetery on "the little spot of level ground where the cabin of the Leather-stocking had so long stood" (449). This piece of land, during the course of the novel the habitation of Chingachgook, Effingham, and Natty—three generations of social history: Indian, British, and American—is now transformed into a memorial not only of what has passed away but also

17. McWilliams, *Political Justice in a Republic*, sees the conflict avoided because Natty and the judge "belong to different stages of settlement" (102).

18. Certainly Natty is in some measure patterned after Daniel Boone, who also headed farther west at an advanced age, but as I argue here, the language of the passage establishes exhaustion, not a hardy old age. See Smith, *Virgin Land*, 51–58, for an account of Boone's reputation and its influence.

of what is left, a cemetery and its inheritors. The entire landscape of the novel—the mountains and streams, the lake, the village and its settlers—is here compressed into a Miltonic image of a garden without its god. Instead of the couple being expelled from Eden, Cooper's Adam and Eve, "the silent pair," are left in Eden's ruins: "[T]he cemetery," Oliver realizes, "was occupied only by himself and his wife" (456). It is Natty, as the expelled god, who looks back with tears in his eyes.

Behind him are the dead letters of the tomb: the cemetery, Templeton, and by implication the novel itself, for Natty remains within the silent garden of writing, his name inscribed not only on the tombstone of Major Effingham but in the novel itself as the memorial of a spirit more safely remembered than encountered. This has been the implication from the very first glimpse we have of Natty trying to read the headstones. *The Pioneers* is a headstone on which are chiseled the words of Cooper's past, which can only be evoked and reclaimed in the written word. Not only is the novel a written memory in the conventional sense, but the memory it calls into being—in a writing within writing—is also one in which writing prevails over, transforms, and expels the voice of immediacy. Thus, buried under this seemingly abstract distinction between speech and writing is something both profound and homiletic. If the social and political world of time is mediated, ordered, and preserved in the written word, then the future, now constituted as writing itself, belongs to those who know what the words mean—or who think they do. This is the precise implication of Natty's soliloquy: "'There's something I suppose is reading; but I can't make anything of it.'"

In granting hegemony to the printed word, Cooper was affirming the medium in which his imagination would have a public life. Clearly he associated writing with spiritual absence and even questioned the word's capacity to preserve and remember the spirit. Still, this was a risk he was willing to take, for the revealing fact of Cooper's "imaginative repossession" is that *The Pioneers* lays no claim to the original promise of the frontier community. The novel argues instead that the continuity of that society, even in his imaginative re-creation, seems to depend upon the eviction, the dispossession, of that very promise. By comparison, the suspicion that the Republic had become merely a dead letter uninhabited by its rightful spirit was for the Transcendentalists a motive for their insistence upon an American expression, and the typical mode of discourse for such men as Emerson, Thoreau, and Douglass was the public speech. The question they raised—that the United States might be building a nation of words alienated from the original meanings of the New World's possibilities—remains alive to this day. For Cooper, on the other hand, it appears that the issue had been decided. From this standpoint, *The Pioneers* seems to be an act of imaginative resignation or stubborn retrieval, a commemoration that is more tomb than temple.

JEAN FAGAN YELLIN

Hawthorne and the American National Sin

Slavery in all its forms, whether in the overworked
Irish girl or the brutalized farmer or the Negro, dis-
quieted . . . [Thoreau]. He had been beset with the
problem of slavery from the time of the Mexican
war—and even earlier if one recalls that his home was
a hotbed of abolitionism—and it had been increasingly
distracting him, until in the Anthony Burns affair the
slavery of Massachusetts itself became unbearable.
His native soil, in which he hoped to plant the seeds
of virtue, had flowered with the rank weeds of
injustice.
                                    —*The Shores of America*

Beguiled perhaps by his brilliant self-portrayal of the artist as politically disengaged, Nathaniel Hawthorne's critics generally have
not examined his failure to participate in the effort to end chattel
slavery. They apparently have assumed that he, unlike his Concord
neighbors Emerson and Thoreau, was largely unaware of the great
moral struggle going on all around him.[1] Yet there is considerable

1. Among critics who have recently examined parallel issues, particularly inter-
esting, in addition to those cited later, are Milton R. Stern, "Conservative After
Heaven's Own Fashion," in Joseph Waldmeier (ed.), *Essays in Honor of Russel B.
Nye* (East Lansing, Mich., 1978), 195–225; and Sacvan Bercovitch, *The American
Jeremiad* (Madison, Wis., 1978).

evidence to the contrary. In the years before he wrote the great romances, Hawthorne became intimately acquainted with the essential facts of chattel slavery, as well as with the debate raging around it. I intend here to establish that he possessed this knowledge, then to explore why it fails to show itself in the great romances, where it might naturally be expected to illustrate their major theme of psychological bondage.

Hawthorne's Notebooks yield a consistent, if partial, record showing his awareness of the issue of black slavery. In his earliest journal (1836–1837), we find: "In an old London newspaper, 1678, there is an advertisement, among other goods at auction of a Black girl of about 15 years old, to be sold."[2] We cannot know why he chose to note this seventeenth-century item from the English press and to ignore a similar American notice from an eighteenth-century issue of the Salem *Gazette*, which he had read in Joseph Felt's *Annals*, a local history: "To be sold . . . a likely, strong and remarkably healthy negro girl, between 11 and 12 years of age; is well acquainted with the business of a family, can knit, spin and sew, etc."[3] Another journal entry, made at Litchfield in 1838, however, testifies to Hawthorne's consciousness of the history of slavery and racial segregation in *New* England. "In a remote part of the graveyard—remote from the main body of dead people—I noticed a humble, mossy stone, on which I traced out—'To the memory of Julia Africa, servant of Rev.' somebody. There were the half-

2. Nathaniel Hawthorne, *The American Notebooks*, ed. Claude M. Simpson (Columbus, Ohio, 1972), 21, vol. VIII of *The Centenary Edition of the Works of Nathaniel Hawthorne*, ed. William Charvat, Roy Harvey Pearce, and Claude M. Simpson, 18 vols. to date. This text is identical in *Hawthorne's Lost Notebook, 1835–41*, transcribed by Barbara S. Mouffe (University Park, Pa., 1978), 28. Unless otherwise noted, references to Hawthorne's writings are to the *Centenary Edition*. I am grateful to the National Endowment for the Humanities for a summer research fellowship that enabled me to work on Hawthorne; to Neal Smith, Executive Director of the Hawthorne Project at Ohio State University; to my colleagues Frederick C. Stern, Roger B. Stein, Gloria Oden, and Rita Gollin for commenting on early versions of this paper; and to Daniel Peck for his indefatigable editing. For biographical information, I have relied on standard works, including Robert Cantwell, *Nathaniel Hawthorne: The American Years* (New York, 1948); James R. Mellow, *Nathaniel Hawthorne in His Times* (Boston, 1980); and Louise Hall Tharp, *The Peabody Sisters of Salem* (Boston, 1950).

3. Joseph B. Felt, *Annals of Salem* (Salem, 1827), 416.

obliterated traces of other graves, without any monuments, in the vicinity of this one. Doubtless the slaves here mingled their dark clay with the earth."[4]

Hawthorne's Salem, like many New England seaports, had fed on slavery. Felt reports on local ships directly engaged in the "Guinea" slave trade in 1773, 1785, 1787, and 1792. In the wake of Jay's treaty curtailing East Indian shipping, a far greater number were involved in the larger "triangular trade" that exchanged New England rum for African slaves and, in turn, slaves for West Indian sugar. In the smaller "triangular trade," they sold New England rum for West Indian slaves and molasses, then sold the slaves in Charleston and other southern ports and carried the molasses back home. Whatever booty Hawthorne's acclaimed privateer forebear, the "bold" Daniel Hathorn, plundered on the high seas remains a mystery, but records show that Hawthorne's father Captain Daniel was briefly involved in the West Indian trade before Hawthorne's birth. Although there is no evidence to suggest that he carried slaves, everyone in the West Indian trade, like everyone in Hawthorne's Salem, understood that the slave trade was a fact of international commerce. Felt writes that at least some of Hawthorne's fellow citizens were as ashamed of Salem's historic involvement in the Guinea trade as they were of Salem's historic involvement in the persecution of "witches."[5]

Like most New England towns, nineteenth-century Salem was home to blacks as well as whites. They had lived there since the first Africans were imported in 1638. A hundred years later, black slavery was still practiced; it is not clear precisely when the com-

4. Between September 9 and 24, 1838, *American Notebooks*, 150. Approximately fifteen years later, when Hawthorne went through the old Gosport church records, among the items he copied without comment were the baptismal records of two black infants (*American Notebooks*, 550).

5. Vernon Loggins, *The Hawthornes: The Story of Seven Generations of an American Family* (New York, 1951), 197–98. Although Captain Daniel was homeward bound from the East Indies when his son was born, the following year he sailed the *Neptune* from Trinidad with a cargo that included slave-produced molasses and sugar. And in 1807 he sailed to French Guiana, where he traded for molasses, cocoa, and cotton (see Loggins, *The Hawthornes*, 203–205). For trade in the years before 1816, see James D. Phillips, *Salem and the Indies* (Boston, 1977). Felt, *Annals of Salem*, 265, 288–89, 291, 296.

munity was established that local historian William Bentley characterized in Hawthorne's youth as "our black town."[6]

Hawthorne mentions the black residents of Salem in "Old News" (1835), an early sketch that describes them as contributing "their dark shade to the picture of society." To his readers, they perhaps served to identify the scene as American in much the same way that the inclusion within a single canvas of representatives of the three races—red, black, and white—identified as American the paintings by Hawthorne's contemporaries.[7]

"Old News," however, presents peculiarly contradictory views of blacks. Hawthorne writes, "[T]he slaves, we suspect, were the merriest part of the population—since it was their gift to be merry in the worst of circumstances; and they endured comparatively few hardships." This sounds very much like the classic plantation novel *Swallow Barn* (1832), in which the slavery apologist John Pendleton Kennedy had recently pictured the blacks as happy and their bondage as light.[8] But while Kennedy had avoided the brutal aspects of slavery, such as the sale of slaves, the breakup of families, and the torture of rebels, Hawthorne specifically addresses them. Commenting that "[t]here seems to have been a great trade in these human commodities," he quotes from numerous advertisements for slaves. Discussing the separation of mothers and their infants, he adopts a manner that fails both as satire and as whimsy: "When the slaves of a family were inconveniently prolific, it being not quite orthodox to drown the superfluous offspring, like a litter of kittens, notice was promulgated of 'a negro child to be given away.'" Later, mentioning that blacks rebelled by escaping and that their masters tried to catch them, he remarks on a repeated run-

6. William Bentley, *Diary* (4 vols.; Gloucester, 1962), quoted in "A Brief History of the Negro in Salem, Prepared for the Salem Committee on Racial Understanding, 1969" (Typescript at the Essex Institute, Salem, Mass.), 1. I am grateful to the Essex Institute for this source.

7. "Old News" first appeared in *New-England Magazine*, I–III (February-May, 1835); it was collected into *The Snow-Image* (*Centenary Edition*, XI, 132–60; quotation on 134). See, for example, John Lewis Krimmel's *View of Centre Square, on the 4th of July* at the Historical Society of Pennsylvania.

8. "Old News," 138. See my *Intricate Knot: Black Figures in American Literature, 1776–1863* (New York, 1972), Chap. 4.

away who "carried with him an iron collar rivetted around his neck, with a chain attached."[9]

Although he touches on the violence of slavery that was routinely omitted from plantation fiction, however, Hawthorne does not urge his readers to act to end human bondage, as the abolitionists were doing with similar accounts. Instead, "Old News"—though published four years after Nat Turner had jolted Americans into an awareness that servile insurrection could occur in this country—ignores the danger of armed conflict over slavery and proposes a peaceful accommodation to it. Hawthorne writes that the fugitives would have done better not to attempt escape but to submit to their condition, "performing their moderate share of the labors of life, without being harassed by its cares." Asserting that the whites included their slaves among the family circle, Hawthorne in his final comment echoes contemporary proslavery accounts, such as *Swallow Barn*, in claiming that the masters' kindness "modified and softened the institution, making it a patriarchal, and almost a beautiful, peculiarity of the times."[10]

By Hawthorne's day, all the black residents of Salem were free, though a number of them had been held as chattel. The presence of this free black population was not as dramatic as the slave trade or domestic slavery had been, but Salem felt it. When Hawthorne was born at the beginning of the nineteenth century, little more than three hundred of Salem's approximately ten thousand residents were nonwhite; by 1840, the white population had grown half again as large while the black population stayed approximately the same. Although small, this black community was stable. During Hawthorne's childhood, black Salem organized and formed an Af-

9. "Old News," 139; note in first publication in *New-England Magazine* (*Centenary Edition*, XI, 467). In *Grandfather's Chair* (1841), Hawthorne wrote, "As for the little negro babies, they were offered to be given away like young kittens" (*True Stories: Writings for Children*, VI, 109). Hawthorne again registered awareness of black slavery in the colonial period in his letter to Sophia of September 16, 1841, in *The Letters, 1813–1843*, ed. Thomas Woodson, L. Neal Smith, and Norman Holmes Pearson, XV, 573.

10. "Old News," 139.

rican Society. By the time he returned home from college, Salem, like Boston, was enmeshed in a series of controversies. The black population, which included the Remonds, a prominent abolitionist family, was asserting its political rights and protesting against segregation in schools, churches, and burial grounds.

Then in 1830, local race relations were strained by the sensational murder of Captain White. Because he had made his fortune in the slave trade, at first it was thought that the captain had been killed by a vengeful black. (Ultimately, the Crowninshields, Hawthorne's distant cousins, were convicted of the crime.) That year, racial tensions surfaced when white Salemites opposed the efforts of their black neighbors to enroll their daughters in the new girls' high school. There were more protests in 1834, when blacks again tried to attend the school. The blacks persisted, however, and finally, in 1843, Salem schools were desegregated.[11]

Although essentially conservative, the town had its share of controversy over abolition. Many local antislavery activists were women. Black Salem women were the first in the nation to create a female antislavery society. Later reorganized to include both blacks and whites, this group sent delegations, some of them interracial, to all three conventions of American Women Against Slavery. In 1835, anti-abolitionist whites protested against the appearance of a prominent abolitionist lecturer by mobbing an antislavery meeting at Howard Street Church. Two years later, however, local abolitionist women scheduled four full days of activities featuring the Grimké sisters, southern aristocrats who had embraced William Lloyd Garrison's doctrine of immediate emancipation. The Grimkés' historic speaking tour made them notorious for defying the ta-

11. For black Salem, see Felt, *Annals of Salem;* Bentley, *Diary;* Lorenzo J. Greene, *The Negro in Colonial New England* (New York, 1942); Dorothy B. Porter, "The Remonds of Salem, Massachusetts," American Antiquarian Society, *Proceedings,* XCV, Pt. 2 (October, 1985), 259–95; Porter, "Sarah Parker Remond, Abolitionist and Physician," *Journal of Negro History,* XX (July, 1935), 287–93; Ruth Bogin, "Sarah Parker Remond: Black Abolitionist From Salem," *Essex Institute Historical Collections,* CX (April, 1974), 120–50; and Gloria C. Oden, "*The Journal of Charlotte L. Forten:* The Salem-Philadelphia Years (1851–1862) Reexamined," *Essex Institute Historical Collections,* CXIV (April, 1983), 119–36. See also Zilpha Elaw, *Memoirs . . .* (1846), reprinted as *Sisters of the Spirit,* ed. William L. Andrews (Bloomington, Ind., 1986); and Loggins, *The Hawthornes,* 244.

boos against women addressing "promiscuous" audiences of both sexes. In Salem, they spoke at the Friends' Meeting House, met with "colored members of the Seaman's and Moral Reform Society," addressed an audience of more than a thousand at the Howard Street Meeting House, and talked with children and adults at the "colored Sabbath School."[12]

Sophia Peabody, the townswoman Hawthorne would marry, did not involve herself in the female antislavery movement in Salem, or elsewhere. She later expressed her growing antipathy toward abolitionist women and their efforts when, married and pregnant, she wrote to her mother from nearby Concord about her arrangements for an inexpensive layette. "The ladies of the antislavery society take sewing in Concord and do it very cheaply. So I shall employ them, for I have no manner of scruple about making them take as little pay as possible; while I could not think of not giving full and ample price to a poor person, or a seamstress by profession."[13]

Like other white Americans of his place and time, Hawthorne interacted with Afro-Americans all his life. Although his casual childhood encounters with the residents of "Little Guinea" or "New Africa" at the Salem end of the turnpike have not been documented, we do know that William Symmes, his friend during the carefree boyhood summers spent in Maine, was black. Further, we know that John Russwurm, who later founded the first Afro-American newspaper, *Freedom's Journal*, was among Hawthorne's fellow students at Bowdoin. Another Bowdoin man later recalled walking with Hawthorne to Russwurm's room outside the village, remarking that their black fellow student had not returned their

12. Although well-documented in the holdings of the Essex Institute, the history of the Salem, Massachusetts, Female Anti-Slavery Society has not been written. See *Liberator* (Boston), January 7, and November 17, 1832; Angelina Grimké to Jane Smith, July 16, 1837, in Grimké-Weld Papers, Clements Memorial Library, University of Michigan, Ann Arbor; and *Proceedings of the Anti-slavery Convention of American Women* (New York, 1837; Philadelphia, 1838 and 1839).

13. Sophia Peabody Hawthorne to her mother, Mrs. Elizabeth P. Peabody, November 15, 1843. Unless otherwise stated, quoted passages from Sophia Peabody Hawthorne's correspondence are from The Henry W. and Albert A. Berg Collection, The New York Public Library, Astor, Lenox and Tilden Foundations, and are used by permission.

visits because of "his sensitiveness on account of his color." Hawthorne later documented his own "sensitiveness on account of . . . color" when, at Brook Farm (which, unlike the Shaker settlements, had no black members), he wrote that a child had an "almost mulatto complexion." In this same Notebook entry, he also attests to his awareness of racial stereotyping—and to the associationists' participation in it—by describing a masquerader who disguised himself as "a negro of the Jim Crow order."[14]

Later, at the Old Manse, Sophia Peabody Hawthorne commented to her mother that she was thinking of hiring as a domestic a mature black woman Mrs. Peabody had mentioned to her. Referring to her former maid, a fresh-faced young Irish woman whom she apparently believed dishonest, she writes, "My husband says he does not want me to undertake to keep anybody who is apparently innocent, after my late sore experience. He says the old black lady is probably as bad already as she ever will be. If you find the blackey not disinclined to come to such poor folks, I will take her in September." Whether this black woman joined the Hawthornes at Concord, I do not know. But when they moved to Lenox after publication of *The Scarlet Letter*, they hired the Afro-American Mrs. Peters as a domestic.[15]

Hawthorne acknowledges her presence in his 1851 journal, which records his brief experience caring for his young son while his wife was away. These entries indicate that in addition to doing the cooking and cleaning and serving unexpected guests, Mrs. Peters had considerable responsibility for little Julian. Although she was feeding and dressing his son, however, Hawthorne ignores the black woman and instead names the child's pet in the title of his journal entry: "Twenty Days with Julian and Little Bunny by Papa."

Hawthorne generally showed little interest in servants, and he

14. For Symmes, see Mellow, *Nathaniel Hawthorne in His Times*, 104–105 n20; for Russwurm, see Horatio Bridge, *Personal Recollections of Nathaniel Hawthorne* (New York, 1893), 30; for black Shakers, see *Gifts of Power: The Writings of Rebecca Jackson*, ed. Jean McMahon Hunez (Amherst, 1981). Hawthorne's comment is in *American Notebooks*, 202, 203. For another reference to skin color in relation to race, see the May 8, [1850], entry, 503.

15. Sophia Peabody Hawthorne to Mrs. Peabody, August 20, [1844], in Rose Hawthorne Lathrop, *Memories of Hawthorne* (Boston, 1897; rpr. New York, 1969), 74; also see *Letters*, XVI, 64.

certainly was not interested in Mrs. Peters. His fullest comment, which describes her exchanges with little Julian, sketches a distanced relationship that follows established patterns of racial etiquette. Even though it defies convention by not using her first name, this passage suggests that Mrs. Peters was careful to adhere to accepted patterns even in her dealings with her employers' child: "Mrs. Peters is quite attentive to him, in her grim way. Today, for instance, we found two ribbons on his old straw hat, which must have been of her sewing on. She encourages no familiarity on his part, nor is he in the least drawn towards her, nor, on the other hand, does he exactly seem to stand in awe; but he recognizes that there is to be no communication beyond the inevitable—and, with that understanding, she awards him all substantial kindness."[16]

Mrs. Peters had evidently taken the job with the Hawthornes as a favor, and the following winter she wanted to quit. Only after Sophia promised to teach her to read did she agree to stay on until after the birth of their third child. Many years later, the Hawthornes' daughter Rose recalled Mrs. Peters as "an invaluable tyrant, an unloaded weapon, a creature who seemed to say, 'Forget my qualities if you dare—there is one of them which is fatal!'" The force of her extraordinary comment suggests to me that Mrs. Peters may have embodied the repressed fury that has fueled much of Afro-American literature. Even after achieving literacy, however, she apparently left no record of her responses to America's writer of moral romances. This—like Hawthorne's failure to explore and to render the distancing and "grim" intensity that he sensed in the black woman—is a loss to our national letters.[17]

Routine exchanges with black New Englanders such as Mrs. Peters—and Prince Farmer, a Salem Democrat and restaurateur whose oysters Hawthorne relished—did not, of course, provide him with information about the slave trade or chattel slavery.[18] But through other sources he became extremely knowledgeable about slave life

16. *American Notebooks*, 462–63.
17. Lathrop, *Memories of Hawthorne*, 161; Tharp, *The Peabody Sisters of Salem*, 196.
18. *Letters*, XVI, 415; Porter, "The Remonds of Salem," 264.

in Cuba, about international efforts to police the outlawed African trade, and about the efforts to colonize Afro-Americans in Liberia.

In 1837, on his first visits to the Peabody house, Hawthorne was shown the Cuba Journals. These were letters written home to Salem by Sophia Peabody, who had gone to Cuba for her health, and by her sister Mary, who accompanied her. During their year-and-a-half residence on a sugar plantation (from 1833 to 1835), the young women recorded impressions of slavery. They commented on the overwhelming black presence, the picturesqueness of the Africans at play, and the oppressiveness of slave labor. They cited evidence of the brutality of the system—a coffle of chained Africans on a road, fiercely trained dogs, and "one poor negro . . . actually bitten to death." They wrote about the sexual exploitation of slave women, noting a slaveholder's double families, one legitimate, free and white, the other illegitimate, slave and black. And they discussed the practice of infanticide—the death of twenty or thirty infants on the plantation where they were staying had resulted in brutal punishment for the slave mothers whose babies died. In the Cuba Journals, Hawthorne was confronted with information as shocking as the exposés appearing each week in Garrison's *Liberator*.[19]

A decade after reading these firsthand descriptions of Cuban slavery, Hawthorne edited an eyewitness narrative describing international efforts to suppress the African slave trade and detailing conditions in Liberia (recently established as a "homeland" for American slaves expatriated by the American Colonization Society). This was the *Journal of an African Cruiser*, written at Hawthorne's suggestion by his lifelong friend Horatio Bridge.[20]

Hawthorne was trying hard to win a federal appointment in the early 1840s. Pointing out the *Journal*'s implicit endorsement of the Colonization Society's efforts to send Afro-Americans "back to Af-

19. Cuba Journal, I (Sophia Peabody letters, December 20, [1833]–July 2, [1834], Mary Peabody letters, January 8–May 31, 1834), Sophia Peabody, January 17 and June 19, 1834, Mary Peabody, March 25 and May 12, 1834, all in Berg Collection. The quotation is from Mary Peabody to Mrs. Elizabeth Palmer Peabody, February 8, 1834.

20. [Horatio Bridge], *Journal of an African Cruiser: Comprising Sketches of the Canaries . . . and Other Places on the West Coast of Africa. By an Officer of the United States Navy*, ed. Nathaniel Hawthorne (1845; rpr. London, 1968).

rica," critic Patrick Brancaccio has speculated that Hawthorne used the book to advance himself with procolonizationist Democrats. This seems to me entirely likely. In its praise for colonization, the *Journal* is completely in accord with Hawthorne's later campaign biography of Pierce. In this biography, Hawthorne's rejection of abolitionist activism against chattel slavery echoes both in meter and in matter the rejection of activism against sexual oppression that he would voice at the end of *The Scarlet Letter*. A wise man, he proposes in the biography, might view "slavery as one of those evils which divine Providence does not leave to be remedied by human contrivances, but which, in its own good time, by some means impossible to be anticipated, but of the simplest and easiest operation, when all its uses shall have been fulfilled, it causes to vanish like a dream."[21]

After winning the Custom House job, he of course became even better informed. As surveyor, in 1846 and again in 1847 he complained to his superiors about the inaccuracy of the hydrometer used to test the proof of export liquor. Ellery Channing, who visited the Custom House during this period, recalled Hawthorne measuring the strength of a consignment of rum and boasting, " 'I am determined the niggers shall have as good liquor as anyone gets from New England.' "[22] This statement establishes Hawthorne's awareness that the rum was destined for Africa and shows that he felt it his moral responsibility to guarantee its purchaser a fair measure. But it also shows him avoiding the larger moral question of what commodities the rum would be traded for. Ivory? Slaves, called "black ivory"?

It was not necessary to work in the Custom House or to read firsthand accounts of Liberia or Cuba, however, to be informed about African slavery during the years of Hawthorne's literary appren-

21. Patrick Brancaccio, " 'The Black Man's Paradise': Hawthorne's Editing of the *Journal of an African Cruiser*," *New England Quarterly*, LIII (1980), 23–41; *Letters*, XV, 683, XVI, 82, 113–14, 126–27, 195; Nathaniel Hawthorne, *Life of Franklin Pierce* (Boston, 1883), 416–17, vol. XII of *Complete Works*, ed. George Lathrop, 12 vols.

22. *Letters*, XVI, 176, 203; Frederick T. McGill, *Channing of Concord* (New Brunswick, N.J., 1967), 103; Mellow, *Nathaniel Hawthorne in His Times*, 630.

ticeship. The controversy over abolition brought the issue home to New England. Along with everyone else, Hawthorne and Sophia were aware, for example, of the mobbing of the Boston Female Anti-Slavery Society in 1835. The Boston women, like the Salem reformers subjected to violence that year, had announced that the British abolitionist George Thompson would address their public meeting. In response, Boston merchants, spurred by anti-British feeling and eager to demonstrate their allegiance to their southern business partners, promoted a riot. Despite this threat, the mayor refused police protection, and the mobbed women evacuated their besieged building, walking out through the crowds in racially integrated pairs. Rioters seized Garrison and had a rope around his neck before he was rescued and taken into protective custody.[23]

Like most Boston publications, the *American Monthly Magazine* denounced the abolitionists, not the mob. Under the headline "Reported Riot in Boston," it asserted that the reformers had organized the meeting "as if to court danger and persecution." Although claiming to deplore public violence, the magazine declared that the abolitionists' "incendiary and revolutionary doctrine" should not be tolerated and warned that if the abolitionists "are so mad and so regardless as to continue . . . they at least cannot complain of any harsh treatment." Hawthorne edited the *American Monthly* the following year. In what may have been another comment on the riot, he printed a piece entitled "Mobs" that he took from another publication. The article states that though "the public opinion in America is law," mobs are not a natural outgrowth of America's democratic institutions, and it blandly expresses confidence that enlightened public opinion will end public disorders.[24]

The violence was viewed differently by abolitionists. Although never one of them, Sophia Peabody was, before marrying Hawthorne, part of a Boston circle that included Maria White, who converted her fiancé James Russell Lowell to abolitionism, and the Sturgis sisters, members, as was White, of the Female Anti-Slavery

23. See Wendell P. Garrison and Francis J. Garrison, *William Lloyd Garrison: The Story of His Life Told By His Children* (4 vols.; 1885; New York, 1969), II, 1–30; Boston Female Anti-Slavery Society, *Right and Wrong in Boston* (Boston, 1836).
24. *American Monthly Magazine*, II (1835), 164, II (1836), 505–506.

Society. To them—and to Sophia's circle at Concord, which included the Alcotts and Lidian Emerson, members of the local Society—the mobbed women were martyrs. British writer Harriet Martineau, who had met the reformers in Boston, would use this term to describe them in the *London and Westminster Review*. Soon after the riot, she cut short her American excursion, in the wake of newspaper attacks on her endorsement of the women's antislavery principles.[25]

New England sensibilities were again aroused more than a dozen years later by the seizure of two young black women taken when officers of the schooner *Pearl* were caught transporting a group of fugitive slaves to freedom. To raise money for the sisters' manumission, Henry Ward Beecher staged a mock slave auction—permitting the congregation to experience the joys of beneficence by helping emancipate slaves while simultaneously experiencing the delights of sin by bidding for females exposed on the block. Captain Edward Sayers and mate Daniel Drayton were convicted after a trial that was widely reported in the press. Sentenced to heavy fines that they could not pay, the men spent four years in jail before being pardoned.[26]

Both of these sensational events personally involved members of Sophia Peabody Hawthorne's family. Hawthorne's future sister-in-law Elizabeth Palmer Peabody had been a guest in the house where Martineau was staying and had burned the Boston newspapers to spare the Englishwoman the embarrassment of reading their attacks. Martineau later wrote that Peabody had begged her to modify her antislavery statements in order to retrieve at least a degree of respectability. When she refused, her American tour collapsed. In the case of the *Pearl*, it was Hawthorne's brother-in-law Horace Mann, the antislavery congressman married to Sophia's sister

25. Sophia Peabody to Dr. Nathaniel Peabody, February 9, 1838, in Berg Collection; Harriet Martineau, "The Martyr Age," *London and Westminster Review* (December, 1838), 43; *The Autobiography of Harriet Martineau*, ed. Maria W. Chapman (3 vols.; London, 1877), I, 347–57.

26. Daniel Drayton later spoke for the abolitionists and published an account of his ordeal in *Personal Memoirs* (Boston, 1855). *Key to Uncle Tom's Cabin* (1853; New York, 1968), 306–30; William C. Beecher and Rev. Samuel Scoville, *A Biography of Henry Ward Beecher* (New York, 1888), 292–300; William G. McLaughlen, *The Meaning of Henry Ward Beecher* (New York, 1970), 200–201.

Mary, who defended Sayers and Drayton in court. As a literate New Englander, Hawthorne was doubtless aware of these highly publicized incidents; as Sophia Peabody's husband, he had direct knowledge of them.[27]

In his Notebooks written between 1842 and 1845, Hawthorne reveals that he considered using the problem of slavery as a literary subject.[28] The references to this theme testify to his fascination with the attempt to manipulate and enslave another morally and psychologically.

To point out the moral slavery of one who deems himself a free man.

A moral philosopher to buy a slave, or otherwise get possession of a human being, and use him for the sake of experiment, by trying the operation of a certain vice on him.

Sketch of a person who, by strength of character, or assistant circumstances, has reduced another to absolute slavery and dependence on him. Then show, that the person who appears to be the master, must inevitably be at least as much a slave, if not more, than the other. All slavery is reciprocal, on the supposition most favorable to the rulers.[29]

Although the origins of Hawthorne's major works are present in these jottings, any recognition of a link between this metaphorical slavery and the literal enslavement of blacks is conspicuously absent. And this, despite analyses of the psychology of slavery by abolitionists like the fugitive slave William Wells Brown. Speaking

27. *The Autobiography of Harriet Martineau,* II, 33–35; Louise Tharp, *Until Victory: Horace Mann and Mary Peabody Mann* (Boston, 1953), 224–34; Jonathan Messerli, *Horace Mann* (New York, 1972).

28. During these early years, Hawthorne testified to the abolitionists' success in establishing their rhetoric as the common discourse of oppression by adopting their language to discuss his own situation. Complaining to Sophia Peabody about his job at the Boston Custom House, he wrote that her "husband" felt "the iron of his chain"; after quitting, he exulted, "I have broken my chain and escaped." Later, planning to leave Brook Farm, he wrote that he was looking forward to being "free from this bondage. . . . Even my Custom House experience was not such a thraldom and weariness; my mind and heart were freer!" (Hawthorne to Sophia, March 26, 1840, to H. W. Longfellow, October 12, 1840, and to Sophia, August 12, 1841, all in *Letters,* XV, 428, 497, 557). Also see Nathaniel Hawthorne to Sophia Peabody, August 22, 1841, XV, 562.

29. Between June 1, 1842, and July 27, 1844, *American Notebooks,* 236, 237; between July 27, 1844, and March 15, 1845, *ibid.,* 253.

before the Salem Female Anti-Slavery Society in 1847, Brown denounced American slavery as a system organized "for the purpose of obliterating the mind, of crushing the intellect, and of annihilating the soul."[30]

Years earlier, in Cuba, Sophia Peabody had articulated her conscious decision not to think about African slavery: "I do not allow myself to dwell upon slavery for two reasons. One is, it would certainly counteract the beneficent influences, which I have left home and country to court, and another is, that my faith in God makes me sure that he makes up to every being the measure of happiness which he loses thro' the instrumentality of others. I try to realize how much shorter time is, than eternity and then endeavour to lose myself in other subjects of thought."[31] And like Sophia Peabody in Cuba, Hawthorne, it appears, deliberately avoided thinking about black slavery in antebellum America. In his major writings, he characteristically defines as sinful the effort of one human being to usurp the will of another. He dramatizes this, not by focusing on an individual madman (as Poe did), but by locating characters within a social context that is inevitably oppressive. Yet again and again, he distances this drama in time and in space, instead of connecting it to the context with which every New Englander of his generation would unavoidably have associated it: American chattel slavery.

One reason for this conspicuous omission may be that though he was well acquainted with the reformers, Hawthorne did not like them much. A journal entry written years before his brief involvement with Brook Farm testifies to his lack of sympathy for them and for their reforms, and demonstrates his failure to distinguish among their causes. "A sketch to be given of a modern reformer—a type of the extreme doctrines on the subject of slaves, cold-water, and all that. He goes about the street haranguing most eloquently,

30. William Wells Brown, *Narrative . . . and a Lecture Delivered before the Female Anti-Slavery Society of Salem, 1847* (Reading, Mass., 1969), 82.

31. Cuba Journal, I (Sophia Peabody letters, December 20, [1833]—July 2, [1834], Mary Peabody letters, January 8–May 31, 1834), Sophia Peabody to Mrs. Elizabeth Palmer Peabody, March 21, [1834], the Berg Collection.

and is on the point of making many converts, when his labors are suddenly interrupted by the appearance of a keeper of a mad-house, where he has escaped. Much may be made of this idea."[32]

Hawthorne included critical presentations of reformers in more than a half-dozen of the short pieces published after he left the farm. The fullest condemnation is in "Earth's Holocaust," which presents a vision of ultimate destruction not uncommon in a period of social change like Hawthorne's (and our own).[33] In this sketch, the final conflagration is fueled, not by an accident or by oppressors desperate to maintain power, but by reformers who move from attacking social corruption to attacking society's most valuable institutions and achievements.

Hawthorne returned to this theme in works as diverse as "The Birth Mark" and *The Blithedale Romance.* He in fact never moved beyond it, never changed his view that reforms are ineffective and reformers are dangerous.[34] His consistent criticism is that they suffer from a false vision of the world. In an early sketch, his narrator asserts that reformers must "cease to look through pictured windows," must cease mistaking their distorted illumination for "the whitest sunshine." More than a dozen years later, he used this same figure of speech in writing to Elizabeth Palmer Peabody. "I do assure you that like every other Abolitionist, you look at matters with an awful squint, which distorts everything within your line of vision; and it is queer, though natural, that you think everybody squints except yourselves. Perhaps they do; but certainly you do."[35]

This correspondence documents Hawthorne's hostility toward abolitionism (and toward Peabody), as well as his proprietary atti-

32. For 1835, *American Notebooks,* 10. For an 1838 entry hostile to reformers, see p. 136.

33. See, for example, the following, all published between covers in *Mosses From an Old Manse* (1846): "The Hall of Fantasy," *Pioneer* (February, 1843); "The New Adam and Eve," *Democratic Review* (February, 1843); "The Procession of Life," *Democratic Review* (April, 1843); "The Celestial Rail-road," *Democratic Review* (May, 1843); "The Christmas Banquet," *Democratic Review* (January, 1844); "The Intelligence Office," *Democratic Review* (March, 1844); "Earth's Holocaust," *Graham's Magazine* (May, 1844); "A Select Party," *Democratic Review* (July, 1844); "The Old Manse" (1846).

34. See "Chiefly About War Matters," *Atlantic Monthly* (July, 1862), in vol. XII of *Complete Works,* ed. Lathrop, 229–345.

35. Hawthorne to Elizabeth Peabody, August 13, 1857, in *Letters,* XVIII, 89.

tude toward his wife. Reading it, we learn that after Peabody sent her younger sister Sophia an antislavery pamphlet that she had written, Hawthorne returned the manuscript to her, commenting, "I do not choose to bother Sophia with it, and yet should think it a pity to burn so much of your thought and feeling. . . . [T]o tell you the truth, I have read only the first line or two." When Peabody mailed the manuscript back to her sister, Hawthorne again responded. He writes that he has now read her pamphlet: "Upon my word, it is not very good; not worthy of being sent three times across the ocean; not so good as I supposed you would always write, on a subject on which your mind and heart were interested." He then concedes, "However, since you make a point of it, I will give it to Sophia, and will tell her all about its rejection and return."[36]

Earlier, in the Berkshires, Hawthorne had contemptuously dismissed the abolitionist press, commenting that since he had not seen "a single newspaper (except an anti-slavery paper) . . . I know no more of what is going on than if I had migrated to the moon." It has been assumed that, during his years abroad, he was unaware of the heightening struggle over abolition. But correspondence testifies that Peabody persisted in her efforts to enlighten the Hawthornes about the slavery controversy. Just as Nathaniel had initially censored her correspondence to Sophia, in 1860 Sophia announced that she would not permit their daughter to read Peabody's letter. Claiming that she can tolerate her sister's antislavery comments, though she will not allow Peabody to inflict them on Una, Sophia asserts that both she and Hawthorne are conversant with the reformers' attacks on American slavery: "[A]s you wrote once that I probably never heard anything that was going on in America, even from newspapers, I told [Una] when she wrote you to tell you that we saw the most liberal newspapers all the time. But we do not allow the children to read newspapers."[37]

If a distaste for the reformers and their tactics perhaps made it

36. Hawthorne to Elizabeth Peabody, August 13 and October 8, 1857, both in *Letters*, XVIII, 89, 115.
37. Hawthorne to Burchmore, June 9, 1850, in *Letters*, XVI, 340; Sophia Peabody Hawthorne to Elizabeth Palmer Peabody, [spring, 1860], quoted in Tharp, *The Peabody Sisters of Salem*, 288, and in Lathrop, *Memories of Hawthorne*, 358.

difficult for Hawthorne to connect the slavery question to his concern with psychological bondage, his racial attitudes perhaps made
it impossible. A clue to these attitudes can be found in his discussion of a racist incident that occurred during an 1838 trip to western Massachusetts. He writes that "some of the blacks were
knocked down and otherwise maltreated," and then describes three
Afro-American men. One is "a genuine specimen of the slave-
negro, a queer thing of mere feeling, with some glimmerings of
sense." A second, who had spoken of "the rights of his race," when
confronted by "a half drunken [white] fellow," suddenly assumed
the role of a clown. The third was drunk. After noting the complex
reactions of one of a group of "well dressed and decent negro
wenches" who encounters this "disgrace to her color," Hawthorne
records his own response. Although the woman's face had expressed "scorn, and shame, and sorrow, and painful sympathy" for
the drunken man, Hawthorne does not share her reactions to the
man's presence, nor does he feel any "painful sympathy" for her.
On the contrary. "I was," he writes, "amused." He then adds, "On
the whole, I find myself rather more of an abolitionist in feeling
than in principle."[38] What are we to make of this self-analysis? Is
he saying that unlike abolitionist "principle," abolitionist "feeling"
may find black degradation amusing? This entry acknowledges
that, despite a lifetime of casual contacts with blacks, he feels no
common humanity either with the drunken black man or with the
"decent" black woman.

A subsequent notation at first appears more sympathetic. Watching a black man who, except for his color, is unexceptional among
the travelers at a tavern, Hawthorne hears a white man comment,
"'I wish I had a thousand such fellows in Alabama.'" Again, Haw-

38. August 15, 1838, *American Notebooks*, 111–12. While editing the *American
Monthly Magazine*, he had included three pieces concerning black skin color. "Effect of Colour on Heat" reports the speculation in a recent issue of a London journal
about the effect of climate on skin color, and discusses Africans' adaptation to heat
by means of "insensible perspersation." It also asserts that this "insensible perspera-
tion" causes "the peculiar odour of the coloured race." A follow-up, "Effect of
Colour on Odours," suggests that "negroes . . . suffer more in proportion to their
numbers, than whites, by all sorts of pestilence and unwholesome smells." "Pie-
Bald Negroes" is a filler describing black people with white spots on their skin.
American Monthly Magazine, II (1836), 386, 486, 511.

thorne records his response. The incident, he writes, "made a queer impression on me—the negro was really so human—and to talk of owning a thousand like him." On examination, however, this comment demonstrates that even here, Hawthorne distances himself. He fails to explore the moral implications of his response, does not begin to examine what it means to write "the negro was really so human." Does this signify that the black man was indeed human? Does it signify that, though inhuman, he was very like a man? [39]

More than a dozen years later, while editing the manuscript of *Journal of an African Cruiser,* Hawthorne responded to Bridge's report of his participation in a punitive expedition. Apparently, Bridge's commander had been meeting with a group of African chiefs to discuss the plundering of an American ship and the murder of its captain and crew, when a shot was fired. During the fight that broke out, the chief of Little Berebree and two other Africans were killed. In retaliation for the attacks on the meeting and on the ship, Bridge's commander ordered that the town of Little Berebree be burned and its population dispersed; later, he ordered four additional towns burned. Hawthorne's letter conveys concern for his friend's safety and expresses pleasure because he thinks that this incident will enliven the *Journal.* Then, recording some reservations about the validity of the American attack, he voices uncertainty about the humanity of Africans:

A civilized and educated man must feel somewhat like a fool, methinks, when he has staked his own life against that of a black savage, and lost the game. In the sight of God, one life may be as valuable as another; but in our view, the stakes are very unequal. Besides, I really do consider the shooting of these niggers a matter of very questionable propriety; and am glad, upon the whole, that you bagged no game on either of those days. It is a far better deed to beget a white fellow-creature, than to shoot even a black one. [40]

Hawthorne's language in a piece written years later, during the Civil War, demonstrates that he was still uncertain about the full humanity of blacks. Describing a group of contrabands in Virginia, he writes:

39. September 9, [1838], *American Notebooks,* 151.
40. Hawthorne to Horatio Bridge, April, 1844, in *Letters,* XVI, 26.

They were unlike the specimens of their race whom we are accustomed to see at the North, and, in my judgment, were far more agreeable. So rudely were they attired,—as if their garb had grown upon them spontaneously,— so picturesquely natural in manners, and wearing such a crust of primeval simplicity (which is quite polished away from the northern black man), that they seemed a kind of creature by themselves, not altogether human, but perhaps quite as good, and akin to the fauns and rustic deities of olden times. I wonder whether I shall excite anybody's wrath by saying this. It is no great matter.[41]

The consistency of Hawthorne's racial responses and of his failure to subject them to analysis is worth noting because he is capable of intense self-scrutiny in relation to other issues. It is also notable because it persists throughout a period when other white New Englanders were systematically examining their responses to slavery and race, making moral judgments on these issues, and acting on their judgments. In 1837, Ralph Waldo Emerson—never a Garrisonian—had speculated about the effect of the abolitionists' agitation against the slave trade.

How can such a question as the Slave Trade be agitated for forty years by the most enlightened nations of the world without throwing great light on ethics into the general mind? . . . The loathsome details of the kidnapping; of the middle passage; six hundred living bodies sit for thirty days betwixt death & life in a posture of stone & when brought on deck for air cast themselves into the sea—were those details merely produced to harrow the nerves of the susceptible & humane or for the purpose of engraving the question on the memory that it should not be dodged or obliterated & securing to it the concentration of the whole conscience of Christendom?[42]

If Emerson's efforts to confront his moral responsibility anticipate the efforts of a later generation adequately to respond to the Holocaust, Hawthorne presents a stark contrast. In 1842 he expressed astonishment at the appearance of Longfellow's *Poems on Slavery*: "I was never more surprised than at your writing poems about Slavery. . . . You have never poeticized a practical subject, hitherto." Nine years later, after the Compromise of 1850 had de-

41. "Chiefly About War Matters," 318–19. For a condemnation of Hawthorne's racism and politics in this piece, see *Liberator* (Boston), June 27, 1862, p. 102.

42. November 16, 1837, *Emerson in His Journals*, ed. Joel Porte (Cambridge, Mass., 1982), 178–79. See George M. Fredrickson, *The Inner Civil War: Northern Intellectuals and the Crisis of the Union* (New York, 1965).

stroyed the Missouri Compromise and promulgated a new fugitive slave law—and, as all around him, northern intellectuals were taking a stand on the slavery question—he wrote that he remained unsure of its moral significance: "There are a hundred modes of philanthropy in which I could blaze with intenser zeal. This Fugitive Law is the only thing that could have blown me into any respectable degree of warmth on this great subject of the day—if it really be the great subject—a point which another age can determine better than ours."[43] In Emerson's terms, he apparently never could stop dodging and obliterating.[44]

In 1863, Emerson and others condemned Hawthorne for dedicating *Our Old Home* to Franklin Pierce, whose recently published correspondence, it was charged, had encouraged Jefferson Davis to commit treason. Following Hawthorne's death, however, most seem to have decided to forgive—or to ignore—his refusal to confront slavery, the great moral issue of their day. But in an essay that Hawthorne's publisher reportedly refused to print, George W. Curtis addressed the problem. Noting that, eight years after the appearance of *Uncle Tom's Cabin*, Hawthorne could still write that it was difficult trying to conceive romances "'about a country where there is no shadow, no antiquity, no mystery, no picturesque and gloomy wrong, nor anything but a commonplace prosperity, in broad and simple daylight, as is happily the case with my dear native land,'" Curtis asked: "Is crime never romantic, then, until distance ennobles it? Or were the tragedies of Puritan life so terrible that the imagination could not help kindling, while the pangs of the plantation are superficial and commonplace?" Pressing his con-

43. Hawthorne to Longfellow, December 24, 1842, May 8, 1851, both in *Letters*, XVI, 664, XVI, 431.
44. Critic Richard Brodhead has suggested that "for Hawthorne, the political is a mode of engagement that generates plural and incompatible outlooks, each with the power, at certain moments, to compel understanding and to motivate action, and each with the power to make the others appear delusory." Again and again, he continues, Hawthorne's prose embodies a paradox: the conviction that politics are delusive, that people engage in political action for reasons they do not acknowledge for ends they do not envision; and at the same time that to be politically disengaged is to lose vitality. Brodhead also acknowledges Emerson's reluctance to entrust social reform to the reformers. See "Hawthorne and the Fate of Politics," *Essays in Literature*, XI (Spring, 1984), 95–96, 102.

demnation of Hawthorne's avoidance, Curtis continued: "That the Devil, in the form of an elderly man clad in grave and decent attire, should lead astray the saints of Salem village, two centuries ago, and confuse right and wrong in the mind of Goodman Brown, was something that excited his imagination, and produced one of his weirdest stories. But that the same Devil, clad in a sombre sophism, was confusing the sentiment of right and wrong in the mind of his own countrymen he did not even guess."[45]

Despite Hawthorne's antipathy for the reformers, however, and despite even his racism, he finally *had* guessed: not the significance of slavery and race in his own day, but their significance in the American past. In the same Civil War essay that contains his speculation about whether blacks are perhaps "not altogether human," he includes this passage:

> There is a circumstance, known to few, that connects the children of the Puritans with these Africans of Virginia in a very singular way. They are our brethren, as being lineal descendants from the Mayflower, the fated womb of which, in her first voyage, sent forth a brood of Pilgrims on Plymouth Rock, and, in a subsequent one, spawned slaves upon the Southern soil,—a monstrous birth, but with which we have an instinctive sense of kindred, and so are stirred by an irresistible impulse to attempt their rescue, even at the cost of blood and ruin. The character of our sacred ship, I fear, may suffer a little by this revelation; but we must let her white progeny offset her dark one,—and two such portents never sprang from an identical source before.[46]

Although this pregnant metaphor locates in the past the vital connections between black and white Americans, although it fails to specify the monstrous element in the second birth (was it blackness? was it slavery?), and although it envisions passive black slaves and active white rescuers who must "offset" them, it nevertheless testifies that Hawthorne finally did respond imaginatively to the centrality of race and slavery in America.

But he wrote this long after he had produced his great romances, in which any recognition of these issues is conspicuously lacking.

45. Claude M. Simpson, Introduction, *Our Old Home*, in vol. V of *Centenary Edition*, xxv–xxviii; George W. Curtis, "Nathaniel Hawthorne," *North American Review*, XCIX (October, 1864), 552.
46. "Chiefly About War Matters," 319.

The studied ambiguity of these works, usually understood as the result of deliberate artistic decisions, must also be considered as a strategy of avoidance and denial. Hawthorne, it appears, could not acknowledge the necessary engagement of politics and art, of life and letters—the engagement that Emerson demanded of his generation, and of all generations. Instead, he devised an elaborate refusal to connect the great moral problem that is his literary subject with what the Garrisonians called the "American national sin."[47]

47. For the classic essay using this phrase, see Sidney Kaplan's "Herman Melville and the American National Sin," *Journal of Negro History*, XLI (October, 1956), 31–38, XLII (January, 1957), 11–37.

HUGH J. DAWSON

The Golden Day at the Golden Doorway:

An Emerson Theme in Veblen, Sullivan,

and Dewey

Man has the power to manipulate and overcome obstacles (Dewey), the power of mind or curiosity which
implements his physical power (Dewey and Veblen),
the power of his emotions which makes him a poet,
the power of vision and dream which makes him a
prophet and interpreter, the power of spirit which
helps him diffuse and concentrate his power, and the
power of moral choice. All of these powers make man
a creator, but the teacher [of *Kindergarten Chats*] emphasizes those that have been neglected by educators:
the power of the emotions, of vision, of spirit, and of
moral choice. He wishes to broaden the student's sym-
pathies and to release the altruistic impulse which he
believes is the normal impulse of the heart.
                                    — *Louis Sullivan*

Addressing an age in thrall to the past, Emerson lamented the failure of history to communicate living truths. For him, experience
had lost its power to instruct and had devolved into mere habit.
The churches rehearsed inherited forms largely devoid of meaning,
and the schools taught the classics—which remained the staples of
education—not for their inspiration but as the revered decretals of
form. Yet Emerson, affirming that all things when rightly understood serve the good, held that the best resources for the future lay

in a study of the past that looked beyond transient conventions to the sustenance nature had, from the earliest time, always provided. Just as natural facts were richly symbolic, so myths were repositories of sublime truth. To tease out their fabulous meanings was, like Champollion's deciphering of the Rosetta Stone hieroglyphs, to enter upon lost realms of genius. Studying the primitive became a twofold enterprise. As incipient cultural anthropology—the formal discipline did not yet exist—that study appreciated the distinctness of the earliest, putatively more spiritual peoples. And, like the psychology that would emerge with Freud, it showed dimensions of the self that had been lost in the human surrender to civilization's strictures.

Throughout the second quarter of the nineteenth century, the noble savage embodied the doctrines of philosophic primitivism. Especially in New England, where the Indian had until recently been a living presence, the primitive gave writers a symbol of what lay beyond—because it had been anterior to—culture. Thoreau experienced the mystery of the primordial in the arrowheads he unearthed at Walden, and he copied into his "Indian Books" the language and pictographs of the first Americans. In his encounters with the Maine Penobscots, Joe Polis and Joe Aitteon, and the French-Canadian woodcutter Alek Therien, he discovered evidence of the native self and recognized the costs exacted by civilization. Bronson Alcott wrote of recovering in farming what to him had been lost and unknown: "I become a primeval man. I restore the age of labor."[1]

By establishing an original relation to the universe, Emerson sought to recover the primal interfusion of signs, objects, and spiritual facts. He eagerly read of Champollion's work. Important as the great Egyptologist's discovery was, it presaged far more, for it marked a further approach to that still earlier, essential self from whom Emerson in *Nature* fashioned a metaphor of the contingent human situation and its potential: "Every man's condition is a so-

---

1. *The Indians of Thoreau: Selections from the Indian Notebooks*, ed. Richard F. Fleck (Albuquerque, 1974), 67; Robert F. Sayre, *Thoreau and the American Indians* (Princeton, 1977), esp. 63–69; Joel Myerson, "Bronson Alcott's 'Scripture for 1840,'" *ESQ*, XX (1974), 247.

lution in hieroglyphic to those inquiries he would put."[2] The person or community that would recover itself needs first to penetrate to the integrity that has survived beneath the deceptions taught by civilization. So the spatial metaphor of entry into the psyche melds with the temporal myth of regression to origins in the imagined encounter with the radical self.[3]

Emerson and the others in the party of Hope he inspired have written out of their sure confidence in the imagination's restorative powers. The relationship between the part and the whole, the mirroring of the little in the large, the correspondence between the "Me" and the "Not-Me," and the reciprocity of each and all were for Emerson variations on a single theme, the recognition of the unity hidden by seeming divisions and the shifting norms of fashion. In the awakening of the human spirit, what had been mere forms would yield up long-unknown meanings. Lost harmonies would be recovered. Personal and collective regeneration would begin with the rediscovery of what Emerson called that "aboriginal Self on which a universal reliance may be grounded."[4]

By the end of the century, the formative stages of the individual and the race, the child and the primitive, had become specialized subjects of psychology and the nascent science of anthropology. The importance attaching to the new disciplines was evident in the places assigned the behavioral and social sciences at the World's Columbian Exposition. Under the auspices of the American Psychological Association, Joseph Jastrow and Hugo Münster-

2. John T. Irwin, *American Hieroglyphics: The Symbol of the Egyptian Hieroglyphics in the American Renaissance* (New Haven, 1980), 8–14; *Nature*, in *Nature, Addresses, and Lectures*, ed. Robert E. Spiller and Alfred R. Ferguson (Cambridge, Mass., 1971), 7, vol. I of *The Collected Works of Ralph Waldo Emerson*, 4 vols. to date.

3. One recalls the photographs of Freud musing upon his Berggasse collection of ancient artifacts, probing their great mysteries, his expression testimony to his reverence for the primitive. In *Totem and Taboo*, Freud writes: "The interpretation of dreams is completely analogous to the decipherment of an ancient pictographic script such as Egyptian hieroglyphs. . . . The ambiguity of various elements of dreams finds a parallel in these ancient systems of writing" (*The Standard Edition of the Complete Psychological Works of Sigmund Freud*, trans. James Strachey [London, 1953], XIII, 177.

4. "Self-Reliance," in *Essays: First Series*, ed. Joseph Slater, Alfred R. Ferguson, and Jean Ferguson Carr (Cambridge, Mass., 1979), 37, vol. II of *The Collected Works of Ralph Waldo Emerson*, 4 vols. to date.

berg assembled a model experimental laboratory.[5] It was at the Fair that Frederick Jackson Turner elaborated the meaning of the closing of the American frontier, an event that—by marking the advance of civilization and the subduing of the Amerinds—brought with it losses that the Anglo-Saxon bias of Turner's lecture ignored. Elsewhere on the fairgrounds, exhibits of exotic cultures so abounded that the curator of the Smithsonian Institution's Bureau of American Ethnology declared that "it would not be too much to say that the World's Columbian Exposition was one vast anthropological revelation. Not all mankind were there, but either in persons or in pictures their representatives were."[6] To whatever degree professionalized study of the psyche and culture differed from Emerson's philosophical speculations a half century earlier, the mirror that the new researchers held up to nature gave back possibilities of personal and societal renewal reminiscent of those proposed by his critique. Thorstein Veblen, Louis Sullivan, and John Dewey were three close contemporaries who drew upon the anthropologist's inquiry into culture and the psychologist's study of the individual to illumine the mystery of the "aboriginal Self."

Among the most popular displays at the Chicago Fair was that of the Kwakiutl Indians, whose tradition of the potlatch Franz Boas would elaborate in a series of papers during the following decade.[7] One can imagine the interest with which Veblen would have studied the exhibit, for the Kwakiutls' competitive gift exchanges had their parallel in the conspicuous consumption he later satirized in *The Theory of the Leisure Class*. There, by appropriating the comparative method employed by anthropologists, Veblen would make telling use of the folkways of the "lower races" to take the measure of the "higher nations." Far from being democratic, he insisted, contemporary society had chosen to live by its own hierarchical deference; its own behavior was irrational, compensatory, and ritualized. In vindication of his method, Veblen wrote that "any theory

5. Sherman Paul, *Louis Sullivan: An Architect in American Thought* (Englewood Cliffs, N.J., 1962), 98.
6. Otis T. Mason, "Summary of Progress in Anthropology," *Annual Reports of the Smithsonian Institution for the Year Ending July 1893* (Washington, D.C., 1894), 605.
7. Joseph Dorfman, *Thorstein Veblen and His America* (New York, 1966), 116.

of culture, late or early, must have recourse to a psychological analysis, since all culture is substantially a psychological phenomenon." However, the future need not be foreclosed, for the means of renewal lay in long-neglected human powers. Veblen epitomized his confidence in the ironic reversal of a platitude: "Invention is the mother of necessity." The self was favored with an instinct for workmanship, an insistent curiosity, and an inclination to beneficence that had been betrayed by what he called "institutions," the cultural accretions that had come to prescribe character.[8] Yet the identity that had enjoyed expression in the earliest stage of the race remained latent in every individual.

The preface to *The Leisure Class* explains that its "premises and corroborative evidence" have been "borrowed from ethnological science . . . of the more familiar and accessible kind." The impress of anthropological researches on Veblen is seen in a letter of 1896, written while he was working on *The Leisure Class*. In it he urges his readings in ethnology on a young friend and predicts that the overdue rethinking of economics will draw upon anthropologists' investigations of social history.[9] Veblen had been interested in primitive cultures since his boyhood, when he had been fascinated by the early experiences of the Scandinavian and Icelandic peoples: studying their customs and literature remained his lifelong avocation. In his later writings, the Plains Indians and the Jews would serve not as historical case studies but as metaphors of the saving remnant in humanity that had survived the demands of the dominant culture.

Veblen's cultural anthropology seems to have been chiefly in-

8. Thorstein Veblen, "Mr. Cummings's Strictures on 'The Theory of the Leisure Class,'" in Leon Ardzrooni (ed.), *Essays in Our Changing Order* (New York, 1964), 17; Veblen, *The Instinct of Workmanship and the State of the Industrial Arts* (New York, 1964), 314, 316n.

9. Thorstein Veblen, *The Theory of the Leisure Class* (New York, 1965), n.p. (subsequent citations of this volume will occur parenthetically in the text and will be identified by *LC*); Veblen to Sarah McLean Hardy, January 23, 1896, Xerographic copy of holograph original in Bancroft Library, University of California, Berkeley. See also Veblen's essay "Why Is Economics Not an Evolutionary Science?" in his *The Place of Science in Modern Civilisation and Other Essays* (New York, 1919), 56–81 (subsequent citations of this volume will occur parenthetically in the text and will be identified by *PS*); and Dorfman, *Thorstein Veblen and His America*, 132–33.

debted to the writings of Edward Burnett Tylor.[10] The most striking resemblances between the theory informing *The Leisure Class*
and Tylor's anthropology are their central concern with animistic
practices and the evolutionary "survivals" discovered by means of
the ethnologists' comparative method. Veblen need only have read
the first paragraph of Tylor's *Researches into the Early History of
Mankind* to have found comparisons between primitive and contemporary cultures of the sort he would employ ironically:

The women of modern Europe mutilate their ears to hang jewels in them,
but the reason of their doing so is not to be fully found in the circumstances among which we are living now. The student who takes a wider
view thinks of the rings and bones and feathers thrust through the car-
tilage of the nose; the weights that pull the slit ears in long nooses to the
shoulder; the ivory studs let in at the corners of the mouth; the wooden
plugs as big as table-spoons put through the slits in the under lip; the teeth
of animals stuck point outwards through holes in the cheeks; all familiar
things among the lower races up and down in the world. The modern ear-
ring of the higher nations stands not as a product of our own times, but as
a relic of a ruder mental condition, one of the many cases in which the result of progress has been not positive in adding something new, but negative in taking away something belonging to an earlier state of things.[11]

"The science of culture," Tylor urged, "is essentially a reformer's
science." Anthropology must serve a social function, working to
"expose the remains of crude old culture which have passed into
harmless superstition, and to mark these out for destruction."[12] As
a reformer, Veblen has too easily been misappreciated as a constitu-
tional malcontent who delighted in attacking the smugness of the
age. However, his challenge to useless survivals was but the prelude to a hoped-for reconstitution of society taking its form from

10. Veblen's friends included W. I. Thomas and Frederick Starr, University of Chicago sociologists who taught its first anthropology courses. While completing *The
Leisure Class*, Veblen rented his apartment from Starr, whose course lectures drew
heavily upon Tylor's researches. "Veblen used to bring it into my room," Starr later
recalled, "and read it aloud chapter by chapter." One can hardly doubt that Starr referred Veblen to the anthropologist he knew best. Dorfman, *Thorstein Veblen and
his America*, 125–26, 174; George W. Stocking, Jr., *Anthropology at Chicago: Tradition, Discipline, Department* (Chicago, 1980), 9–15.
11. Edward Burnett Tylor, *Researches into the Early History of Mankind and the
Development of Civilization* (London, 1878), 1–2.
12. Edward Burnett Tylor, *Primitive Culture* (2 vols.; New York, 1889), II, 453.

the triad of drives that had inspired the primitive. For him, instinct psychology and anthropology had established as essentially human the traits that he had glimpsed in his studies of pre-Christian Scandinavia and that he believed had enjoyed expression in the innocent beginnings of the race. Despite the long reign of "institutions," a term in many ways equivalent to Louis Sullivan's "feudalism," these suppressed traits had survived and remained accessible to those who would work toward the renewal of contemporary society.

Although Veblen is remembered for his critique of American universities, his indictment of education extended to the conventional pedagogy's inhibition of the schoolchild. He began where Emerson and Dewey had: "The point of departure of modern psychological inquiry is the empirical generalization that The Idea is Essentially Active."[13] Against the entrenched associationist view, modern studies in instinct psychology had revealed that the long-suppressed dynamic of the primitive survived, still eager to declare itself:

The later psychology, reenforced by modern anthropological research, gives a different conception of human nature. According to this conception, it is the characteristic of man to do something, not simply to suffer pleasures and pains through the impact of suitable forces. He is not simply a bundle of desires that are to be saturated by being placed in the path of the forces of the environment, but rather a coherent structure of propensities and habits which seeks realisation and expression in an unfolding activity. . . . The activity is itself the substantial fact of the process, and the desires under whose guidance the action takes place are circumstances of temperament which determine the specific direction in which the activity will unfold itself in the given case. (*PS*, 74)

In an environment of choice the individual would discover his or her true potential as a "centre of unfolding impulsive activity" and know new dimensions of fulfillment (*LC*, 15). But the end Veblen proposed raised the question of means: How was it possible to break free of institutions' self-validating and mutually reinforcing categories of worth? Veblen found a promise of a new orientation

13. Review of G. Tarde, *Psychologie économique*, in Thorstein Veblen, *Essays, Reviews and Reports: Previously Uncollected Writings*, ed. Joseph Dorfman (Clifton, N.J., 1973), 497. See also Veblen, *The Place of Science*, 5.

in technology's economy and efficiency of action. The machine "throws out anthropomorphic habits of thought" and "inculcates thinking in terms of opaque, impersonal cause and effect, to the neglect of those norms of validity that rest on usage and on the conventional standards handed down by usage."[14] The machine would thus shame institutionally prescribed waste and contradiction. It would be the means of unlearning imposed patterns of thought and provide the model for the reengagement of the instinct of workmanship and disinterested curiosity.

Sociology—the social science rubric under which anthropology was being taught during the University of Chicago's first years— was for Louis Sullivan "the heart of our inquiry into Democracy. . . . This is the unitary science . . . the precursor of Democracy—its explorer, its evangel." Like Tylor and Veblen, he insisted upon the moral dimension of social science: "It is the business of democratic sociology to simplify and clarify all things, to exhibit and elucidate these powers of man which energize his power of choice and the dramatic consequences of such choice."[15]

Whitman's *Leaves of Grass*, which joined self-discovery and democracy in a secular testimony of hope, had first mediated the Emersonian faith for Sullivan. The thirty-year-old architect's chance encounter with Whitman's poetry elicited a grateful letter of resolve: "You then and there entered my soul, have not departed, and never will depart."[16] The reader of *The Autobiography of an Idea* feels the constant presence of Whitman—and behind him, of Emerson. In prose suffused with the ambition and energy of Whitman, *Democracy: A Man-Search* projects a mythic exploration of his-

14. Thorstein Veblen, *The Theory of Business Enterprise* (Clifton, N.J., 1973), 310. See also p. 374.

15. Louis Sullivan, *Kindergarten Chats and Other Writings* (New York, 1947), 102 (subsequent citations of this volume will occur parenthetically in the text and will be identified by *KC*).

16. Quoted in Paul, *Louis Sullivan*, 1. Paul's study of the continuities between the American Renaissance and Sullivan has been followed by Narciso Menocal, *Architecture as Nature: The Transcendentalist Idea of Louis Sullivan* (Madison, Wis., 1981); and Lauren S. Weingarden, "Naturalized Technology: Louis H. Sullivan's Whitmanesque Skyscrapers," *Centennial Review*, XXX (1986), 480–95.

tory.[17] Sullivan's social vision—its anthropological, psychological, and political dimensions—is announced at the outset. The work's title describes the environment of possibilities discovered at the quest's end, and the subtitle represents "man" as both the seeker and the subject of the "search." Read one way, the subtitle calls the fully human agent to the task of overcoming dualism: the Kingdom of God that is within has been present from the beginning, "a solution in hieroglyphic to those inquiries he would put." Read another way, it alludes to the book's imaginative retracing of the racial past by translating "anthropology" into the American vernacular.

The theme of alienation from the instinctual self had already been set out in *Kindergarten Chats*: "Long, long ago in the dawn of proto-man, when the function, man, was seeking form and power within a hostile world, it sent forth out of the abysm of instinct a sub-function which we now call intellect." As though restating Veblen's account of the evolution of institutions, Sullivan tells how intellect, which first promised to "assist in the self-preservation and self-assertion of the ego," became "more and more dominant, while instinct as steadily declined." Out of fear, ego yielded to intellect, and "feudalism began its long career." Through the "sin of intellect . . . man parted . . . company with himself . . . and became a wanderer and then a seeker . . . seeking himself—seeking man" (148).

Feudalism, however, had not been fatal, for rediscovery of the human self was to occur by means of a return to nature: "Democracy and the oneness of all things are one. Thus, even within the depths of historic feudalism, one perceives the primal urge of man's spirit toward Democracy." In Sullivan's telling, self-estrangement took the form of a journey-narrative in which the Romantic myth of primal innocence merged with a variant of the Prodigal's exile: "So, if feudal man has been a wanderer and a seeker, far from him-

---

17. Sullivan regularly writes in the optative and hortatory subjunctive moods. While recognizing that his call for an architecture "of the people, by the people, and for the people" is—like Whitman's democratic faith—an "abstract hope," Alan Trachtenberg faults Sullivan for not providing a closer analysis of the "new social realities" (*The Incorporation of America: Culture and Society in the Gilded Age* [New York, 1982], 228–29).

self, far from man, far from the earth and far from his God—Democracy is but his home-coming."[18]

The loss of confidence in the native powers of humanity was manifest in America's desperate adoption of reassuring forms. Sullivan's insight that "if a building is properly designed, one should be able with a little attention, to read *through* that building to the *reason* for that building" restated a pre-feudal semiotics of architecture (*KC*, 46). His denunciation of New York's Church of Saint John the Divine, begun according to a Romanesque plan that was shifted to Gothic, echoed Veblen's attack on the eclectic Gothic that Henry Ives Cobb fashioned for Rockefeller's university, which Veblen had characterized as "bastard antique." Both programs, like the classical façades dear to bankers in the Middle West, revealed a culture fearful of expressing its own identity (*KC*, 75, 35–40).

Sullivan proposed that young architects restudy the first elements of building, the bare truth of the pier and lintel, and the strong beauty of the arch that timid, deceived generations had surrendered to feudalism. Dimitri Tselos and Robert Twombly have identified the adaptation of Moorish architecture in such different Sullivan projects as the Wainwright Memorial and the Golden Doorway in the Transportation Building at the World's Fair.[19] In the austerity of the Arab saint's tomb that he drew upon for the St. Louis mausoleum, Sullivan found a unity of essential forms that would affirm the lives of the Wainwright family. Economy was nature's lesson; more would have been less. The great Chicago Doorway told its own simple truth. Whatever its exultant Orientalism owed to the Islamic design in Marrakesh, Sullivan's design had none of the slavish imitation of the academic trophy architecture that surrounded it. From his source, Sullivan had reclaimed the elemental power of the arch. Set into a polychromatic façade of Nietz-

18. Louis Sullivan, *Democracy: A Man-Search*, ed. Elaine Hedges (Detroit, 1961), 151 (subsequent citations of this volume will occur parenthetically in the text and will be identified by *D*); M. H. Abrams, *Natural Supernaturalism: Tradition and Revolution in Romantic Literature* (New York, 1971), 141–324, esp. 154–69.

19. Dimitri Tselos, "The Chicago Fair and the Myth of the 'Lost Cause,'" *Journal of the Society of Architectural Historians*, XXVI (1967), 264; Robert Twombly, *Louis Sullivan: His Life and Work* (New York, 1986), 280.

schean boldness that looked east toward the lake, the Doorway resembled the portal of a primitive sun temple, responding to each dawn with its radiant celebration of a new age. As his skyscrapers imitated the upward thrust of vegetative growth, Sullivan's Wainwright Memorial and Golden Doorway followed other of nature's forms in responding to the exigencies of social history. Sullivan, as if reaffirming Emerson's "solution in hieroglyphic," found those demands salutary. By the operation of "natural law," he wrote, "the very essence of every problem . . . contains and suggests its own solution" (*KC*, 203).

Sullivan, who looked for a reform of architecture that would be exemplary for the larger transformation of society, reinvoked the organic metaphor to describe the truth, beauty, and strength that issue from within. This metaphor described as well a genuine education, during which the child would discover "the psychic foundation of Democracy—the living simple germ of Natural Thinking."[20] Employing the image of efflorescence, Sullivan wrote: "It should be clear . . . that a system of education, to be democratic, must be based on the unfolding of these natural powers in the young, and the power of choice clearly impressed and defined" (*KC*, 102). If his expression recalled Veblen's description of the psyche seeking "realisation and expression in an unfolding activity," it also echoed both Emerson's idea of correspondence and the philosophy of Dewey: "The average man needs . . . to see complicated things in a simple way, that their underlying simplicity may reveal itself to him, and he thus acquire the rudiments of the great and only art of plain-seeing, plain-feeling, plain-thinking, and plaindoing" (*D*, 172). By rediscovering elemental truths, such as Veblen's belief in the priority of "invention," the individual would emerge stronger than circumstance: "Man is seemingly driven by necessity,—but all notion of harsh necessity vanishes when he chooses to choose aright" (*D*, 263).

---

20. "Selections from *Natural Thinking*," in *The Testament of Stone: Themes of Idealism and Indignation from the Writings of Louis Sullivan*, ed. Maurice English (Evanston, Ill., 1963), 119. On the corrupting nature of traditional educational practice, see Sullivan, *Kindergarten Chats*, 221–22.

At a centenary commemoration of Emerson's birth, John Dewey responded to the reluctance of some to regard Emerson as a philosopher. If, in Emerson's writing, abstract thought had been given an uncommonly imaginative expression, Dewey "would not make hard and fast lines between philosopher and poet." He declared his expectation that "the coming century may well make evident what is just now dawning, that Emerson is not only a philosopher, but that he is the Philosopher of Democracy." Dewey not only shared Emerson's spirit but deeply identified with him. Looking back in later years, he recognized that, like Emerson's own, his need for the unification of experience had been a reaction to his early life: "The sense of divisions and separations that were, I suppose, borne in upon me as a consequence of a heritage of New England culture, divisions by way of isolation of self from the world, of soul from body, of nature from God, brought a painful oppression—or, rather, they were an inward laceration."[21]

In the decade after its founding, the University of Chicago was distinguished by its close connections with the surrounding community and its body of outstanding representatives of the reform-minded "new psychology" and "new sociology," disciplines influenced by Darwin and committed to social meliorism. These progressive emphases were formative in the civic commitment of Dewey, who arrived in Chicago in 1894. In the preceding year he had published a short essay, "Anthropology and Law," which acknowledged his debt to Holmes's *The Common Law*, a work that had been influenced by Tylor's studies of primitive culture and was already recognized as a seminal text of legal realism.[22] Dewey's work extended far beyond teaching and writing. Besides founding the University Laboratory School, he worked with Jane Addams'

21. John Dewey, "Emerson—The Philosopher of Democracy," in Dewey, *The Middle Works, 1899–1924*, ed. Jo Ann Boydston *et al.* (15 vols.; Carbondale and Edwardsville, Ill., 1976–83), III, 185, 190; John Dewey, "From Absolutism to Experimentalism," in Dewey, *The Later Works, 1925–1953*, ed. Jo Ann Boydston *et al.* (14 vols. to date; Carbondale and Edwardsville, Ill., 1981–), V, 153.
22. John Dewey, "Anthropology and the Law," in Dewey, *The Early Works, 1882–1898*, ed. Jo Ann Boydston *et al.* (5 vols., Carbondale and Edwardsville, Ill., 1967–72), IV, 37–41; Oliver Wendell Holmes, *The Common Law*, ed. Mark DeWolfe Howe (Cambridge, Mass., 1963), 13, 19; Morton G. White, *Social Thought in America: The Revolt Against Formalism* (New York, 1952), 17–18.

Hull-House and involved himself in movements for educational and social reform in Chicago and elsewhere in Illinois. Meanwhile, his professional eminence earned him election to the presidency of the American Psychological Association.

Dewey's educational philosophy required that the child's impetus to creativity be encouraged in every way. He related this creativity to "interest" and—out of the confidence he shared with Emerson, Veblen, and Sullivan—insisted that exercise of natural aptitudes be made the core of schooling. In striking contrast to the pedagogy of coercive instruction, Dewey's philosophy valued the child's interests for their recognition of correspondences: "The genuine principle of interest is the principle of the recognized identity of the fact or proposed line of action with the self; that it lies in the direction of the agent's own growth, and is, therefore, imperiously demanded, if the agent is to be himself. Let this condition of identification once be secured, and we neither have to appeal to sheer strength of will, nor do we have to occupy ourselves with making things interesting to the child."[23]

Dewey's curriculum focused upon what engaged the child's interest. Primal concerns, he believed, excited the natural curiosity of the young mind, which recognized their contemporary relevance. "Starting with the most primitive ways of living, [the first years of the Laboratory School program] took up the beginnings and growth of industry through discovery and invention and their effect on social life." The plan was "to make the study of social life the center of attention and to follow its development, in part at least, from its earliest beginnings through the barbaric stage to the opening of authentic history."[24]

In April of 1899—the year *The Theory of the Leisure Class* appeared—Dewey gave the series of lectures later published as *The*

23. John Dewey, "Interest in Relation to Training of the Will," in *The Early Works*, V, 117–18. Edith Cobb describes the experience of this potential in the "middle age of childhood, approximately from five or six to eleven or twelve . . . when the natural world is experienced in some highly evocative way, producing in the child a sense of some profound continuity with natural processes and presenting overt evidence of a biological basis of intuition" (Cobb, "The Ecology of Imagination in Childhood," *Daedalus*, LXXXVIII [1959], 538).

24. Katharine Camp Edwards and Anna Camp Edwards, *The Dewey School* (New York, 1936), 46.

School and Society. He urged that the schools reflect the natural social development of the community. Such a curriculum would allow the child to appreciate his or her present circumstances through study of the cultural past. The activities of sewing and weaving, for example, provided "the point of departure from which the child can trace and follow the progress of mankind in history, getting an insight into the materials used and the mechanical principles involved." The educational psychologist was to construct a curriculum that capitalized upon the true affinity the child discovered with the primitive.

Many anthropologists have told us there are certain identities in the child interests [*sic*] with those of primitive life. There is a sort of natural recurrence of the child mind to the typical activities of primitive peoples; witness the hut which the boy likes to build in the yard, playing hunt with bows, arrows, spears, and so on. . . . The children begin by imagining present conditions taken away until they are in contact with nature at first hand. That takes them back to a hunting people, to a people living in caves or trees and getting a precarious subsistence by hunting and fishing. . . . Then they go on in imagination through the hunting to the semi-agricultural stage, and through the nomadic to the settled agricultural stage.[25]

Thus the child would become aware of what is constant in human nature and what in the personality derives from social nurture. In this way, history ceased being mere antiquarianism; it became a relational study in which the past was studied for its service to the present and the individual came to appreciate the social contexts of human life.

Veblen, Sullivan, and Dewey, like Emerson and Thoreau before them, looked inward and backward in order to look outward and forward. Nearly a century after the Chicago critics drew on the "new" social sciences' affirmation of a long-suppressed integral personality, the example of the primitive has again quickened American writing. The endeavors of a later generation of anthropologists "to define a primary human potential"—the phrase is Stanley Diamond's—have energized poets urgently aware of the

25. John Dewey, *The School and Society*, in *The Middle Works*, I, 13–14, 31–32.

ecology of the self, society, and art.[26] Contemporary anthropological poetics (or ethnopoetics) proposes a revolutionary critique of
culture: by turning back to nature and the primordial, humanity
will find what is truly sustaining. Its address, as Sherman Paul has
remarked, is both personal and social:

> Primitive simply means first, earliest, original, basic. Historically it refers
> to a way of life prior to civilization—that is, the city-state—but to evoke
> it now is, as Kenneth Burke says, to temporalize the essence, essence, in
> this instance, being the fuller human nature, the first nature, to which we
> aspire. Since it asks us to view ourselves in light of all human history, it is
> a term of manifold critical uses. . . . The primitive, in being prior to the
> city-state, may have been nonpolitical, but to those who now search for
> the primitive, the search is clearly political.[27]

It was in the same spirit of renewal that Emerson looked to the
primitive. His essay "Politics" begins by viewing the recent expedi-
ent of government in the distant mirror of prehistory: "In dealing
with the State, we ought to remember that its institutions are not
aboriginal, though they existed before we were born: that they are
not superior to the citizen: that every one was once the act of a
single man."[28] Counsel that speaks so directly to the present owes
much of its force to the voices that have reaffirmed its truth.
Veblen, Sullivan, and Dewey made Emerson's aboriginal reference
point their own. His themes—the inherent vitalism of human nature, the tyranny of institutions, the genius of the individual, the
open possibilities that await those of good hope—became theirs
and recur in the poets who now find inspiration in the primitive.
The primordial, the essential state of nature, ever opens onto
democratic vistas.

---

26. Stanley Diamond, *In Search of the Primitive* (New Brunswick, N.J., 1974),
119. See also the review by Dan Rose, "In Search of Experience: The Anthropological Poetics of Stanley Diamond," *American Anthropologist*, LXXXV (1983), 345–55;
and Victor Turner's appreciation of the 1975 Ethnopoetics symposium proceedings
published in *Alcheringa*, n.s., II (1976)—his review is in *boundary 2*, VI (Winter,
1978), 583–90.

27. Sherman Paul, *In Search of the Primitive: Rereading David Antin, Jerome
Rothenberg, and Gary Snyder* (Baton Rouge, 1987), viii.

28. "Politics," in *Essays: Second Series*, ed. Joseph Slater, Alfred R. Ferguson, and
Jean Ferguson Carr (Cambridge, Mass., 1983), 117, vol. III of *The Collected Works of
Ralph Waldo Emerson*, 4 vols. to date.

II / Clinging to the Advance:

The Green Tradition and Modernism

VIRGINIA M. KOUIDIS

Prison into Prism: Emerson's "Many-Colored Lenses" and the Woman Writer of Early Modernism

Emerson, in a way, viewed spiritual truth pragmatically, as something discovered in an activity, in process. His theory of the moment and therefore of symbolism recognized the fragmentary, perspective grasp of truth and the necessity of continually taking new positions and sights.
— *Emerson's Angle of Vision*

In Kate Chopin's novel *The Awakening*, published at the close of the nineteenth century, Edna Pontellier grows sleepy while reading Emerson.[1] Her somnolence poses for the dawning twentieth century the question—raised earlier by the careers of Margaret Fuller and Emily Dickinson—of Emerson's relevance to the woman writer. Fuller's life and writing bear witness to the social prejudice awaiting the woman who desired to unify, as Emerson taught, the spiritual, sexual, social, and vocational aspects of the self. In remaining unpublished, Dickinson closed the door on the public disapproval and personal failure that Fuller braved, choosing from the shelter of her father's home alternately to celebrate and to deconstruct Emerson's challenge to their common Puritan heritage. In

1. The novel was published in 1899. Citations in this essay are to Kate Chopin, *The Awakening*, ed. Margaret Culley (New York, 1976). References to the novel are included parenthetically in the text.

the new century the question of Emerson's relevance to women's lives and art is taken up by three of the most revolutionary writers of Anglo-American modernism. The English novelist Dorothy Richardson (1873–1957) and the American poet Marianne Moore (1887–1972) acknowledge Emerson's influence upon their thought and writing. Mina Loy (1882–1966), an English poet and painter discovered by the New York avant-garde, alludes to him in her thematic and structural linkage of the I-eye.

Although it is doubtful that these writers read *The Awakening*, they must certainly have been reading each other. The matter, however, is not one of direct influence among themselves or, perhaps, even among themselves and Emerson. The similarity of the individual spiritual and social quest(ion)ings of Richardson, Loy, and Moore testifies to women's shared dissatisfactions as well as to the exhaustion of old literary forms. Their Emersonianism may well have been updated by their reading in the vitalistic philosophy of Henri Bergson and William James.[2] Certainly, the diffusion of Emerson's ideas throughout turn-of-the-century England and America would have made him a common cultural reference.[3]

How to interpret Edna Pontellier's reading of Emerson and her subsequent drowsiness remains an issue of critical debate that also addresses the moderns' response to his ideas. Is Edna following Emerson's example in rejecting the strictures of her father's Presbyterianism and *les convenances* of New Orleans society? Is she too vague of purpose and undisciplined to take up Emerson's legacy? Or is this legacy boringly irrelevant to the social and biological realities of her life? Is she—like Becky Sharp, who, at the outset of *Vanity Fair*, flings Dr. Johnson's Dictionary from the carriage window—rejecting the dominant culture's oppressive and moribund gentility? Perhaps we are simply meant to smile at the

2. Richardson and Loy acknowledge their familiarity with Bergson's ideas, and Moore cites James in her prose and the notes to her poetry. For the influence of Bergson and other nonrationalist philosophers on twentieth-century American literature, see Paul Douglass, *Bergson, Eliot, and American Literature* (Lexington, Ky., 1986).

3. William J. Sowder surveys Emerson's popularity in England during the period from 1840 to 1903 in *Emerson's Impact on the British Isles and Canada* (Charlottesville, 1966).

staunch New Englander's presence in the Creole's library and to wonder if the pages had been cut.[4]

Edna's encounter with Emerson follows her return from a summer at Grand Isle, where her dalliance with young Robert Lebrun has awakened an unfulfilled sensuality. Having sent her father home and packed her husband and two small sons off on extended visits, she determines "to start anew upon a course of improving studies" and settles down, in her husband's library, with a volume of Emerson (73). But she grows sleepy and abandons the book for the pleasure of a refreshing bath and bed. There is no further mention of Emerson, and Edna is left without a guide through her fluctuating moods and perceptions. Awakening to the sexual double standard underlying the sun-dappled canvas of her New Orleans life, she attempts to turn her hobby of painting into a vocation and, in a declaration of personal freedom impossible for a respectable woman of her class, departs her husband's elegant home for a modest cottage. Her desire for freedom is one with a yearning toward spiritual illumination that she variously experiences as athletic prowess, sexual passion, and "life's delirium" (56). She expects this illumination to accompany her sexual union with the beloved, but she comes to understand that any earthly "marriage" would be transitory, except for the children it would inevitably produce. In her progress toward this knowledge, the inchoate need directing her to Emerson's spiritual guidance leads her to the arms of the no-

---

4. A surprising number of critics ignore the allusion to Emerson. Among those who discuss it, Kenneth Eble, "A Forgotten Novel: Kate Chopin's *The Awakening*," *Western Humanities Review*, X (1956), 261–69, interprets the incident as Edna's reaction to her father's Presbyterianism. George Arms, "Kate Chopin's *The Awakening* in the Perspective of Her Literary Career," in Clarence Gohdes (ed.), *Essays on American Literature in Honor of Jay B. Hubbell* (Durham, 1967), says that "to grow sleepy over a Transcendental individualist . . . hints that Edna's individualism lacks philosophical grounding" (219). Donald A. Ringe, "Romantic Imagery in Kate Chopin's *The Awakening*," *American Literature*, XLIII (1972), reads the novel "in terms of the romantic concept of the self," as an Emersonian correspondence in which inner and outer worlds are mediated by the eyes (582). Charles W. Mayer, "Isabel Archer, Edna Pontellier, and the Romantic Self," *Research Studies*, XLVII (1979), sees Edna's sleepiness as a sign that Emerson confirms rather than challenges what Edna already desires—a surrender of the self to the unconscious in order to be "free from all authority, and be guided by the spirit" (91).

torious womanizer Alcée Arobin and then to the ultimate embrace of the sea.

The difficulty readers have had in deciding whether Edna's suicide is cowardly or heroic may rest in the possibility that Chopin uses Emerson both as representative of the system that denies Edna's aspiration and as a judgment on the narrow vision by which Edna defeats herself. Early in the novel, Chopin indicates that Edna has intuited for herself the situation that attracted Fuller, and has proverbially attracted young men, to Emerson's life and writing. From an early age "she had apprehended instinctively the dual life—that outward existence which conforms, the inward life which questions" (15). In seeking a unified self, Edna would have followed her male predecessors and contemporaries in turning to such famous Emersonian essays on self-realization as "The American Scholar" (1837) or "Self-Reliance" (1841). But either of these would have confronted her with the emphatic gender bias of the Emersonian tradition. From his use of the masculine pronoun to his substantive distinction between male and female vision, Emerson shapes and reflects the sexual chauvinism against which women have had to defend and define themselves.[5] Emerson laments the restricted field for a Margaret Fuller's talents, but otherwise he offers young women the old marriage plot wherein they fulfill their destiny as wife and muse. An example of the attitude informing the sexual double standard of the essays appears in an 1843 journal entry that follows upon a conversation with Fuller: "For me today, Woman is not a degraded person with duties forgotten, but a docile daughter of God with her face heavenward and endeavouring to hear the divine word and to convey it to me." In his journal for 1841 he makes it clear that his vision of culturally redeeming speech precludes woman's voice: "Give me initiative, spermatic, prophesying man-making words."[6]

5. For an overview of Emerson's sexual politics and metaphysics, see Erik Ingvar Thurin, *Emerson as Priest of Pan: A Study in the Metaphysics of Sex* (Lawrence, Kan., 1981), esp. Chap. 2.
6. *The Journals and Miscellaneous Notebooks of Ralph Waldo Emerson,* ed. William H. Gilman (14 vols.; Cambridge, Mass., 1960–78), VIII, 372, 148. The second quotation is included in "Inspiration," in *The Complete Works of Ralph Waldo*

There is, of course, more to the Emersonian legacy, and Edna may have been unfortunate in her selection of texts. Chopin's presentation of Edna's plight suggests that in "Experience" (1844) she might have found the consoling wisdom of a fellow sufferer. This essay presciently glosses her sleep, her awakening, and her suicide, as well as the themes and structures of the three modernist writers. Its delineation of humanity's rite of crisis might serve as the archetype for all four writers' exploration of woman's awakening to her cultural and psychological otherness. They point to a common ancestry in their use of Emerson's image in "Experience" of the "many-colored lenses" that limit and empower perception: "Dream delivers us to dream, and there is no end to illusion. Life is a train of moods like a string of beads, and, as we pass through them, they prove to be many-colored lenses which paint the world their own hue, and each shows only what lies in its focus."[7] The image, looking back to Shelley's *Adonais* with its "dome of many-coloured glass" that "stains the white radiance of eternity," is part of the Romantic legacy that comes to these writers, as to Chopin, in recognizably Emersonian form.

"Where do we find ourselves?" begins "Experience." The question emerges when a personal crisis disturbs the comfortable dream of our life, and "[w]e wake and find ourselves on a stair" of uncertain origin and destination (*RWE*, 471). It voices our recognition of the discrepancy between the fixed world we had dreamed and the opaque shifting surfaces exposed by our pain. Our awareness of discrepancy Emerson calls "the Fall of Man"; it is the knowledge "that we exist" (487). In despair, he says, we locate the reality and permanence we seek in death. "We look to that with a grim satisfaction, saying, there at least is reality that will not dodge us" (473). We are led to this impasse by individual temperament. It "is the iron wire on which the beads are strung . . . [and] shuts us in a

---

Emerson, ed. E. W. Emerson (12 vols.; Boston, 1903–1904), VIII, 294. Citations of *Journals* will appear parenthetically in the text and are identified by *J*.

7. Joel Porte (ed.), *Ralph Waldo Emerson: Essays & Lectures* (New York, 1983), 473. References to this volume are included parenthetically in the text and are identified by *RWE*.

prison of glass which we cannot see." And we remember Edna Pontellier in Emerson's question, "Who cares what sensibility or discrimination a man has at some time shown, if he falls asleep in his chair?" (474).

As in earlier essays, Emerson resolves the question "Where do we find ourselves?" with a reaffirmation of the inner fire of the Eternal that we share with the world: "Underneath the inharmonious and trivial particulars, is a musical perfection, the Ideal journeying always with us, the heaven without rent or seam" (*RWE*, 484). Illumination comes in the solitude of reading or thinking, "as it were in flashes of light, in sudden discoveries of its profound beauty and repose, as if the clouds that covered it parted at intervals, and showed the approaching traveller the inland mountains" (484–85). Against those who despair at life's oscillations Emerson re-images the stairs of our perplexity as a sliding scale along which the consciousness of each man moves, identifying him "now with the First Cause, and now with the flesh of his body; life above life, in infinite degrees" (485). We hope to earn "an insight which becomes the light of our life." Although history offers no example of anyone successfully realizing his private world, genius attempts to transform this private light "into practical power" (492).

In this assertion of practical power, Emerson concludes "Experience" with a somewhat forced return to his optimistic privileging of active, masculine perception.[8] Throughout his writing he distinguishes between masculine and feminine perception and understands each I-eye to have its masculine and feminine aspects. The masculine eye sees abstractly and actively; the feminine, specifically but passively. In the man of genius, feminine attention to detail is exceptionally strong. He sees "the plaid of a cloak, the plaits of a ruffle, the wrinkles of a face"; but unlike a predominantly feminine perception, genius pursues daily trivia to its roots "in Universal Laws" (*J*, VII, 310).

When Emerson uses the image of colored subjective vision in

8. Joel Porte, *Representative Man: Ralph Waldo Emerson in His Time* (New York, 1979), 179–86, reads "Experience" as a fall into confusion that permits only "obligatory" final affirmations.

earlier essays, it typically is proof of genius. In "The American Scholar," he says that our inevitable coloration of the world can certify the attainment of worldly power: "They are the kings of the world who give the color of their present thought to all nature and all art" (*RWE*, 65). In "Self-Reliance," such personal coloration is to be trusted as product and evidence of divine grace: "[W]hen the devout motions of the soul come, yield to them heart and life, though they should clothe God with shape and color" (265). In "Experience," however, colored perception becomes restrictive and normative, and in later writings it is increasingly associated with inferior feminine vision. In a journal entry for 1851, Emerson notes of the recently deceased Margaret Fuller that her "habitual vision was through coloured lenses" (*J*, XI, 335). A passage in the essay "Woman" (1855), adapted from the 1851 journal, makes it clear that he did not mean to compliment Fuller, even though he is attempting to flatter his audience, a women's rights convention. Women, he says, "emit from their pores a colored atmosphere, one would say, wave upon wave of rosy light, in which they walk evermore, and see all objects through this warm-tinted mist that envelops them."[9] Feminine perception clouds and distorts, be it ever so attractively.

In her struggle to escape this stereotypical feminine mist, Edna Pontellier arrives at the Emersonian truth that most of life is illusion, but she is too much the product of her culture and servant of her body to heed his advice that, though earthly marriage, in the spiritual sense, is impossible, "[t]he universe is the bride of the soul" (*RWE*, 488). On the one hand, Edna cannot dissociate spiritual ecstasy from the image of the loved one. On the other, as her musician friend Mlle. Reisz suspects, she lacks the discipline and the courage to choose the solitude of the truly awakened soul. In deciding for suicide, she yields to the sleep that has dogged her fitful awakening and whispered promises in the white light of the moon at Grand Isle. The memories that overcome her consciousness as she takes her final swim mark her suicide as a defeat, not

9. Emerson, "Woman," in *Complete Works*, ed. E. W. Emerson, XI, 412.

as a heroic existential choice. In terms of the Emersonian commentary implicit in the novel, she refuses to undertake the stairs leading to Mlle. Reisz's lonely and shabby artist's attic.

To the extent that Edna's defeat involves her limitations as an artist, a scene near the beginning of *The Awakening* provides a point of departure for considering how Richardson, Loy, and Moore aesthetically exploit the Emersonian legacy.[10] At Grand Isle, Edna sketches her friend Adèle Ratignolle, whom she sees as a Creole mother-woman, and then destroys the sketch because it does not resemble its subject. The scene indicates that Edna has neglected her talent, but it also suggests the limitations of her perception. Her dissatisfaction with her sketch may result from her inability to see or express Adèle's shifting and complex reality. Edna seems to be in error in wanting for her sketch a conventional realistic likeness and for herself a linear plot that proceeds to resolution. When, as foretold by Emerson, she awakens to the surety of life's permutations, the cultural moment and her own temperament are not propitious for entertaining Emerson's speculation in "Experience" that "[p]erhaps these subject-lenses have a creative power" (487).

However, by the new century's second decade, the three moderns are able to act upon this speculation. Each makes the necessity of honest, unresolved perception her main subject and theme, and each shapes that necessity—Loy calls it "the crisis in consciousness"—into revolutionary literary form.[11] Their combined accomplishment is to unknot the paradox of "feminine genius" inherent in Emerson's apotheosis of active, masculine perception. If, as Emerson claims in "The Poet" (1844), "[w]ords are also actions" (450), and action is requisite for genius, then they lay claim to genius with literary forms that metamorphose the colored prison of subjectivity into prisms of understanding. In contrast to the sper-

10. Wayne Batten, "Illusion and Archetype: The Curious Story of Edna Pontellier," *Southern Literary Journal,* XVIII (1987), also finds this scene suggestive of Edna's failure to resolve "the inevitable tension between illusion and reality" (85).

11. Mina Loy, "Aphorisms on Futurism," *The Last Lunar Baedeker,* ed. Roger L. Conover (Highlands, N.C., 1982), 273. References to this volume are included parenthetically in the text and are identified by *LLB*.

matic, bardic proclamations of masculine genius, these women involve language in complex, twisting observations that refuse the finality of the declamatory stance.

This commitment to the act of observation places Richardson, Loy, and Moore among the legatees of what George Santayana in his definition of the genteel tradition calls the Emersonian "method," even as they, like Edna, are victims of Emersonian subjectivity petrified to the transcendental "system." In satisfying the religious instinct in an increasingly secular world, the system supplanted or justified discredited Calvinism with subjective vision. Socially and artistically, it defended tradition and inherited privilege against the pressures of burgeoning democratic culture.[12]

Like other modernist writers, these women employ the Emersonian method of perception, often applied to realities excluded from genteel drawing rooms, in order to resist the stultifying decorum of the genteel tradition. However, their close observations exist in tension with a strong religious inclination toward mystic transfiguration. Each in her private life finds institutional expression for this inclination: Richardson for a while in Quakerism, whose inner light resembles Emerson's "inner fire"; Loy in Christian Science, with its systematization of Emersonian self-reliance; and Moore in the Presbyterian heritage of divine grace she shares with Emerson. Their writings are interspersed with visionary illuminations that it is important to distinguish from the secular epiphanic moments found in other modernist writings.[13] Richardson, Loy, and Moore desire to shatter the colored glass of subjectivity and attain the unifying vision Sherman Paul ascribes to Emerson: "[T]he apprehension of unity, represented by the moral sentiment in Emerson's thought, fused subject and object with a religious warmth, and by

12. George Santayana, "The Genteel Tradition in American Philosophy" (1911), in *The Genteel Tradition: Nine Essays by George Santayana*, ed. Douglas L. Wilson (Cambridge, Mass., 1967), 37–64.

13. The distinction between mystical vision and the epiphanic moment in nineteenth- and twentieth-century literature is made by Morris Beja, *Epiphany in the Modern Novel* (Seattle, 1971), esp. 13–70; and Robert Langbaum, "The Epiphanic Mode in Wordsworth and Modern Literature," *New Literary History*, XIV (1982–83), 335–58.

uniting man with God, sanctified perception as a moral duty."[14] Richardson and Loy, however, are unable to situate their mystical illuminations in a metaphysics that would sustain the perceptual act. Emerson characterizes a similar inability in Margaret Fuller as "female mysticism." In Fuller's expression, he says, the mere good feeling of a man who has dined well "exaggerates a host of trifles . . . into a dazzling mythology; but when one goes to sift it, and find if there be a real meaning, it eludes all search. . . . [One] can connect all of this or any part of it with no universal experience" (*J*, XI, 293–94). Richardson ultimately blames her failure on the coldness of Emerson's thought, while Loy ironically undercuts the Emersonian expectation of cosmic unity and her own failure to relinquish the quest for unity. Only Moore approximates Emerson's cohering vision, probably because she follows Emerson's direction in focusing so many of her meticulous observations on nature's splendors and because she projects her own vitality into Presbyterian doctrine.

In *Pilgrimage* (1915–1967), Dorothy Richardson explores the choices Edna Pontellier did not make in her life and art. Richardson's thirteen-book künstlerroman presents the struggle of Miriam Henderson to find an alternative to the culturally sanctioned marriage plot and her family's Anglicanism. Miriam's qualified victory proceeds from her use of Emerson as a guide, a touchstone, through much of her quest.

Her father's bankruptcy forces Miriam and her three sisters to support themselves. Two marry, but Miriam and Eve, by choice and necessity, enter the economically marginal world of female white-collar employment in late nineteenth-century England. Miriam, about eighteen years old in the first book, teaches at girls' schools in Germany and London, serves a stint as a governess, then settles into the poorly paid occupation of dental assistant in London's Harley Street. As was true of Edna, the substance and symbol of her freedom is independent lodging. But whereas Edna's Thoreau-like move to the little cottage is supported by a legacy from her

14. Sherman Paul, *Emerson's Angle of Vision: Man and Nature in American Experience* (Cambridge, Mass., 1952), 35.

mother, Miriam struggles for subsistence.[15] She lives in the un-heated attic of a Bloomsbury rooming house and is constantly hun-gry, often cold, and perpetually embarrassed by the shabbiness of her clothing. Throughout the approximately twenty years encom-passed by the novel, she eludes a number of marriage opportuni-ties. She wants to experience life directly and early understands as illusion Edna's dream of spiritual marriage with another human being.

Emerson enters Miriam's story in *Deadlock* (1921), book six in the series. Established in London, she is caught between her desire for independent selfhood and the bodily and social realities of sex and marriage. The conflict is amusingly presented as a contest of books. Miriam has agreed to teach English to another roomer, the Russian-Jewish emigré Michael Shatov. She chooses a volume of Emerson to begin the lessons, believing that he would be perfect reading: "[H]e [Shatov] would see that there was an English writer who knew everything. . . . He *must* read Emerson; one could insist that it was the purest English and the most beautiful." More im-portant, Miriam builds her ideal of an independent, fully realized self upon Emerson's loftiest sentiments: "'If I have shrunk unequal from one contest, the joy I find in all the rest becomes mean and cowardly.'"[16] In return for Miriam's gift of Emerson, Shatov intro-duces the provincial English girl to Tolstoy's study of sexual pas-sion in *Anna Karenina*. Emerson and *Anna*: how to reconcile spiritual and sexual desire?

Thematic questions become structural problems. First as a reader and then as a novice writer, Miriam seeks a fictional structure that accurately expresses the interpenetration of feminine conscious-ness and the external world. The typical male novelist (she men-tions Balzac) is preoccupied with externals. However, in Emerson's emphasis on the inner life and Henry James's psychological novels, she discovers possibilities for proving Emerson's conjecture that

15. Peter Conn, *The Divided Mind: Ideology and Imagination in America, 1898–1917* (Cambridge, England, 1983), compares Edna's "pigeon house" to Tho-reau's cabin (166).

16. Dorothy M. Richardson, *Pilgrimage* (4 vols.; London, 1979), III, 23, 20. Subse-quent references to *Pilgrimage* will give volume and page parenthetically in the text.

"these subject-lenses have a creative power." Whether or not Richardson had Emerson's image specifically in mind, it does in fact account for her experiments in what has come to be known as the stream of consciousness novel.

The overall movement of *Pilgrimage* is easily understood as Miriam's rapid, often abrupt, passage through a succession of sometimes radically opposed moods. The structure embodies an awareness that we know the world primarily through the colors we give it and that the colors of feminine perception are unique and valid. However, a stream is perhaps too linear an image to describe Miriam's perceptual process. Her transformation in *Honeycomb* (1917) of Emerson's string of beads into the erratic movement of billiard balls seems more apt: "the gentle angular explosion of pieces into a new relation and the breaking of the varying triangle as a ball rolled to its hidden destination, held by all eyes in the room until its rumbling pilgrimage ended out of sight in a soft thud" (I, 434–35).

Revolving Lights (1923) transforms the colored beads into the city lights of the book's title. These lights have a particularly social hue, recalling Emerson's similar transformation of the image: "[I]t needs the whole society, to give the symmetry we seek. The particolored wheel must revolve very fast to appear white" (RWE, 477). The city offers Miriam independence, anonymity, unconventional friends, solitude, and intellectual stimulation. Included in that last are reform movements, such as feminism and socialism, in which Miriam unsuccessfully searches for a "system" that would bring her pilgrimage to conclusion.

However, Richardson's emphasis is on Miriam's own shifting perception. The whiteness she seeks comes in visionary illuminations that momentarily validate the self. Her life is composed of erratic horizontal movements and spiritual ascents, the latter often imaged as the stairs of "Experience." For Freud, stairs symbolized the sexual act, but Richardson's stairs ascend toward a more purely spiritual experience.[17] Thematically and structurally, they tie her mysticism to daily routine. Poverty requires her to live in attic

17. Thomas F. Staley, *Dorothy Richardson* (Boston, 1976), 48.

rooms, her dental assistant's job sends her repeatedly from the up-
stairs offices to the downstairs lab and sitting room. Through the
ascents and descents during the day's routines, her consciousness
alternately penetrates the heavens and becomes a slave to bodily
fatigue.

In her greatest enthusiasm, Miriam has not felt totally at one
with Emerson's ideas. She is disturbed by his privileging of mas-
culinity: "Even Emerson . . . positive and negative, north and
south, male and female . . . why *negative?*" (III, 50–51). In *Dimple
Hill* (1938), the penultimate volume, she muses on the tranquillity
of Emerson's genteel New England life, unharassed, she imagines,
by the exigencies that fence her own freedom. Spiritually, she feels
"something missing from Emerson's scheme, whose absence left
one alone with serenely burning intellectual luminosities in a universe whose centre was for ever invisible and inaccessible" (IV,
420). For a while the Quakers' inner light seems to offer a correc-
tive to the cool abstraction of Emerson's Eternal fire. Miriam is
living with a Quaker family in rural England when she has one of
her archetypal Emersonian illuminations. She has retreated to the
solitude of a hillside and is reading a book that ten years earlier
Shatov gave her, with the comment that its author's ideas resembled Emerson's. A forgotten amuletlike phrase gives her a
physical shock. Looking up, she sees a "golden light," and rapture
fills her previously empty being. The light dissolves, and she hears
herself exclaim, "I have seen the smile of God." As earth consciousness returns, Miriam understands that human warmth is what is
lacking in Emerson, and she literally and figuratively runs home to
her Quaker friends (IV, 415–21). They offer community and the divine still center of being, as opposed to Emersonian individuality
and becoming.

But Miriam is never able to deny Emerson's attraction. He is still
a disturbing presence at the end of the posthumously published
final volume, *March Moonlight* (1967). Here Miriam remembers an
earlier visit with Shatov and his wife Amabel, a couple she brought
together to evade the demands of both upon herself. The marriage
was troubled, and before Miriam was well into the house, Amabel
declared, " 'Mike has done with Emerson. We both find him trite'"

(IV, 658). She seems to have meant (and Miriam by her silence seems to acquiesce in this) that Emerson is irrelevant to the realities of sex and marriage, to the compromises of domestic life. Amabel may also have been trying to distance Miriam from Michael and accusing her of betraying her friends to serve her own end of Emersonian self-reliance.

A similar judgment might be applied to the novelistic structure Richardson devises to convey the process of her protagonist's subjectivity. Aspiring to self-realization but excluded from or rejecting the culture's plots for male and female lives, Miriam emerges unrealized, unfocused by her Emersonian quest. The absence of the structure and thematic resolutions required by a traditional narrative caused even the sympathetic Virginia Woolf to express reservations. Of *The Tunnel* (1919) she complains that while we are given the "helter-skelter" reality of Miriam's mind, "sensations, impressions, ideas and emotions glance off her, unrelated and unquestioned, without shedding quite as much light as we had hoped into the hidden depths. . . . The old method [of narration] seems sometimes the more profound and economical of the two."[18]

The conclusion of *Pilgrimage* substantiates Woolf's assessment of *The Tunnel*. Richardson seems not to know how to end her novel and give meaning to Miriam's quest. (Even the Quakers disappoint her with their adherence to conventional social and sexual mores.) In the ambiguous final scene, or memory, Miriam ecstatically embraces the Shatovs' baby in a luminous epiphanic moment. Her gesture suggests that she will henceforth exchange her Emersonian self-absorption for the cohering principle of maternal affection, exchange relentless becoming for "the complete stilling of every one of my competing urgencies" (IV, 658). Such a shift is vaguely anticipated by the suicide of Miriam's mother early in the story, the unexplained termination of Miriam's pregnancy, and a series of intense female friendships. However, there has been little of the maternal in Miriam's character, and the ending seems imposed upon the eternal transitions of the stairs of "Experience." The con-

18. Virginia Woolf, "Dorothy Richardson," in Michèle Barrett (ed.), *Women and Writing* (New York, 1979), 190–91.

cern for perceptual process has generated an exciting new poetic that is not necessarily, or finally, a congenial mode of living.

Mina Loy never expresses a debt to Emerson. The pervasiveness of Emersonian themes and images in her poetry may simply reflect the diffusion of his ideas throughout the culture as well as the synoptic wisdom of "Experience." However, there is sufficient internal evidence in Loy's poetry to suggest Emerson as a vital presence; and from the Emersonian formulations she shares with Richardson, Moore, and Chopin there begins to emerge a distinct conjunction of metaphysics, aesthetics, and feminist concerns within early modernism.[19]

Loy's insignia might well be an Emersonian I-eye, fringed with *fin de siècle* lashes, afloat in cosmic mystery. She is obsessed with connecting the act of perception to self-and-world cohering vision, though she often treats her obsession ironically and balances it with the knowledge expressed in "Human Cylinders" (1917) that to answer cosmic mystery would "Destroy the Universe / With a solution" (*LLB*, 13). "Magasins du Louvre" (1915) expresses Loy's characteristic application of the truths of "Experience" to female sexuality: "All the virgin eyes in the world are made of glass" (41). Like "Magasins," "Virgins Plus Curtains Minus Dots" (1915) is typical of the early poetry's distinction between male and female perception:

Men's eyes   look into things
Our eyes   look out   (36).

Ultimately, it is not sex but artistic genius that is the crucial distinction. Only artists, such as Loy's friends Gertrude Stein, James Joyce, and Constantin Brancuşi, possess the gift of visionary trans-

19. Joanne Feit Diehl, "In the Twilight of the Gods: Women Poets and the American Sublime," in Mary Arensberg (ed.), *The American Sublime* (Albany, 1986), 173–214, proposes such a tradition based on the poetry of Dickinson, Moore, H. D., Elizabeth Bishop, and Adrienne Rich. She also emphasizes the woman poet's refuge in the complexities of language: "[T]he highly experimental and difficult cast of poetry by American women reflect[s] their individual sense of alienation and, consequently, their need to employ language that proves its own defense" (210). Feit Diehl views Emerson as the opposition without the qualification that he may also be a source for the woman poet's alternative to the bardic tradition.

formation. Their dedication to the process of perception enables them momentarily, and eternally, to arrest the life-flux in divine form. Loy's interest in the visionary quests of women and artists culminates in the poetic künstlerroman *Anglo-Mongrels and the Rose* (1923–1925), a satire of the obstacles to the female child-artist's perceptual growth. In the less formally expressive poetry of 1930 and after, she offers a series of proletarian portraits whose protagonists too often settle for false Nirvanas.

Loy most tantalizingly hints at an Emersonian ancestry in *Love Songs to Joannes* (1915–1917), a thirty-four-poem collage of love's failure that rewrites "Experience" in flamboyantly sexual imagery (*LLB*, 91–107). The speaker is a woman who, like Edna Pontellier, is disillusioned by the fairy-tale expectation that the lover will be a liberating god. Instead, she awakens to "Pig Cupid" (poem 1), "The skin-sack / In which a wanton duality / Packed / All the completions / Of my infructuous impulses" (poem 2), "a butterfly / With the daily news / Printed in blood on its wings" (poem 3), and other deflationary images of romantic love. She has expected "Eternity in a skyrocket" (poem 1), but the earth-bound beloved moves linearly. He is "More of a clock-work mechanism / Running down against time / To which I am not paced" (poem 2).

The difficulty of the *Love Songs* derives from the modernist compressions and fragmentations that restructure the colored sequential beads of "Experience" into a complex collage that spatializes the traditional narrative of failed love. Each of the thirty-four poems kaleidoscopically re-figures the failure as pieces of "Coloured glass," the elliptical concluding image fragment of poem 1. Implicitly, Loy accepts Emerson's statement that women emit "wave upon wave of rosy light" and follows the permutations of that rosiness in the "bellows / Of experience" (poem 1). The speaker has begun life with rose-colored illusions, but the bellows' heat intensifies rosiness to the blood red of sexual combat, and bleaches it to the insipid pinkness of the game of love and the scummy whiteness of "saliva" (poem 1) and "spermatozoa" (poem 9). Repeatedly, the fragments of love shift into new patterns of limitation. Poem 28 summarizes the process in an imagistic compression of "Experience":

The steps go up for ever
And they are white
And the first step   is the last white
Forever
Coloured   conclusions
Smelt   to synthetic
Whiteness
Of my
Emergence

The whiteness of mystic transfiguration dissipates to post-coital depression: "I am burnt quite white / In the climacteric / Withdrawal of your sun." The speaker retreats from her foray into perceptual dislocation to the protective irony of literary cliché: "Love—the preeminent littérateur" (poem 34).

Appearing at the same time as Loy's *Love Songs*, the "Love Song" (1915–1917) by William Carlos Williams is also structured by the Romantic, perhaps Emersonian, image of the world colored by sexual ecstasy: "the stain of love / is upon the world! / Yellow, yellow, yellow / it eats into the leaves."[20] The coincidence is a reminder that the image of colored illusions was a common literary property of elusive origin. More important, the contrasting versions of the self in the two love songs exemplify the very different sexual realities that energize masculine and feminine poetics. Williams' poem carries on the self-affirmation of Whitman's Emersonian beads in "Crossing Brooklyn Ferry": "The glories strung like beads on my smallest sights and hearings."[21] Loy mines the tradition's core of doubt.

Marianne Moore's poetry and prose are luminous with manifold allusion to Emerson.[22] Her admiration for the Emersonian spiritual

20. *The Collected Poems of William Carlos Williams*, Volume I, *1909–1939*, ed. A. Walton Litz and Christopher MacGowan (New York, 1986), 53, 107. M. L. Rosenthal, "Is There a Pound-Williams Tradition?" *Southern Review*, XX (1984), 282–83, reads the poem as descended from Shelley's *Adonais*. Williams' "Weasel Snout" (1937; *Collected Poems*, 450–51) is a straightforward adaptation of the Shelleyan and Emersonian image of colored subjectivity.

21. *Walt Whitman: Complete Poetry and Collected Prose*, ed. Justin Kaplan (New York, 1982), 308.

22. John M. Slatin, *The Savage's Romance: The Poetry of Marianne Moore* (University Park, Pa., 1986), offers an in-depth examination of Moore's debt to Emerson.

principle is evident in the prickly individuality and moral fastidiousness of her poetic I-eye. She disdains the shockingly "modern" sexual honesty characteristic of Chopin, Richardson, and Loy; and when she (infrequently) writes about sex, it is with a wry indirection and decorum resembling Emerson's cautious approach to this treacherous subject. It is significant, then, that in the poem "In the Days of Prismatic Color" (1919–1921) she, like the other writers, implicitly associates Emerson's subjective colored lenses with sexual distortion and defines her poetics as resistance to the obfuscations of truth created by the sexual relationship. The poem allegorizes the other writers' life-studies of sexual awakening and disillusion, exemplifying at the same time the perceptual process by which the self avoids despair.

The crisis of "In the Days of Prismatic Color" is nothing less than woman's existence. The union of the masculine and feminine by definition becomes the Fall, forever distorting the pure color of original creation. Moore begins the poem by imagining the clarity of perception before the Fall, "not in the days of Adam and Eve, but when Adam / was alone." Then, "obliqueness was a variation / of the perpendicular, plain to see and / to account for"; now, the "blue-red-yellow band / of incandescence that was color [does not] keep its stripe." Moore's own perceptual strategy is to reject both the murky overrefinement of sophisticated seeing and the Apollonian abstraction of reality into formal order. Truth exists somewhere between complexity and form, a nebulous place she knows only in the act of attention to the "short-legged, fit- / ful advance, the gurgling and all the minutiae" of whatever she fixes her sight upon.[23] She echoes Emerson's warning in "Experience" that "for practical success, there must not be too much design" (483).

"Marriage" (1923) unites complexity and form in one of the female modernists' most witty and complex analyses of the marriage plot. Here Moore offers her bemused observations on specific and general causes of the Fall and its ambiguously comedic aftermath.

He also emphasizes the importance for Moore's poetics of the "colored and distorting" lenses of "Experience" (166, 173).

23. *The Complete Poems of Marianne Moore* (New York, 1967), 41. Subsequent references to this volume are included parenthetically in the text.

Her method is to assemble a collage of closely observed details and shifting perspectives that reinvigorate the clichés of irreconcilable sexual opposition. She gives us Eve, "equally positive in demanding a commotion / and in stipulating quiet" (62); and Adam, "a crouching mythological monster / in that Persian miniature of emerald mines" (63); and their union, "'Married people often look that way'"— / "'seldom and cold, up and down, / mixed and malarial / with a good day and a bad'" (66). The poem seems to resolve these contraries in its reassertion of Daniel Webster's entreaty for "'Liberty and union / now and forever.'" But perhaps the concluding images—"'the Book on the writing table; / the hand in the breast pocket'"—express indeterminacy (70). The commitment implied by the book and the gesture may just as well suggest fossilized language and a hand withheld from communication.[24] Such nonresolution, reminiscent of the endings of *The Awakening, Pilgrimage,* and the *Love Songs,* recalls the discomfort we feel with Emerson's affirmations at the end of "Experience."

Moore's "The Pangolin" (1941) reminds us that the hope of "Experience" resides in Emerson's speculation that the colored prison of subjectivity might be transformed into a prism. In those moments when divine light strikes pure, true color in us, we enjoy what Moore's Presbyterian heritage calls grace. "The Pangolin" understands grace to be the fleeting reward for the pain and absurdity of humanness. Naked man possesses none of the external armor and physical grace of Moore's admired animals. He blunders about the world, "slaving / to make his life more sweet," often "capsizing in / / disheartenment" (119). His saving graces are perceptual, a sense of humor and an ability to write his world. "Always / curtailed" and "thwarted," he attains spiritual grace in the pursuit of his daily labors: "'Again the sun! / anew each day; and new and new and new, / that comes into and steadies my soul'" (120). In these repetitions, grace appears not as mystic transfiguration but as courage to venture forth again among the world's impediments. The allusion is to "The American Scholar": "Every day, the sun; and, after sunset, night and her stars. Ever the winds

24. Taffy Martin, *Marianne Moore: Subversive Modernist* (Austin, 1986), 24.

blow; ever the grass grows . . . always circular power returning into itself" (55).

In "Experience" Emerson re-images glass-imprisoned man as "a bit of Labrador spar, which has no lustre as you turn it in your hand, until you come to a particular angle; then it shows deep and beautiful colors" (477). For Emerson, the outflow of colored light becomes a charged current of correspondence between this world and divinity. The moderns are less sure of their ability to ignite such a connection. They pursue Emerson's qualification, noted in the epigraph to this essay, that the *process* of perception may be as important as the cohering vision. Borrowing an image from "The Pangolin," we can say that in the sparks emitted as their words slide against each other into new literary forms, Richardson, Loy, and Moore prove themselves "writing master[s]" of the world.

JEFFREY BARTLETT

"Many Loves": William Carlos Williams and the Difficult Erotics of Poetry

The affirmation of love is neither as easy nor as sentimental as we usually believe it to be. Williams earned
it, honestly and courageously, in the face of death—his
and the world's.

— *The Music of Survival*

When I first began reading William Carlos Williams, I wasn't excited by him. The cat poem, the wheelbarrow, the swiped plums—
these were good poems, of close observation exactly stated. But I
thought Williams not very passionate. This notion was encouraged
by the first book of his I owned, *The Autobiography*, which in-
structs us in its foreword not to look for intimate revelations, especially of sexual life. *The Autobiography* still seems to me tame and
evasive, but about the passionate, even erotic nature of Williams'
poetry, I was seriously mistaken.

Williams is in fact one of our most passionate poets; for him, poetry at its root is sensual. But his passion resides in the structure of
his poems, not in what they "say." He insists that a poem is an *object* made of words—by which he means that it is constructed of
materials arranged in so particular a form that it cannot be altered
in any way, or the whole poem is lost.[1] For him, paraphrase is point-

1. For Williams' most succinct articulation of this, see "Author's Introduction"
to *The Wedge* in *Collected Later Poems* (New York, 1950), 3–5. Subsequent refer-

less, as is explanation of the poem's "meaning." From this radical position, Williams attempts to prohibit understanding of the poem in terms other than its form prescribes. Form itself, he believes, is created primarily by feeling, as it expresses itself in the action (as opposed to the embedded content) of the poem. His single most sweeping achievement is to restore human feeling to the poem, and to us, straight as it comes from within the poet to the page. He brings poetry back to its senses.

We cannot say that Williams became a poet in order to restore love, in so many words; the driving ambition of his life was simply to be a poet. Yet, born of the Romantic tradition, his vision of poetry is fundamentally related to love between men and women—which remains among his strongest lifelong concerns. He always felt an intimate association between love and poetry. Speaking of the poem, he feared that we "die miserably every day / for lack / of what is found there."[2] And what is found there is the healing force of relation to self, others, and world, called love.[3]

By the time he published *Spring and All* in 1923, Williams was aware of the mannered excesses of the Romantic lyric and its futility for his own day and place, at least partially because he had committed these errors himself. *Spring and All* is something of a culmination, because it unites the poetics announced in the Prologue to *Kora in Hell* and statements for his *Contact* magazine with the direct expression and speech-determined rhythms and

---

ences to this volume will be identified by *CLP* and include page references parenthetically in the text.

2. William Carlos Williams, *Pictures from Brueghel* (New York, 1962), 161–62, hereinafter cited as *PB* in the text.

3. Williams uses the word *love* in the titles of numerous individual poems and of his two most accomplished plays, one of which, *Many Loves,* has supplied the title for my essay. He associates poetry with love in the early poem "Riposte" (*Collected Earlier Poems* [New York, 1951], 156):

Love is like water or the air
my townspeople;
it cleanses, and dissipates evil gases.
It is like poetry too
and for the same reasons.

This volume is hereinafter cited as *CEP* in the text.

lines of *Al Que Quiere!*. That volume (1917) holds evidence that his desire to "sing" of love has undergone modifications of formal necessity that will change his sense of love's nature and lead him to revalue it, as well as the poet's right to express it.

He did not achieve this breakthrough easily. Poetic love, with its Romantic singer swearing fealty to his beloved on her balcony, has failed to be proven in experience. It has given us the illusion of love, a strange ideal we can neither recognize nor touch. But this was Williams' model, in society as well as poetry. His admitted early influences are the English Romantics, particularly Keats (and not at his best—*Endymion*), and Shakespeare in the sonnets and songs. Both these examples require an object-person to address, a loved one removed from the poet by circumstance or her own caprice. The poet must speak from mixed feelings of longing and frustration, pouring out his earnest desire but enduring its unfulfillment. His loved one is, of course, also his muse, his inspirational source. Love in this tradition is characteristically ideal and unreachable; the poet is debarred from satisfaction except in the sensuality of his song and in his imaginative "fancy."

The poems in Williams' first published book, *The Tempers* (1913), follow almost sheepishly the role of Romantic singer. "First Praise," popular today with anthologists, represents the volume's archaic diction, syntactic inversions, and bent-knee posture, which only "Mezzo Forte" avoids. Yet much was in the air at this time: just as romance became a pale form of love in a time of increasing physicality and the boyish guise of beseecher grew ridiculous in a generation soon to fight the first modern war, so had fixed forms and lilting melodies begun to appear rigid and precious. Enter Ezra Pound.

Williams' first magazine publication was six poems that later appeared in *The Tempers*; Pound wrote a brief preface for the first group and also reviewed the entire volume. His reserved and mildly condescending approval suggests, as do the poems themselves, that Pound felt he had here a promising follower of his own example.[4]

4. Pound's introductory note is reprinted in William Carlos Williams, *I Wanted to Write a Poem*, ed. Edith Heal (New York, 1978), 12; part of his review is reprinted in Emily M. Wallace, *A Bibliography of William Carlos Williams* (Middletown, Conn., 1968), 10.

Pound's influence is in fact heavily evident, even to the use of personae, "lusty" declamation, and the measured (not metrical) cadences prescribed in "the musical phrase."

All this is history, and so far William Carlos Williams hardly figures in it except derivatively. No doubt he recognized this and did not enjoy it. His apparent standards were English, like his publishers. Then came *Al Que Quiere!*, which he had considered calling *The Pleasures of Democracy*—an American volume, defiant of all proprieties, literary and mannerly, of the overseas master culture. He did not need Pound to introduce him this time; he wrote his own greeting, aggressive, vernacular, reckless of its reception, and addressed to the "gentle reader" who "will probably not like it, because it is brutally powerful and scornfully crude. Fortunately, neither the author nor the publisher care much whether you like it or not. . . . [W]e have the satisfaction of offering that which will outweigh, in spite of its eighty small pages, a dozen volumes of pretty lyrics. We have the profound satisfaction of publishing a book in which, we venture to predict, the poets of the future will dig for material as the poets of today dig in Whitman's *Leaves of Grass.*"[5]

Few of the poems that follow express such antipathy for their readers, yet the preface is not uncharacteristic of the book. Williams always is willing to take chances, to speak extravagances in prose that he will seldom dare in poems (for example, *Spring and All*), probably because he has less to lose and is less restrained by formal considerations. At this time, prose has for him pragmatic ends, as "statement of facts concerning emotions, intellectual states, data of all sorts." On the other hand, poetry produces "new form dealt with as a reality in itself."[6]

The opening announcement in *Al Que Quiere!* voices its author's conviction (and underlying worry) about rejecting the old poetic forms and vision. Williams believes that, within itself, form implies content, and he begins to oppose the critical complaints he

5. Wallace, *Bibliography*, 11–12.
6. William Carlos Williams, *Spring and All*, in *Imaginations*, ed. Webster Schott (New York, 1970), 133. Hereinafter cited as *SA* in the text.

knows will follow his poems. He makes an explicit attack on traditional critics two years later (1919):

But all thought is ugly to the American critic—especially if it come from the left. And since in a work of art the form of the composition bespeaks the thought, then all new forms are inevitably anathema and this is not alone true of America.

So let us take off our undershirts, my friends, and scratch our backs in good company. At least we will not be praised because of our loveliness.[7]

Williams' hostility toward conservative critics who arbitrate polite taste continues throughout his career, though its violence lessens in his later years. He invariably takes the side of the New, the colloquial, the local, and the actual in such debates; often he must pay for it by being thought simpleminded, imitative, and provincial. He is none of these things. Although his important place as a Modernist has been recognized widely in the last ten years or so, there persists among some critics a tendency to patronize Williams as a sort of innocent, somewhat ignorant when compared to Pound, Yeats, and Eliot.

Williams is a serious aesthetician, though not a brilliant one; he is a premier practitioner. He is not primarily an "intellectual" poet, in the way that Eliot or Stevens may be said to be. Rather, he directly transmits sensory perception (as opposed to describing it) and so frees us to feel directly, necessitating an equally forthright response. He does not often prescribe how we are supposed to feel, or legislate our emotions, as do Pound and Eliot, hence the confusion of overly mental readers in regard to what his poems "mean." He is an anti-academic writer, the very opposite of a poet of ideas, as his dictum, "No ideas but in things," insists. Most of all, Williams means to elicit our senses, and our intellects in their service. Demonstrably, his various poems appeal to all five senses and the sixth, the mind's sense—the imagination.

Al Que Quiere! as a whole exhibits many qualities typical of Williams: no capital letter to begin a line unless the sentence re-

7. William Carlos Williams, A Recognizable Image, ed. Bram Dijkstra (New York, 1978), 60–61.

quires it; breaking the line according to the order of the poet's perception; preoccupation with the visual sense, and direct rendering of the stimuli it receives; rhythm, diction, and syntax taken from the spoken, common language; specific, natural images local to the poem's context; the poet's absorption with flower images, and his equating them with a woman or some feminine element.[8] The volume contains three different poems entitled "Love Song," each of which possesses characteristics of form, address, and voice that demonstrate the poet's drive toward a modern American expression of love.

The first, "Daisies are broken," marks a significant advance in poetic technique partly by what it does not do. The love expressed is not of devotion to a lady, but of the simple beauty of relation—of man to woman, of human to nature, of words to feeling and memory. It is a poem of understatement, both subtle and private. Only in the title is love named, yet the emotion is presented amply. Williams realized that this poem "is cryptic, shy";[9] nevertheless, it is a direct rendering close to the conditions of experience.

As do many of Williams' poems, this one opens with observation of natural fact; the poet's eye registers, and language precisely records, what it sees. His reactions complicate and personalize as the poem progresses from the fragmentary observations "Daisies are broken / petals are news of the day" (CEP, 125). The other four lines of the stanza introduce the human presence, telling us how the daisies may have been broken ("they catch on shoes") and who it is that sees petals as "news." Further observation follows in the second stanza; the poet, looking at the arching branches, sees—more likely, he imagines after the fact; either way, the event is actual in the poem—that

They hold firm
break with a roar
show the white!

---

8. Syntactic studies of Williams pay great dividends, as those of us who have taught his poems can testify. Hugh Kenner devotes a chapter to this in *The Pound Era* (Berkeley, 1971). However, he literally misreads "Young Sycamore," damaging his claim to close analysis (see pp. 402–403).

9. Williams, *I Wanted to Write a Poem*, 23.

All ten words have one syllable each, both simple and sensual, emphasizing the solidity of the branches and the "roar" of destructive energy when one is split off from the trunk. This action excites the poet to exclamation and, in the rest of the poem, to commentary on spring and his own life. Williams' insistence upon the destruction complementary to all creation is well known ("descent" and "ascent"); he learned it from nature's processes and from the turbulence of his own personality. This is no source of dismay to him, rather an assurance of cyclical continuity, affirmed in the poem's third stanza; it, too, makes him exuberant.

Just as the revelation of white gum-fiber stimulates him to sing "the return in May" of spring, so that transition moves him to the personal remembrance with which the poem ends. There are but three personal possessives in the poem, and the repetition of "your" identifies the season ("Your moods are slow") with his wife ("your father's grove"). They are made indivisible by this pronoun and form the association that, along with the previous broken branches, completes the poet's song of love. Although the great oaks had been "ripped from the ground," he responds to them now (in memory: the fourth stanza is in the past tense) in wonder at the natural power that did this and with implied faith that their life will be in some way renewed. Again, spring and love are joined in his mind. By the unintrusive presentation of the various details, Williams has created for Flossie an avowal of the binding relation they share and of his belief that love (theirs) is a force in human life as strong as the cycle of seasons. He has not said, "I love you," for love is not a mere matter of declaration or sentiment for Williams. He has objectified the emotions of love and, in the last five lines (i.e., "Remember this?"), the shared moment by which she will know what he feels.

This final stanza employs a technique by which Williams frequently closes his earlier short poems. It reverses or expands previous types of statement or styles of address, in a sense opening the poem to a further insight or occasion for thought, and so cannot strictly be called closure, though it is the poem's end. For example, "Chicory and Daisies" (part one) is a lyrical invocation to the chicory to grow and so realize its nature; such fulfillment of natural purpose is so important to Williams that he believes "the sky goes out / if you should fail" (*CEP*, 122). Yet part two shifts entirely to a vision of innocent destructiveness that we are meant to see also as natural and as a source of wonder:

I saw a child with daisies
for weaving into the hair
tear the stems
with her teeth!

The purity of scene and the excited tone of these lines express the poet's amazement at the processes of life, the innocence and the necessity of such action. Like the last lines of "Love Song," they affirm life by an outpouring of feeling that expresses love, of which joy is a form, not by worshipping it but by living and by making a poem that re-creates the emotion for readers.

The three "Pastorals" in *Al Que Quiere!* use this technique or a variation of it. "If I say I have heard voices" functions as does "Chicory and Daisies," presenting a visual image that stops all argument by the sheer fact of its being:

If I say I have heard voices
who will believe me? . . .
I looked and there were little frogs
with puffed-out throats,
singing in the slime. (*CEP*, 161)

The other two reverse this order, offering brief personal statements on common observations; they argue no cases, simply state positions. Life is better revealed because more itself by "the old man" who cleans up dog shit than by the "Episcopal minister / approaching the pulpit," though Williams does not press the qualitative judgment: "These things / astonish me beyond words" (*CEP*, 124).

Both versions of this "clincher" means of ending, which summarizes and/or redirects an impression yet does not "finish" it, are examples of Williams' desire for *contact*, direct sensuous relation to objects of perception, material for poetry. Contact is erotic. It gratifies the senses and realizes desire, and so overcomes the isolation of the Romantic singer. Williams is a sensualist, in that he cares more for his own feelings and perceptions than for ideas. Feeling, for him, is always immediate—it must come *now* and therefore must be *local.* He trusts his feelings, but only as they are expressed, made tangible through the formation of the poem. Writing a poem is a way of feeling, and direct presentation keeps it *new,* stops it from falling into falsifications such as sentimentality. Contact generates creation, which in turn validates it. As Williams says, "How else to derive benefit from that which I love, unless I create a new thing of my own."[10]

And how can we love what we have never known, at least in imagination. Contact is a way to love and may be accomplished through two means, perception and language, unified in the poem. Pertinent to this relation is Pound's aphorism gleaned from Richard of St. Victor: "*Amare videre est.* To love is to perceive." Williams agrees that the active senses potentiate love, as does Zukofsky, who applies this Chinese proverb: "*What the eyes cannot see, the heart cannot crave.*"[11] For Williams, contact with the world is also contact with himself; even the most objectified poems are self-expressive, by their attention to things tacitly proving the poet's intimate connection with them. The words are Williams', not the objects', and we must hear them spoken, even when they create a purely visual effect. The poem, itself an object, implies by its nature the perception of its author and its readers, as well as the environmental matrix in which all things coexist.

It is difficult to overestimate Williams' emphatic need for contact in the early poems. A relatively inexperienced poet, uncertain of his talent and direction, he turns outward to seek in the world around him objects, people, and language that may help him create the kind of poetry he feels he must write. He must not only make the form new, fit for its time, but make poetry yield the substance of his own life. Only in poems can he admit this—not, for example, in his essays, in which he suckers himself into arguing ideas. When he stays on the true ground of feeling, Williams refutes intellectual complaints by the proof of his example. His anger

10. William Carlos Williams, "America, Whitman, and the Art of Poetry," *Poetry Journal,* VIII, No. 1 (November, 1917), 28.
11. Ezra Pound, *Selected Prose, 1909–1965,* ed. William Cookson (New York, 1973), 71; Louis Zukofsky, *Bottom: On Shakespeare* (Austin, Tex., 1963), 266.

is aroused by critics who, in questioning his practice, in effect cast doubts upon the truth of his emotions.

Williams felt deeply the need for release from the frustrating contradictions of his personality. Although not given to confessional intimacy, he aches to project his feelings; he insists upon directness and actuality, yet longs for revelation. As a late poem has it, "In our family we stammer unless, / half mad, / we come to speech at last" (*PB*, 77). Many of the dualisms of Western life may be found in his poems, whose actions attempt to unify them.

"Danse Russe" exemplifies the poems announced in Williams' defiant preface. It is a poem about self-love and freedom, yet whimsical and circumspect. Representing the sexual aspect of Williams' poetry, it portrays the physical expression of a man blocked from its outlet in another way. Williams was acutely aware of and frequently defended the conventionality of his life in Rutherford, especially when he compared himself with the bohemian artists he knew in New York and Europe. However, his regular visits to those sources of cultural revolution signify his desire to break out of the restrictions of small-town respectability in which, more than anything else, the decisive forces of his personality kept him.[12]

This life provides the backdrop against which the sensual outburst of "Danse Russe" occurs:

If when my wife is sleeping
and the baby and Kathleen
are sleeping. (*CEP*, 148)

The conditional "If" renders the entire dance hypothetical but also challenges the would-be censors (readers) of the final lines. To sing and dance naked, to celebrate oneself, enacts self-identification, even it it happens behind "the yellow drawn shades" and the song's subject is loneliness. It parodies the melancholy Romantic bard yet simultaneously revalues the function of poet/singer in language fit for the modern age. It accepts its condition as well: "'I was born to be lonely, / I am best so!'" And the poem ends with a two-line

12. With some bitterness, Williams recalls this conflict between the freedom of writing and the responsibility of work in *The Autobiography* (New York, 1951), 48–49.

clincher that dares the world to deny him: "Who shall say I am not / the happy genius of my household?"

Notice that the poem does what the action it recounts does not: It raises the blinds and brings the song and dance of the happy/ lonely naked man into the light of day. It liberates the poet's sexual energy, as the dance puts him (literally?) in touch with himself. The lone action is purged of its solitude, making a place for itself in the varieties of experience.

"Danse Russe" also introduces the second of Williams' three important structural analogues for his work: a poem may be a song, or a dance, or both, as this one is. Song is the musical element, voice its articulation. Dance is the movement expressed by the body and perceived by the eye. Of course, music accompanies dance, or vice versa, but for Williams (unlike Pound or, in another way, Zukofsky) music is not a means of formal measurement applied by the ear but an instinctual sense of progression choreographed by the eye and the natural order of language (later, "idiom") as it is spoken. Williams' music of perception is determined by bodily intuition.

The visual dance of words asserts primacy over the song in the later work, especially in *Paterson* and the poems of old age that follow it. Yet Williams never ceased to write "songs," though his conception of what kind of singer he had to be would change as he developed his ideas of the dance of imagination. His songs remain vocally expressive, but they grow less effervescent as he grows older. These quiet lines from a "Song" in his last volume summarize his attempt to unify the senses of the poet and aspects of the various arts:

undying accents
repeated till
the ear and the eye lie
down together in the same bed. (*PB*, 15)

In fact, Williams' faith in the possibilities of a new poetry goes so deep that, at one time or another, he authorizes it to assume functions of all major arts, to use their materials or perspectives and to represent them. He writes "songs" and "dances" and also "portraits" (all are contained in *Al Que Quiere!* and all are in *Pic-*

tures from Brueghel). Such absorption with "art" poems belongs to his plan to mirror modernity and so produce forms to record accurately the perceptions and stated values of each prospective occasion.

Conversely, Williams knows how seriously the language has been traduced, how strong the temptation to "answer in the smart language."[13] The creation of new poetry requires a sweeping re-valuation of language and its uses. Feelings lie locked inside us, needing new words and contexts to liberate them because the old are dead and we cannot feel honestly with them. Knowledgeable of the advances in modern painting and music, Williams adapts them to his verse, with the result that things and emotions are not de-scribed or explained but presented (hence, for one thing, the vi-tality of his images). His poems do not primarily uphold moral values; like the works of painter and musician, they serve the forms of human feeling. "Della Primavera Trasportata Al Morale," one of his earliest experiments with typography and spacing (pub-lished in the *Imagist Anthology* of 1930), demonstrates his convic-tion that life, clearly perceived, has a moral nature prior to all codes:

Moral
   the redhead sat
   in bed with her legs
   crossed and talked
   rough stuff
Moral
   the door is open
Moral
   the tree moving diversely
   in all parts—
—the moral is love, bred of
the mind and eyes and hands—. (*CEP*, 60)

As a whole, the poems in *Al Que Quiere!* move toward the pre-cise integration of form and voice found in *Spring and All*. Some of these earlier poems succeed in applying the modern method Wil-liams was developing; others, like "A Portrait in Greys," remain

13. William Carlos Williams, *In the American Grain* (New York, 1956), 215.

tentatively transitional. Regardless, formal experimentation is always used by Williams as a means to bring himself more fully into a situation—and closer to himself.

Like perception and desire, love cannot exist without an object. Both naturally and traditionally, we immediately assume that this object will be another person. In a poem we first expect the lover to address or speak of the beloved one. Isn't that what a "love song" is? The most common concern of such love is romance or sex, or both.

In his first poetry, William Carlos Williams follows this line of desiring lovers and, throughout his life, associates love with the feminine. As I have said, the issue of male-female love remains imperative for him, deepening to include marriage and family in the late poems. His sense of love as striving also endures. The residue of romantic longing, frankly tinged with sexual interest, subsists in the poems of solitary "girl watching" that are plentiful in the *Collected Earlier Poems*, including "The Young Housewife," "The Right of Way," and "In the 'Sconset Bus."[14] To some extent, these poems are voyeuristic, products of Williams' lustful eye, but like other poems of close visual observation, they arise from his intense curiosity about living things he contacts—old people, children, animals, plants. Erotic love, sexual and bodily in the early work, is transmuted later into the sensuous idea of Beautiful Thing in *Paterson*. She may be seen as a composite of the various objects of love found in his poetry: woman, nature, the modern environment, and ideal beauty (which is revealed only in its actual embodiments, supplemented by the imagination).

Williams loves his own senses and loves experience because it stimulates them, excites him, and thereby leads to the marvelous. His willingness to embrace and respond to physical stimuli reveals the essentially healthy outlook that stands as one of Williams' most engaging qualities as a poet and as a man. It is summarized perfectly in this note from 1928: "A piece of experience—of any kind—but especially of love is meat that enriches the whole

14. Other such poems may be found in *Collected Earlier Poems*, 101, 253, 369, 462; in *Collected Later Poems*, 70, 86, 123, 166; and in *Pictures from Brueghel*, 46, 50, 123.

body."[15] Although he knows the difficulty and transience of the sensual/spiritual ecstasy of love, Williams never abandons his faith in it. Like D. H. Lawrence, he believes in duality, as a potential bond for overcoming the split that it itself represents. So whatever he, a man, loves, must be feminine—to him (perceptually, not absolutely).[16]

His many flower poems span Williams' entire career and provide his most memorable affective images. He repeatedly goes to them because of the nurturing affirmation he finds there. Williams is no sensitive "nature poet"—he does not "appreciate" flowers from afar. He is moved sensually by them as objects of contact. The resultant relation is a form of love, enacted in numerous poems. Through the flower poems, as through the portraits of natural scenes and poems of the seasons in process, Williams is able to bridge the gap between man and nature, which rationalism and industrial blight have exacerbated and widened in this century. In these poems he revalues the Romantic tradition's approach to nature.

Sour Grapes (1921), which follows *Al Que Quiere!*, is overlooked as a volume, but it abounds in poems of exactly this passionate involvement of the poet with his environment. Near its center lies a vibrant quartet of flower poems in which the human and the natural intertwine, even to sharing personal pronouns. These are not the sighing recollections of Wordsworth over his daffodils, but active possession of experience in the present. For example, sight of the primrose leads him to recognition of natural interconnectedness, which is a fact and a feeling rather than an idea:

Yellow, yellow, yellow, yellow!
It is not a color.
It is summer!
It is the wind on a willow,
the lap of waves, the shadow
under a bush, a bird, a bluebird,

15. William Carlos Williams, *The Embodiment of Knowledge* (New York, 1974), 35.
16. Of course, this does not apply to masculine friendship, which is not a major theme of Williams as it is, for example, of Herman Melville and Henry Miller.

three herons, a dead hawk
rotting on a pole—
Clear yellow![17] (*CEP*, 209)

In his effort to equal the demands of modernity without being untrue to his own romantic feelings for nature, Williams takes the large step of embracing the contemporary city and the machine. In 1932, he states this modern interrelation in the most direct manner:

Would you consider a train passing—or the city in the icy sky—a love song? What else? It must be so.

And if I told you the dark trees against the night sky and the row of the city's lights beyond and under them—would you consider that a love statement?

This is what my poems have been from the first.[18]

More than a few poems of the 1920s and the 1930s show his wish to unite the objects of modern social life with human feeling in a single vision integrated by the relational force of love. "Brilliant Sad Sun" (1927) combines his mother's nostalgia for her past with lines spaced to approximate restaurant signs, giving us at once her feeling ("sad"), the location and the time of year ("Restaurant: Spring!"), and observation of an action (familiar from "The Red Wheelbarrow") by which he hopes to cheer her up and bring her from the past into the present:

Look!
from a glass pitcher she serves
clear water to the white chickens.

What are your memories
beside that purity?[19] (*CEP*, 324)

17. Compare the repetition of "yellow" here with that in "Love Song" ("I lie here thinking of you"). This device, used for emphasizing emotional intensity, is one of Williams' primary means of showing that he feels good. To the end of his life, he continues, with variations, to apply such repetition for exultation and/or insistence, as in the crucial line near the end of "The Desert Music": "I *am* a poet! I am. I am. I am a poet, I reaffirmed" (*Pictures from Brueghel*, 120).

18. Williams, *A Novelette and Other Prose*, in *Imaginations*, 298–99.

19. This poem combines techniques used singly elsewhere, for example, the sad memories of "All the Fancy Things" (with which it was published in the *Dial* in 1927) and the electric soda sign of "The Attic Which is Desire" (1930).

Alfred Stieglitz, "Reflections: Night—New York," 1896–97
Gravure, 8 5/16 × 10 3/4"
Collection, The Museum of Modern Art, New York

The poem presents an entire complex of events, objects, and emotions without unnecessary comment by the poet; as such, it may be called a highly advanced form of the Imagist poem defined by Pound.

Other city poems rest side by side with poems of nature, such as "Overture to a Dance of Locomotives" and "The Great Figure" in *Sour Grapes.* In Williams' terms, a flower is not "like" a woman, nor is a city "like" either; such correspondences do not depend on metaphor. They show that the poet contacts the objects in the same sensuous manner and that the emotion produced and expressed in each case is the same: call it love.

Williams' career really begins with *Al Que Quiere!* and, after the flourish of successful experimentation in the early 1920s, proliferates in a diversity of forms and genres. Despite the later expansions of focus, it remains true that the deepest account of Williams' life is to be found in his poetry, with its continuing theme—the search for love, for whole relation to others and the world. We must take Williams at his word, that poetry is revelation, and that, for him, so shy of confession, the mystery of personality is bared *in* the poem.

The finest articulation of his effort to clear poetic ground and then live in it, comes in *Spring and All*. In this book, he first becomes himself, integrating the violent quest for clarity of intention and stance that also marks the Dadaesque prose styles of *Kora in Hell* and *The Great American Novel* with the formal precision of perception in the poems. By juxtaposing the two genres, he expresses—and, at the same time, contains—the dualistic tensions of his own mind. In *Spring and All*, prose carries the fight of descent, of revolt against the dead old, while poetry provides the affirmation of ascent into new form. This does not necessarily imply that their contents are placid, for, as Williams says in poem XV, "destruction and creation / are simultaneous" (*SA*, 127), and the anguish of his troubled self is not to be excluded from (or permanently settled by) the poem. Nevertheless, both discursive and polemical, it is a triumphant book, a breakthrough to expression and his most complete effort before *Paterson*, whose major advance from *Spring and All* is compositional, in the addition of material by direct presentation within a more elastic, open structure.

The convoluted, destructive process of the prose, "dedicated" to the "imagination," forces itself through the dense stupidity of modern times, clearing ground for the emergence of spring. Williams characterizes his prose in its "hard battle" as "notes jotted down in the midst of action" (*SA*, 98). The opening sequence, uninterrupted, is more than twice as long as any other. Leading into the first poem, it stops, "Suddenly it is at an end. THE WORLD IS NEW" (95). The book has prepared its own birth, which occurs in this poem. The precise moment when the reborn plants "enter the new world" is spatialized to hold the movements within a sequence that, by virtue of the syntax, the watching eye also joins. By virtue of the poem, spring in the world is spring in the imagination; in the context of the entire book, the awakening of the world is also the poet's awakening to his task of expression.

In the opening poem and the second poem, with which it is paired, one of Williams' "still lifes," the poet is not obviously present. They are acts of perception of natural objects and processes, directly carried over into words. Likewise, the third, except that in the final lines the farmer is explicitly called "the artist figure . . . composing" (*SA*, 99), because he faces the new work that springtime brings. The poet, who has been addressing us between poems, speaks directly of himself in the fourth one, which follows immediately. Because there is

> Nobody
> to say it—,
> he must
> Burst it asunder
> break through to the fifty words necessary—.

In poem V, set against wintry "winds from the north," he is ready to deal with his own trouble, having for inspiration the examples of nature and the farmer. He cries,

> Black wind, I have poured out my heart
> to you until I am sick of it—
> Now I run my hand over you feeling
> the play of your body—the quiver
> of its strength—. (103)

This powerful emotion includes and dramatizes the artistic statements of the prose while, typically for Williams, equating a natural object with a loved person. The certainty of his assertions is diffused, for poetics is one thing and the act of the poem another. After obliquely rejecting the transformed classicism of Pound ("the grief of the bowmen of Shu"), Williams concludes worriedly,

How easy to slip
into the old mode, how hard to
cling firmly to the advance—.

Spring and All (like all Williams' writing) attempts exactly this, the advance into the New, a matter of personal liberation and vitalization of living forms. The former issue is the subject of poem VI ("To Have Done Nothing"); the latter, of poems VII ("The Rose") and VIII ("At the Faucet of June"). The book moves on, fluctuating between extremes of perceptual contact without intrusive comment (for example, XXII, "The Red Wheelbarrow") and intensely personal expressions (such as IX, "Young Love"). Themes and images that recur throughout Williams' poetry surface repeatedly here, including flowers, woman, the modern city, lower-class life, painterly observation, and the poet's role, as well as the fear that American life now is empty. Yet progressively his reach grows, as shown by the poems that divide the whole group into thirds, numbers IX, XVIII, and XXVII.

Poem IX, after a culminating purge of shame and impotence, brings the poet to a kind of acceptance of his past failure in love and prepares the reader to see the urgent truth that initiates the next prose segment: "Understood in a practical way, without calling upon mystic agencies, of this or that order, it is that life becomes actual only when it is identified with ourselves" (*SA*, 115).

His failure is America's, a failure to love, to touch and mingle. This is why "The pure products of America / go crazy—" (131) and why the modern world has

No one
to witness
and adjust, no one to drive the car. (133)

The last stanza summarizes the persistent negative state also prominent in poems V, VI, and XXV, which confront as well the poet's dilemma in a culture that does not want him and, if he could not write, would make him crazy, too. The function "to witness / and adjust" is the poet's; by his use of language driven by feeling, he hopes to speak for people who have no other outlet for expression. Seen this way, "To Elsie" is another of Williams' love songs (though one of unfulfillment). The car, Williams' favorite vehicle for observation, is no symbol, rather a fact of contemporary life that, by its very nature, isolates people from contact with others. Williams likes to look at women, as in poem XI ("The Right of Way"), and believes it to be a sort of outreaching, but there is a tinge of sadness as well as desire in that act of passing.

Williams does not minimize this dis-ease, for the most pessimistic poems are laid next to brighter visions throughout. However, he chooses to conclude with a poem to the "black eyed susan," just as the prose concludes with a prospect of freedom for both man and word. Poem XXVII seems almost to answer XVIII. Despite the maddening pressures of America, the "dark woman" (who is a flower, which is a woman, says Williams) stands at the end of the book as a promise of what one may break through toward, if he can cling firmly enough to the advance.

Spring and All itself offers the same prospect, though without easy solution; readers too must undergo the incessant struggle it enacts. The number and frequency of poems increase as the book progresses, from eleven in the first half to sixteen in the second, and conversely the amount of prose exposition decreases. By this transformation, the book's open form also moves us toward Williams' vision of poetry as a healing release.

Williams offers us the brave example of a poet who refused to be thwarted, despite all difficulty, by forces of society and self, who refused to be blocked from the contact with life that poems can celebrate. In 1952, crippled but not stopped, he reasserted this impetus: "The best of modern benefits are rooted in us. . . . [W]hen an impasse in modern art is encountered the clarification of it is found in the path of our advance, close to hand in our familiar environment. This is my theme; we may lose our lives in pursuit of it."[20] We may gain our lives from it also. By determinedly clinging to the advance, Williams proved his contention. For it, we have no better word, made new, than love.

20. Williams, *A Recognizable Image*, 210.

EDWARD BRUNNER

"The Farewell Day Unkind": The Fragmentary Poems of Hart Crane's Last Five Years

Crane's definition of the poet's concern—"self-
discipline toward a formal integration in experience"—also tells us of the function poetry had for
him. He was a poet by necessity, having need of a discipline, not of denial but inclusion, that provided
enough security to permit the risk of growth.
                              —*Hart's Bridge*

Given the physical and mental pressures on Hart Crane between
1928 and 1932, in what would be the last five years of his life, it
should be surprising that he was able to complete any poetry at all.
By and large, he did not. In 1929 he added one long and two short
sections to *The Bridge,* and a few weeks before his suicide in April,
1932, he finished "The Broken Tower." Apart from these, he rarely
saw a poem through to its final form.[1]

Crane's mental and physical deterioration during these years has
been documented by eyewitnesses. Yvor Winters recalls the shock
of meeting Crane "during the Christmas week of 1927, when he
was approximately 29 years old; his hair was graying, his skin had

---

1. In the latest edition of the poems, *The Poems of Hart Crane,* ed. Marc Simon
(Liveright, 1986), the majority of works labeled "Incomplete Poems" and "Fragments" date from 1928 to 1932. Except where otherwise cited, texts are from this
edition and page numbers occur parenthetically in the text.

the dull red color with reticulated grayish traceries which so often
goes with advanced alcoholism, and his ears and knuckles were
beginning to look a little like those of a pugilist." Susan Jenkins
Brown registers surprise on greeting him after his return from
Paris: "His eight months' absence had made a change in his appearance: complexion red and somewhat mottled, hair grayer, figure
slightly puffy—this at twenty-nine." She also reports an "[i]ncreas-
ing inability to tolerate alcohol," which Peter Blume confirms:
"Sue Brown used to say that she tried to leave the party just as
Hart was getting 'lit up' because she knew 'what followed.' 'What
followed' happened rather suddenly. His exhilaration turned into a
sullen sputtering. A repetition of some personal slight to himself,
some critical injustice, some dislike or frustration, which would go
on and on to everybody's discomfort and misery, turning sometimes
to violence." To Blume, Crane suffered the bouts of a manic de-
pressive as well as those of an alcoholic. And in Malcolm Cowley's
description of a 1931 party—one of many that Cowley recalls—
Crane's behavior deteriorates no less rapidly.[2]

Such harrowing accounts have been considered more than sufficient to explain the sudden drop in both the quantity and quality of
Crane's work after 1927. But this explanation, considered by itself,
may be too simple. A more convincing reason for his collapse is
that in his final years he consciously set out to write a poetry of a
kind new to him. As it happened, this poetry proved unusually
difficult for him to compose, even though it was far less complex
than any of his previous work, because it was at odds with so
much in his own life. Yet he was strongly attracted to this new
poetry, and mastering it may have seemed essential if he was to
continue as a poet.

An example of this new poetry is "A Name for All," written in
October-November of 1928, published in the *Dial* of April, 1929,
and one of the few late poems to appear in Crane's lifetime. With-

2. Yvor Winters, *In Defense of Reason* (Denver, n.d.), 589–90; Susan Jenkins
Brown, *Robbers Rocks* (Middletown, Conn., 1969), 117; Peter Blume to Warren
Herendeen and Donald Parker, May 31, 1977, in *Hart Crane Newsletter*, II (Sum-
mer, 1978), 18 (but see his "A Recollection of Hart Crane," in *Yale Review*, LXXVI
[March, 1987], 152–56, for a less dramatic portrait of Crane's later years); Malcolm
Cowley, *A Second Flowering* (New York, 1973), 214.

out drawing upon unusual diction or disruptive rhythms, the poem unfolds in three 4-line rhyming stanzas and proceeds steadily and confidently to its close. It is a piece that directly conveys a message:

I dreamed that all men dropped their names, and sang
As only they can praise, who build their days
With fin and hoof, with wing and sweetened fang
Struck free and holy in one Name always.   (119)

Thomas Parkinson described this as "a poem so dull that it is hard to believe Crane could have written it and astonishing that he should have published it."[3] "A Name for All" appears to be true to a new set of aesthetic principles that aim for purity, as distinct from the daunting complexity of his previous work. If these principles could be enacted, they would produce a poetry that would be both uplifting and solemn. Unlike some of the lyrics in *The Bridge*, set in a South Street speakeasy ("Cutty Sark") or in the National Winter Garden burlesque house, this would be an impersonal poetry that would depend on the strong authority of the poet's clear perceptions rather than on the wrenching personal struggles that had informed his previous work.[4]

Why would Crane want to alter his poetics at this time? There are several answers to this question. For one thing, in 1927, laboring to complete *The Bridge*, he must have been aware that he stood before an important threshold, where some of his immense ambitions might be realized: he published more poems in that year—nineteen—than in any other year of his life, and his work was being

3. Thomas Parkinson, *Hart Crane and Yvor Winters: A Literary Correspondence* (Berkeley, 1976), 130.
4. At this time, Crane was disinclined to express pleasure at the complexities of his earlier work. "My White bldgs, now out," he writes to Winters on January 3, 1927, "shocks me in some ways. I think I have grown more objective since writing some of those poems—more sympathetic with the reader. 'Make my dark heavy poem light—and light' is a line from Donne which has always haunted me" (Parkinson, *Hart Crane and Yvor Winters*, 29). Crane's friendship with Winters begins in 1927, about the same time that he starts to shift away from original experimental poetry. The destructive effect of Winters, the stringent moralist, on Crane is left unexplored by Parkinson, who is concerned primarily with restoring Winters' reputation.

actively sought by editors. It may have been permissible for him to compose extravagantly when he was an unknown beginner struggling for recognition, but he was now on the verge of becoming the Bard, the master poet of America whose appearance Emerson had predicted—a new Whitman. But this opportunity could still elude him. Because he had allowed so many portions of his epic to be published (virtually everything that he had completed was in print by 1927 and in conspicuous places—the *Dial, Poetry,* the *Criterion*), he was obliged to produce additional sections for the book version. But in 1926, *The Bridge* had grown suddenly in unexpected directions; what he had written was, in fact, not what he had planned.

He had planned a cultural epic that would dramatize the growth of America from the time of the first settlers through the upheaval of the Civil War to the crisis of the machine age. That crisis had already been resolved in the drafts from "Atlantis" written as early as 1923. In this finale, the poet's vision, establishing a panoramic perspective with the Brooklyn Bridge as a focusing lens, harmonized in suitably lavish language the discord between the machine and nature. That framework, however, was awkwardly stretched by what he actually composed in 1926, a sequence that reflected his personal predicament. In exile on a Caribbean island and isolated from that urban setting whose anonymity had granted him such freedom, nostalgic for friends and lovers, and unable to find emotional release in the reckless ways that the city had characteristically allowed him, he wrote a series of poems that captured the disrupted and undirected vitality of urban New York with a stunning brilliance.

The implicit question that these poems ask is, What holds one together in this setting that is all motion and energy? The answer, Crane understood as he evoked the frenzied swirl of the modern city, is that here one could pursue a genuine love. The key word is pursue; pursuit of love is what compelled one to go to the city, and this pursuit is itself Crane's "eternal" theme. He could depend upon it, as a constant through history, even to help him visualize the lost world of the Indian. But love was not so easily found, and what Crane came to understand, in a final twist that contributed to the complex brilliance of these 1926 poems, was that often the city's allure became a substitute for genuine love. Its bright lights and motion were attractions that had to be seen through, much as Columbus had to see through his own desire for Cathay and wealth and fame to discover what he could not have known he would find until he actually found it.

The Bridge in 1926 had become a wonderfully complex and energetic series of insightful poems that located Crane himself at the center of the modern city. After 1926, though, when he began to sort through the work he had produced so effortlessly, he no longer had the eye to see what he had accomplished. Indeed, the one section he completed in 1927, "The River," built upon a fragment composed the year before, "Calgary Express." Blending the music of Afro-American spirituals with the southward roll of the Mississippi, the fragment offered a sympathetic portrait of the American black who, despite his oppressive circumstances, transformed his anger into acceptance, his resentment into submission—at least for the moment. In his revision of this material, however, Crane suppressed its radical theme and produced a pleasant and rambling testament to the vagabond life. By 1927, then, Crane was already beginning to undermine the originality of what he had achieved only a year earlier.[5]

Perhaps what argued most insistently for a change in poetics, however, was Crane's personal life; that is, how he might draw upon it as a subject for poetry. He could willfully propose to move away from avant-garde experimentalism, attempting to convince himself that his readers should be treated with more sympathy. He could see himself moving away from his penchant for obscurity by embracing more public themes, ones commensurate with the expectations of notable critics. But there remained the problem of his homosexuality. Had his personal life been even marginally acceptable, like that of a creative bohemian, this would have been one thing. In fact, however, he lived far beyond the pale of what would be acceptable to his family and their friends. He could decide to write a new kind of poetry, but he could not change his identity.

5. Crane's revisions of "Calgary Express" are explained in detail in my *Splendid Failure: Hart Crane and the Making of "The Bridge"* (Urbana, 1985), 187–201.

For most writers, a larger expanse of their personal life becomes available to them as subject matter for poetry as they mature. What Crane had to face as he began to feel an increasing confidence in his own abilities was that to include material from his own life was to risk devastating exposure. At the height of his powers, then, able to see into himself as never before, Crane could not use his life in his poetry.

Because of the vicious circle into which he had fallen—barred from personal subject-matter and encouraged to produce a verse suitable for an American bard—Crane's problems were imposing before he even put a word on paper. One way to understand the work of his last five years is to see it as veering wildly between verse that was agonizingly personal and almost confessional, and verse that aimed to speak in lofty generalities with the voice of a high-minded observer. In fact, "A Name for All" has the virtue of merging these two apparent opposites. Its message is that people should refrain from categorizing others, but the hidden context is suggested by the fact that Crane wrote the poem shortly after he had confronted his mother with the truth of his homosexuality. Her response had been devastating; though accounts vary, it appears that her reaction lay behind Crane's decision abruptly to leave the West Coast, where he had been visiting her, and return to New York. (One version is that his mother, hearing the news, insisted on moving to a hotel.) Thus "A Name for All" carries within its surface generalities a pointed message addressed to his mother, centering on an episode in his personal life.

The extraordinary circumstance that produced "A Name for All" was not to be duplicated. In other poems of this time, the opposing features divide. The result is work that is either intensely personal or patently public. On the one hand, Crane composed dense fragments that ached with pain, such as "The Visible the Untrue" (dedicated "to E.O.," the subject of *Voyages*). Only the final stanza of this work falls within sure understanding:

The window weight throbs in its blind
Partition. To extinguish what I have of faith.
Yes, light. And it is always

Always, always the eternal rainbow
And it is always the day, the farewell day unkind. (198)

Essentially the poem says that Crane's dream of love is still alive,
even though it apparently will never be realized. The "eternal rainbow," a sign of hope, is there "always / Always, always." Yet at the
same time it is met with "the day, the farewell day unkind." There
are at least two personal allusions in this final stanza. The rainbow
echoes the "White rainbows" in the farewell of "Voyages VI," from
the sequence written in homage to E.O. The window in its blind
partition recalls the window that "goes blond slowly" in "The Har-
bor Dawn" from *The Bridge*—the singular love poem of that sequence that describes dawn over Manhattan from the room in
Brooklyn where Crane and E.O. had embarked on their affair.

These two allusions suggest that other parts of "The Visible the
Untrue" have their own private significance:

> Forthright
I watch the silver Zeppelin
destroy the sky. To
stir your confidence?
To rouse what sanctions—? toothaches? (198)

To identify the Zeppelin as a homoerotic symbol and to see it as
rendering obsolete the leisurely traffic of the steamship (E.O. was a
ship's purser) is a likely explanation of the significance embedded
in these lines. And the question "What about the staunch neighbor
tabulations, / With all their zest for doom?" may lead into speculation about friends and neighbors who predicted the failure of his
relationship with E.O. and thereby helped to destroy it. But the interest of such poetry is, needless to say, extremely narrow. It is
unmistakably poignant, yet it serves primarily as a release for Crane.
Its message is a private one delivered in a public medium (the poem
was located among Crane's manuscripts after his death and had
never been submitted for publication).

"To Shakespeare" is the opposite of "The Visible the Untrue."
Instead of bearing a personal message, it refuses to deliver anything; instead of twisting its words uniquely to evoke a particular
instant, it sets out to be almost entirely self-sufficient; instead of

unfolding in its own measure, it takes the conventional form of a sonnet. Its characteristics prefigure the approach Crane would take in composing his homage to Whitman in "Cape Hatteras" (1929). The method is to ascribe extraordinary powers to the subject being addressed, in order to hold together apparent contradictions. "Who shall again / Engrave such hazards as thy might controls—" (131), Crane asks of Shakespeare; he asks Whitman: "But who has held the heights more sure than thou, / O Walt!" (81). Shakespeare is "pilot,—tempest, too!" and is capable of taking "laughter, burnished brighter than our fate" and blending it "with such tears" (131). Whitman is seen operating "at junctions elegiac, there, of speed / With vast eternity" yet at the same time answering "deepest soundings" (82). In both cases, the general reader need not be familiar with the writer to understand the basis for Crane's enthusiasm.

This, then, was the strategy of such poems: to write in homage to another poet whose historical stature was well established. In such a way, he might satisfy a portion of his own urge to write about himself without dropping his guard. Another safe subject, which he explored in France in 1929, was local color. A Caribbean setting had served him well in 1927, in the picturesque "Carib Suite," which contained several brief works, and in Martinique he tried the same with "To the Empress Josephine's Statue." His address is a supplication to the muse, but one marked by a straining toward the impersonal and the public. The poem is an odd variation on a theme in "Carib Suite" that insists that both Europeans and then Americans have exploited the natives, dominating their local culture. Here, though, Crane is defending the European colonists as preferable to their American successors. The statue, for example, "looked back to Leda, who [has] seen the Swan" and "Outdid our spies and hoodwink sputum" (195). The meaning of these lines is by no means clear, but they suggest a contrast between the culture imposed on the West Indies by Europe—the tradition of Leda and the swan reaches back to ancient mythology and allows for the presence of sexuality in human affairs—and the culture imposed by American forces, a combination of spying and "hoodwink sputum," far less tolerant, far less sophisticated than its European predecessor.

Europe, in fact, provided Crane with a vantage point from which to excoriate or appreciate American qualities, depending on his inclinations. In either case, he would write as the Bard who has words of wisdom his countrymen should hear. He had left for Europe in 1929, after receiving a small inheritance, to pursue his next long poem, a blank-verse tragedy based on Aztec mythology.[6] But he remained preoccupied with the problem of how to complete *The Bridge.* Both his urgent need to write as a bard and his preoccupation with his epic poem surface in a fragment, "I Rob My Breast . . . ," which begins as a confession, swerves toward local color, and ends as a homily. Its three stanzas of five, five, and three lines are each different in tone.[7] In a confessional mode and speaking as the frustrated epic poet, he admits that his own outpourings leave him exhausted because "My vision is a grandiose dilemma"

6. This long poem never went anywhere and was, in a sense, preempted in March, 1932, when Archibald MacLeish published *Conquistador,* a long poem based on historical chronicles of the conquest of Mexico. Although MacLeish's epic reveals no influence from Crane—its singularly flat style resembles *in our time* crossed with the Malatesta cantos—the acclaim with which it was greeted (third printing, April, 1932) must have reached Crane in Mexico, at the end of his unproductive year as a Guggenheim fellow. Its success would be one more shame he would have to endure if he arrived in New York.

7. Simon's text differs from that cited by R. W. B. Lewis (in *The Poetry of Hart Crane* [Princeton, 1967], 387–88) and described by Kenneth Lohf (in *The Literary Manuscripts of Hart Crane* [Columbus, Ohio, 1967]). Simon adds four extra lines to the final stanza:

> But I believe that such "wreckage" as I find
> Remaining presents evidence of considerably more
> Significance than do the cog-walk gesture
> Of a beetle in a sand-pit. (219)

In his note to the poem, Simon explains that "the lowercase first letters of lines 14–17 are altered to capitals." The manuscript shows, that is, that what Simon prints as the last four lines did not have uppercase first letters, as did lines one through thirteen. Moreover, Lohf's description of the actual manuscript, item D39, in *The Literary Manuscripts of Hart Crane,* 96–97, cites "13 lines on recto and 4 lines on verso." Although I have not inspected the manuscript, my sense is that Simon has erred in concluding that the four lines on the back of the page are a continuation of the thirteen lines on the front of the page. In turning the manuscript over, Simon did not uncover a new treasure but simply a fragment of prose, a piece of scrap paper that Crane picked up on March 26, 1929, when he began to write "I Rob My Breast . . .".

(219). In stanza two, though, as the observing reporter, he recalls fighting the crowds at the Place de la Concorde to view "the stricken bones, the noble / Carcass of a general, dead Foch," borne to his rest as "Defender, not usurper," a striking contrast to the arch-imperialist Napoleon, who lies in a "defunct pit." This glimpse into the patriotic wisdom of the French launches him upon his third stanza:

My countrymen,—give form and edict—
To the marrow. You shall know
The harvest as you have known the spring

At this point, the poem breaks off, as complete as it could be, though perhaps two lines short. Crane may have seen that whatever he wrote next would be mere filler. The poem has an energy rare in Crane's late work, but even this is misleading; for the source of the energy is Crane's rapid-fire swerve from one mode to another.

The paradox of Crane's final years is that much of what he was experiencing deeply he could not transform into poetry because it was far too personal in its reference. At the same time, he was striving for themes that might be of interest to a wider audience. Two versions of an unpublished work, "A Traveller Born," vividly underscore this struggle. One version, assembled by Marc Simon for the 1986 edition of the collected poems, is indiscreet; the other, presented by Waldo Frank in his 1933 edition, is circumspect. Frank's version is presented as a finished poem:

Of sailors—those two Corsicans at Marseilles,—
The Dane at Paris, and those weeks of May
With distance, lizard-like, green as Pernot . . .
This Connecticut rain, its smashing fall, its wet inferno—

Enforces memory—prison, perfume of women, and the fountain—
Oh, final apple-math of ripe night fallen!
Concluding handclasp, cider, summer-swollen,
Folds, and is folden in the echoing mountain . . .
Yields and is shielded, wrapt in traffic flame.[8]

8. Frank's version appears in *The Collected Poems of Hart Crane* (New York, 1933), 143. It was not collected in Brom Weber's *Complete Poems of Hart Crane* (New York, 1966).

Home in rainy Connecticut, Crane reaches back to pleasant souvenirs of Europe (the "Dane at Paris" is almost certainly another reference to E.O.). But mixed in with the pleasantries of recollection is the sense of memory as a prison. The rain "Enforces memory," leads into a train of thoughts that begin with "prison," and tends toward the finality of a "Concluding handclasp." The poem ends vaguely, but appropriately, summarizing recollections as both yielding and shielding, echoing the doubleness they have demonstrated throughout.

Frank's version exhibits saving details, such as the "perfume of women," which work to allay doubts set in motion by the opening reference to sailors. The version by Simon is far more provocative:

> Of sailors—those two Corsicans at Marseilles,—
> The Dane at Paris and the Spanish abbé
> With distance, lizard-like, green as Pernod;
> Its cargo drench, its wet inferno
> Condenses memory. The abbey colonade, the vesperal fountain—
> Oh, sudden apple-math of ripe night fallen!
> Concluding handclasp, cider, summer-swollen
> Folds, and is folden in the echoing mountain . . .
> Yields, and is shielded, wrapt in traffic flame,
> The One, this crucifix that bears a name . . . (199)

This version continues for several more lines. The differences are telling. Rhyming with "Marseilles" is "Spanish abbé" instead of "those weeks in May." And the "perfume of women, and the fountain" have become "the abbey colonnade, the vesperal fountain"— a scene that pointedly recalls the specific characters introduced earlier. Moreover, all its figures are male. Whereas Frank's version launches into a generalized reverie that turns on the understanding that memory both releases and imprisons, Simon's version introduces a larger number of specific characters, and even returns to them by supplying a background that suggests the occurrence of some particular event. In Simon's version, there is no "Connecticut rain" that "Enforces memory." Instead, we have an unspecified referent that "Condenses memory." The emphasis falls on actually reliving the past, experiencing the merging of events in memory, rather than, as in Frank's version, commenting upon the way memory operates as it discloses a vista from which one is distant.

"A Traveller Born" delicately displays Crane's major dilemma at this time. When he escapes the inclination to compose a public poetry—a hymn that will uplift (or excoriate) America or praise the wisdom of an alien civilization—then he is prohibited from giving undivided attention to his personal experience because aspects of it must remain guarded. In aesthetic terms, the best that can happen occurs in Frank's version, which may have been edited quite thoughtfully: memory is both an expansion and a contraction, a yielding and a shielding. It may be more pertinent to say that, for Crane, in his dilemma, the personal lyric *itself* is both a yielding and a shielding, an admission and an omission. But Crane's profound longing is divulged in Simon's version, where the emotions he experienced in Europe are relived again, almost indulgently, in a series of tantalizing phrases.

The one outlet that remained open to Crane becomes increasingly evident in his very last works: committed to write a public poetry that makes large-scale observations about culture, he feels most comfortable accusing others of a narrow-mindedness that prevents them from appreciating diversity of any kind. Such a position reaches all the way back to his first—and, arguably, only—successful example of his new poetics, "A Name for All," which adopted a critical stance against narrow-mindedness. This theme, thin as it is, is all that he has left, but it allows him to express some of his dark pessimism in "Quaker Hill" and to undermine the possessiveness of the mother who speaks in "Indiana," the last two sections of The Bridge, both composed in 1929. Unfortunately, it can also surface in a tone of bitter anger, as in the unpublished and probably incomplete "The Pillar and the Post." Playing on disruptive meanings in the word Yank, Crane goes on to villify American culture, describing it in terms of defiant oxymorons such as "clean-limbed taint." Crane's struggle to seek out the positive qualities in American life may, by this point, have created a backlash; the bard has turned to crying in the wilderness. Addressing the American as a "Midas of motion," the poet is content to castigate a stereotype:

and ask the sun what time it is
before your fingers lose their ten—in biological
and betrothed answer to the ambitious monkey synthesis that you
    adore. (197)

While Crane's anger is obvious, its cause remains obscure. By admiring technology, he seems to say, Americans too easily lose touch
with natural events, no longer telling time by the sun. And he may
also be trying to say that American faith in evolution displays at
least two evils: first, a commitment to an empty scientific model,
a "biological . . . answer"; second, an arrogant belief that the future
belongs to them and their progeny as the world evolves into the
USA, that "ambitious monkey synthesis."

This tone of angry chastisement, directed against those who remain complacent, surfaces again in the few works that Crane completed in his year in Mexico. These fragments from the last year of
his life are all that remain of his ambition to write of the Aztec civilization. Of the five pieces written (one of which is only a two-line
epigram), perhaps the clearest is " 'They Were There . . .'". It portrays natives as virtually invisible to tourists—a theme Crane earlier explored in a "Carib Suite" poem, "Bacardi Spreads the Eagle's
Wings." Although little more than a sputtering tirade, it at least
employs rhymes cleverly:

And all the missions and the votaries
And old maids with their chronic coteries
Dispense in the old, old lorgnette views
What should have kept them straight in pews.
But doesn't confuse
These Indians, who scan more news
On the hind end of their flocks each day
Than all the tourists bring their way. (225)

This verse, edging toward doggerel, displays all too clearly the ingredients of a late poem by Crane: a generalized theme with a hidden personal reference (in this case, the elevation of the "hind end"
over the "lorgnette views"); a slap at those whose narrowness
blinds them to appreciating the uniqueness of an alien culture; and
a sympathy for those whose existence remains simple in contrast
to those who build institutions such as "missions." Another poem,

"The Sad Indian," presents similar themes but without the angry sputter of the disgusted poet. The Indian is the vestige of the proud Aztec civilization, overwhelmed by the Midas motion of the twentieth century. He views the "new hum in the sky" as a step backward, though he himself "looms / / Farther than his sun-shadow" (188) because his own shadow reaches back to his powerful ancestors.

What is most disappointing in Crane's Mexican poems is that, in their repetition of old themes, they are so utterly accessible. The single exception is "The Circumstance (To Xochiphili)," a poem in which Crane displayed greater interest than he did during most of this period, working on it up to the time of his leaving Mexico and just prior to his suicide.[9] It mixes its themes in a way more daring and more courageous than appears in the other Mexican poems. Beginning from a tourist's point of view, the poem cites the attributes of the Aztec civilization, but instead of proceeding to exalt these characteristics in the easy manner of his other late poems, Crane recoils from them because of their strangeness. He is struck into thoughtfulness, perhaps by the force of their violence. A reference to "bloody basins" recalls the human sacrifice at the center of that civilization, though an earlier reference to "a bloody foreign clown" suggests that the Spanish conquerors may have been the more evil of the two races. But the obvious theme at hand, concerning the foreigners' exploitation of the natives, is not developed here, but it

9. Lohf, *The Literary Manuscripts of Hart Crane,* 87, dates a working typescript draft as "March-April 1932" and notes: "Written on bottom half of sheet of typewritten 'memoranda' relating to debts and transportation indicating that draft was made shortly before Crane left Mixcoac [Mexico] in April 1932." Simon's edition of "The Circumstance" agrees with Lohf's dating, but interferes with Crane's punctuation. The manuscript had a parenthetical phrase in lines 21–22: "(shave lightning, / Possess in halo full the winds)." Simon extends the parentheses to include the next two words, "of time." He maintains that Crane left his alteration "incomplete": "He did not delete the parenthesis at 'winds)' and add the closing parenthesis after 'time)' for coherent syntax" (254). But this alteration plays havoc with Crane's syntax. If the parenthesis remains, as originally written, then Crane has joined two natural forces, the lightning and the wind, and given each its own verb: "shave lightning" and "Possess . . . the winds." The passage creates a series of quasi-parallel clauses centering on repetitions of the word *time*: "You could *stop time, give* florescent / *Time* a longer answer back . . . *of time* / A longer answer *force* [emphasis added]." Simon's version creates a cliché, "winds of time," that leaves the poem's meaning unclear.

could have been. Instead, the poem turns upon the perceptions of the narrator, who, significantly, draws closer to the artifacts and ruins. As a result, the verse has a beguiling movement to it, a twisting and turning like a vortex that pulls us closer. It offers a new uncertain rhythm unlike the stolid blank verse in which most of the late poems are safely constrained.

As the poem develops, the ruins of the Aztecs seem to be not broken fragments of stone but remnants of a lost dream. The change begins after "If you could buy the stones" (Crane is still mocking the tourist's viewpoint) and is under way with the shift in the lines "If you / Could drink the sun." In the final stanza, the poem gains further momentum as the poet realizes that the massive stonework is an attempt to erect such permanence that it could "stop time"—or at least, more realistically, slow time and give it "a longer answer back," even to force from time "A longer answer . . . [a] more enduring answer." He is also recalling the calendars of the Aztecs and their experiments with measuring the passage of time, but in the course of introducing this achievement, he begins to meditate on the powerful human wish to control natural events, to shape a culture that would be able to escape from the flow of time and master it. The desire to be "sus- / Taining nothing in time but more and more of Time"—a desire somewhat ineffectively mimed through the line break—is the positive aspect that emerges from ruins that at first seemed only fragments. For if Crane, centuries removed from the civilization, can understand this belief of the Aztecs, then they have indeed lived beyond and mastered time. But it is not just the idea that makes this poem singular. It is the fact that Crane has, at least momentarily, broken away from his commitment to conventional verse. Moreover, his engagement is new. Here he has made an effort to see himself as a tourist, instead of merely castigating the tourist's point of view. For him to acknowledge that the Aztec is in some way alien to him, that he must struggle to understand this difficult culture, is a breakthrough. He may be able to bridge this gap because, as a poet, he sympathizes with the longing to build an enduring monument, an edifice that will last eternally. Although the ruins seem to mock his ambition, he is eager to find that some spirit persists, despite the overwhelming evidence of the civilization's destruction. This realization, too, has a particularly personal relevance.

"The Circumstance" is not a hidden masterpiece, but it escapes from the absolute dilemma that Crane had locked himself into in so many of his other late poems. In his last five years, Crane was pursuing an impossible program, attempting a kind of poetry for which he had no particular skill and in which he could rarely invest his own feelings. Its effect was to add one further element of complexity to a life that was already straining in too many different directions. By imposing a set of poetics that prevented him from being himself even in his poetry, he had already guaranteed that a large part of him had died—clearly the most important part—before his own death.

JAMES GUIMOND

The Green Tradition: Found and Lost in Edmund Wilson's *I Thought of Daisy* and *Memoirs of Hecate County*

Memoirs of Hecate County belongs with those works
which Wilson calls night thoughts. It is the product of
the dark depressing nightmarish world, the hades, usually kept from public view.
                                    —*Edmund Wilson*

In a 1933 letter to Louise Bogan, Edmund Wilson suggested that
she should write a *"confession d'un enfant du siècle,"* which would
enable her to express her "internal conflicts and ranklings," because "once you get [the] experience out of your system in a sat-
isfactory literary form, you can thumb your nose at the world."
Wilson himself started to write what might have been his own
confession in the early 1940s, during a period in his life when he
had a variety of inner and outer conflicts to rankle and motivate
him. Disturbed by the deaths of his close friends F. Scott Fitzgerald
and John Peale Bishop in 1940 and 1944, troubled by his difficult
marriage to Mary McCarthy, which ended in divorce in 1946, and
confronted by economic problems as he searched for secure literary
employment, he sketched out the characters and plot for a novel
entitled "The Story of the Three Wishes." In the course of this
novel, a dissatisfied man—whose personal experiences in the 1930s
are quite similar to Wilson's—is "transformed" magically into

three other men whose lives would have encompassed the major experiences of Wilson's own generation, the creative young people of the 1920s. Each episode, Wilson wrote in his notes, "seems a different world in which [the hero] is hoping to find something new. . . . But now the reader is to find out . . . that they have all been the same thing—the modern world."[1]

Instead of writing this novel, however, Wilson wrote a somewhat different book, *Memoirs of Hecate County* (1946), a series of six short stories that deals primarily with the "dark depressing" social history of his generation and their efforts to confront the vicissitudes of "the modern world." Even more than Wilson's critical writings of the 1940s, Diana Trilling said in her review, the *Memoirs* expressed his "unhappy response to the contemporary social and cultural situation of this country." She shrewdly noted that the book should be read as a sequel to his 1929 novel, *I Thought of Daisy*, since that "earlier book was Mr. Wilson's record of American artistic and intellectual life" in the 1920s, and the *Memoirs* dealt with the country's artistic and intellectual development during the 1930s and the 1940s. "The cultural alterations he notes . . . are numerous and significant," Trilling commented, and "the two books together make an enormously valuable document of social change."[2]

In the 1920s, Wilson, who greatly admired Emerson's *Essays*, had felt some of the same "exhilaration in the air of the time" that Emerson had felt in the 1830s and the 1840s, for he had believed that the United States was on the verge of a cultural renaissance in which American writers would supply the world with some badly needed "sensible ideas about society and life in general." As he summarized the conclusion to *Axel's Castle*—his major critical study of the 1920s—in a 1928 letter to Maxwell Perkins, the pessimism of European literary attitudes was "principally the result of the exhaustion of the war," and he hoped a reaction against this pessimism would begin in America, because "in another genera-

1. Edmund Wilson, *Letters on Literature and Politics, 1912–1972*, ed. Elena Wilson (New York, 1977), 234; Wilson, *The Forties: From Notebooks and Diaries of the Period*, ed. Leon Edel (New York, 1983), 10, 16.
2. Diana Trilling, "Fiction in Review," *Nation*, March 30, 1946, p. 380.

tion or two, we may be leading the world intellectually. I feel that Europe is coming now to look to us for leaders while we are still respectfully accepting whatever they send us. I don't expect to wave Old Glory quite as openly as this, but I want to make this point at the end." But besides leading Europe intellectually, Wilson and his fellow American writers would, he assumed, be helping their countrymen to become more sensitive and sophisticated. Both the current quality and the future development of American culture were the subjects of intense, and sometimes acrimonious, debates among intellectuals throughout the 1920s. As an editor and contributor to several of the more ambitious and intelligent magazines of the decade—*Vanity Fair, New Republic,* and the *Dial*—Wilson expressed a cautious, qualified optimism in this controversy. He admitted in a 1921 letter to Fitzgerald, for example, that American literary standards were not very high and "the commercialism and industrialism . . . impose a terrific handicap upon any other sort of endeavour," but he also believed there was "a great hope for New York as a cultural center. . . . America seems to be actually beginning to express herself in something like an idiom of her own."[3]

Like Emerson, Wilson had believed that this new American idiom, this new expression of what Paul Rosenfeld called the green tradition, would be created by a fusion of high art and popular culture, by the discovery that art and creativity existed in even the most commonplace facts and activities of American life.[4] Thus Emerson had claimed in "The Poet" that "the schools of poets, and philosophers, are not more intoxicated with their symbols, than the populace with theirs," and he had illustrated this assertion by pointing out the "poetry" of the 1840 presidential campaign— "Witness the cider-barrel, the log-cabin, the hickory-stick. . . . The

---

3. Wilson, *Letters,* 151, 64. "I feel very strongly," Wilson told Walter Lippmann in 1928, "that America has been unfortunate since the war in being obliged to take over all the indifferentism and defeatism of Europe, and that it is high time we set out ourselves to supply some sensible ideas about society and life in general" (*Letters,* 145). For Wilson's comments on Emerson, in 1923, see *ibid.,* 110.

4. Paul Rosenfeld, *By Way of Art: Criticisms of Music, Literature, Painting, Sculpture, and the Dance* (New York, 1928), 303.

people fancy they hate poetry, and they are all poets and mystics!"[5]
Wilson did not make similar claims for the 1928 Al Smith–
Herbert Hoover campaign, but in *I Thought of Daisy*, his novel
about Greenwich Village life in the 1920s, he described his narrator
as "noticing with a new attention the way . . . Americans talked"
and as reading "with astonished gratification, the first books of
those American writers who seemed to be making a new kind of
literature out of that sprawling square-syllabled speech."[6] Considered in this context, *Daisy* is an essentially affirmative book in
which Wilson had dramatized his feelings about America's "general
life" and culture by having the narrator gradually overcome his
doubts about American life as he encounters an assortment of
poets, radicals, and advertising men, a wise old professor from England, and Daisy, a pretty young chorus girl from Pittsburgh who
represented, Wilson later said, "American reality" and "ordinary
human life undirected by special ideas."[7] Thus he ended the novel
with the narrator spending a day with Daisy at Coney Island and
then making love to her, presumably to suggest that the narrator
accepted the synthesis between ideas and "ordinary . . . life," at
least temporarily. At Coney Island with Daisy, the narrator can re-
lax from his efforts to be a part of the Greenwich Village "artistic
and intellectual life"; and, seeing his own reflection in a penny-
arcade mirror, he can imagine he is "a figure from the funny papers:
Mr. Suburban American, at the seaside, with packages and a straw
hat" (297). Confronting this new facet of his identity surprises the
narrator—he does not recognize himself at first—but he does not
reject the image. As Wilson wrote in his foreword to the 1967 edition, by this stage of the novel the narrator has effected "a real
union" with Daisy, and his "point of view" has become "instinc-
tive, democratic, [and] pragmatic. My hero has at last, for the moment, made connections with the common life" (v, vi).

Accepting the "common life" of America in the twentieth century means, among other things, accepting mass culture. Near the

5. Emerson, "The Poet," *Essays: Second Series*, in *Ralph Waldo Emerson: Essays and Lectures* (New York, 1983), 454.
6. Wilson, *I Thought of Daisy* (1929; rpr. New York, 1967), 66. All later citations of this novel are included parenthetically in the text.
7. Wilson, *Letters*, 176.

end of the novel when he hears "Mamie Rose"—a popular song—
on the radio at Coney Island, Wilson's narrator speculates on how
its composer, a young New Yorker, might have created this song—
"carrying us beyond expectation, by breaking into that new accent"—by fusing his childhood memories of what he had heard in
a synagogue with New York street sounds, German music, jazz
rhythms, and even the modernism of Schönberg and Stravinsky to
produce a new kind of art that the narrator compares to the works
of Sophocles and Dostoevsky (300). Indeed, the narrator becomes so
enthusiastic about the possibilities of combining high art with
popular culture that he speculates that he himself might become a
creative writer without suffering "that dreadful isolation," so often
the fate of the serious artist. "Such pictures as I imagined of Daisy
would grow directly and freshly from life," he believes. "And it
seemed to me . . . that literature was as amiable as writing ballads,
as necessary as making tables," because "there was really no difference in kind between carpentry and literature" (313).

Most of the characters in the six stories that make up the *Memoirs*
are suburban Americans, but they are not figures from "the funny
papers." As its title implies, *Hecate County* is a grimmer and more
sinister work than *Daisy* is, and in it Wilson expressed a much
more pessimistic vision of America's mass media, popular culture.
Hecate is the Greek goddess of witchcraft, prophecy, nightmares,
and the underworld; and, according to Wilson, his book was intended to be a "suburban inferno" populated by "different kinds of
people . . . [who] all have . . . a kind of odor of damnation." Near
the end of the book, his narrator explains ingenuously that the
county's name "was merely one of those many classical place-
names, like Syracuse, Hannibal and Rome, that the early inhabitants . . . picked at random out of Plutarch." But nineteenth-
century Americans had expressed their optimism about their nation by choosing heroic or pretentious classical names for their
communities—and Hecate was exactly the sort of name they did
not choose.[8]

8. Wilson, *Letters*, 433; Wilson, *Memoirs of Hecate County* (Garden City, N.Y.,
1946), 322. All later citations of this book are included parenthetically in the text

Alfred Kazin has pointed out that by 1946, when the *Memoirs* was published, Hecate had become a very "congenial" symbol for Wilson. His county was "clearly meant to be [seen as] the landscape of a type of middle-class mind in this country," because in it "we see . . . the acute period of the American crisis, between Hoover and Hitler."[9] Actually, the *Memoirs* deals with a variety of crises in American life during that period—the depression, the collapse of the brief alliance between American liberals and communists, and what one character, citing Thurber, calls "the war between men and women." However, the crisis that most consistently concerns Wilson throughout the book is the breakdown of the cautious rapprochement between high and popular culture, between the "superior individual" and the "common life" of America, which he had achieved in the final section of *I Thought of Daisy* and his critical writings in the late 1920s. From his reading of Flaubert's *L'Education sentimentale* in the 1930s, he had derived the "suspicion" that a middle-class, acquisitive civilization might decline and fall, because "our middle-class society of manufacturers, businessmen and bankers . . . so far from being redeemed by its culture, has ended by cheapening and invalidating all the departments of culture, political, scientific, artistic and religious, as well as corrupting and weakening the ordinary human relations: love, friendship and loyalty to cause—till the whole civilization seems to dwindle."[10] When one reads the *Memoirs*, it is difficult to avoid the suspicion that this book is Wilson's *L'Education* and that he too is describing a society that has begun to "dwindle" because it has devalued its own culture and human relationships.

---

and identified as *MHC* as necessary. According to a 1966 *Hammond Atlas*, there are no counties or towns in the United States named Hecate, though Canada does have a Strait of Hecate near the coast of British Columbia.

9. Alfred Kazin, "Le Misanthrope," *Partisan Review*, XIII (Summer, 1946), 376.

10. Wilson, *The Triple Thinkers* (New York, 1948), 81. Wilson phrased this indictment a little differently in the 1938 edition of *The Triple Thinkers* (113). My use of the term *superior individual* is derived from Kazin's insight that most of Wilson's best books are "overtures to the conflict between the superior individual and society that is his main subject" ("Le Misanthrope," 375). Sherman Paul has pointed out the connections between Hecate County and Flaubert's works, particularly *L'Education sentimentale*. See *Edmund Wilson: A Study of Literary Vocation in Our Time* (Urbana, 1965), 148–49.

In *Daisy* the narrator's growing interest in American mass culture was synchronized with his growing emotional involvement with Daisy herself, and these two developments merged in the final section of the novel as he speculated on how the song "Mamie Rose" might be a work of art and then made love to Daisy after their day at Coney Island. The same two subjects are present in the *Memoirs*, but they are not integrated. In that book, Wilson's interest in mass-media culture has become negative and cynical, and it is expressed in three stories that are satires or exposés and deal primarily with themes out of mass culture—"The Man Who Shot Snapping Turtles," "Glimpses of Wilbur Flick," and "The Milhollands and Their Damned Soul."

Throughout these stories, Wilson ridiculed and sniped at ideas, mores, and magazines that have been mainstays of American middle-class, mainstream culture ever since the 1920s. Thus in "The Man Who Shot Snapping Turtles," he satirized the "romance of American business" success stories that have been so popular in magazines such as the *Saturday Evening Post* and *Fortune*.[11] Or in "Glimpses of Wilbur Flick" the title character, a wealthy nonentity, parrots ideas from Nietzsche and confides that he thinks Mozart is "an aristocratic soul. . . . I go back to the great ones more and more. What else have you got in these times?" as he sits down at his "desk, on which was a silver writing set, a neat little pile of letters and a copy of the *Reader's Digest*" (*MHC*, 66).

Wilson's most extensive and bitter satire occurs in "The Milhollands and Their Damned Soul." In what is ostensibly a version of the Faust legend, the Milhollands, a clan of literary hacks and entrepreneurs, sell their souls and those of their colleagues to the devil so they can be more successful. The story is essentially a fictionalized exposé in the style of Budd Schulberg's *What Makes Sammy Run?* or Jerome Weidman's *I Can Get It for You Whole-*

---

11. The phrase "romance of American business" is from Wilson's 1930s play, *Bebbo and Beth*, in which he satirized American Big Business in his characterization of Luke Bostock (Wilson, *Five Plays* [New York, 1954], 342). "The Man Who Shot Snapping Turtles" can be interpreted as another, more deadpan satire on American business in which Asa Stryker is paternalistic industrialism and Clarence Latouche represents advertising and Madison Avenue.

sale—except that the subjects of Wilson's satire are not the hustlers who run the nation's movie and garment industries. Instead, they are a group of reviewers, publishers, and editors who pretend to be arbiters of good taste.[12]

Besides satirizing the Milhollands' greed and their sleazy behavior, Wilson also described the process through which they had commercialized and corrupted a belief he himself had taken seriously in the 1920s. As he had told Fitzgerald in 1921, Wilson believed that America was "beginning to express herself in . . . an idiom of her own" and that there was a "growing public for really good stuff." But in the 1920s and the 1930s this growing interest in culture and creativity had begun to be exploited by editors and media entrepreneurs who promoted what Alice Marquis has described as an "optimistic American prognosis for the common man": not only that "anyone could become a millionaire, but also that anyone could become cultivated." Radio stations began broadcasting operas and classical music, Hollywood studios hired famous writers to produce scripts for film versions of "literary classics," and book clubs began selling supposedly good literature to people who were too "busy" to select books for themselves or who lived in towns that did not have book stores.[13]

Much of Wilson's story deals with the techniques that editors, reviewers, and book club executives use to inflate the reputations of the books they want to promote. They coordinate their efforts to make sure that these books receive "preferential treatment . . . [so] that one could be sure, any given week, of finding the same new book featured in all" the literary periodicals (*MHC*, 268). But he also implied that this process started with what had been a positive development in American culture in the 1920s, the discovery of the value of modern literature. Warren Milholland, the head of a book club called the Readers' Circle, had begun his career as an En-

12. In a letter to Louise Bogan, Wilson said the story's characters were based on Charles Van Doren, Henry Seidel Canby, and Harrison Smith of the Book-of-the-Month Club and the *Saturday Review*. Interestingly enough, Smith gave the *Memoirs* a moderately favorable review, a response Wilson considered "very sporting" (Wilson, *Letters*, 437).

13. Wilson, *Letters*, 64; Alice G. Marquis, *Hopes and Ashes: The Birth of Modern Times 1929–1939* (New York, 1986), 5.

glish professor by defying the staid tastes of his department and teaching his students to appreciate writers such as Henry James and George Bernard Shaw. After becoming editor of a literary magazine, however, Milholland began inflating the reputations of American mediocrities, claiming that "Carl Van Vechten was the American Congreve, Joseph Hergesheimer the American Flaubert, and James Branch Cabell the American Anatole France." After that, it was a short, insidious step for him and his reviewers to boost the reputations of the second-, third-, and fourth-rate writers whose books were being promoted by his club. Instead of raising the level of American culture, the Milhollands had begun to lower literary values, since they were quite willing "knowingly to feed back to the public its own ignorance and cheap tastes" (263). In one scene, Wilson implied that what "the public" really wanted in literature was a kind of peep show in which the entertainment was other people's neuroses and sexual activities. "The whole damned literary racket—when you come right down to it, what is it but huckstering in a lot of greasy daydreams?" declares one of the Milhollands' publishers in a moment of cynical candor. "You take fantasies that people have made up because they can't travel as much as they want to or haven't got anybody to sleep with, and you get them set up by a printer and . . . organize a business to distribute them" (279).

But besides debasing their readers' tastes, the Milhollands also—by implication—destroy their own and their associates' creativity and sensitivity. Virtually every character in "The Milhollands and Their Damned Soul" becomes more sterile or inept, as well as more corrupt, as the story goes on. Warren's younger brother, Spike Milholland, for example, begins his career as a "very Left" radical poet. Then he starts reviewing books on the radio and in a newspaper column as a "barker for Parnassus." Finally he ends up promoting books on television, earning sixty or seventy thousand dollars a year, and trying to ignore or despise literature that is not salable. "[T]he very mention of *Finnegans Wake* makes him foam at the mouth," since he is infuriated by "the idea that Joyce took seventeen years to write it!" (292–93). Si Banks, an alcoholic poet who is a friend of the narrator's, becomes so sterile as a poet that he can only complete the first lines of poems as he helps to ghostwrite the horrible historical novels the Milhollands peddle through their book club and on television. But all of this warped or thwarted intelligence and creativity does express itself in an "almost apocalyptic manner" in the last scene when Spike Milholland has a kind of nervous-cultural breakdown during his television show. Spike hates *Finnegans Wake,* but he begins making Joycean puns about the historical novel he is promoting: "[O]ur own American *War and Police,"* written by a novelist who "was a freight clerk and serda-joker" until he "conceived a creapive [*sic*] dream. . . . That dream . . . was Yale in China. It began with Dick Pratt of the class of '84 saying grace over a bowl of chop suey and it ended with the expulsion from China of the competitive Japanese invader.—And now, folks, I want to say a word about Gluko jelly desserts" (295–96). The final irony is that no one, except for the narrator and Si Banks, seems to notice that Spike is talking gibberish. This might be interpreted as Wilson's comment on the quality of television as a medium and the intelligence of its audience.

To use terms that Wilson applied to Kafka's "Investigations of a Dog," we can say that these three satiric stories are his equivalents of Flaubert's *Bouvard et Pécuchet,* his works that have "something in common with Flaubert's most contemptuous indictment of the pettiness and ineptitude of the modern world." Each of these stories ends with an emphatic "Flaubertian irony," and all of them are characterized by the detachment of Wilson's narrator, which is also quite Flaubertian. The follies of creatures such as Wilbur Flick and the Milhollands are so obvious, Wilson seems to imply, that it would be inappropriate for any intelligent person to do more than report on their actions in a crisp, sophisticated way.[14]

In contrast, the narrator does have some respect or even affection for the subjects of the three other stories in the *Memoirs*—"Ellen Terhune," "The Princess with the Golden Hair," and "Mr. and Mrs. Blackburn at Home." Instead of being detached from these subjects, he tries to involve himself with them. These three stories also resemble one another because they share a theme that occurs

14. Wilson, "A Dissenting Opinion on Kafka," *Classics and Commercials: A Literary Chronicle of the Forties* (New York, 1950), 389.

in "The Story of the Three Wishes," the book Wilson did not finish in the 1940s. The hero in that novel was a dissatisfied man seeking "something new" to revitalize his life, and in these three stories in the *Memoirs* the narrator can also be considered a person who is seeking newness. In each story he becomes fascinated with persons or places that have the potential to create "something new"—new art in "Ellen Terhune," new social allegiances in "The Princess with the Golden Hair," and a new vision of America in "Mr. and Mrs. Blackburn at Home." However, none of these involvements is successful, and his life in Hecate County remains as sterile and "demonic" as ever.[15]

The narrator's involvements are most elaborate in "The Princess with the Golden Hair," which is by far the longest story in the book. Its erotic passages were explicit enough, in 1946, to make the *Memoirs* sell very briskly and to cause the book to be banned in several cities. (This much annoyed Wilson, who resented the idea that his book "was an unsuccessful attempt to rival *Fanny Hill*.")[16] But underneath the "superstructure" of this eroticism, as a Marxist might comment, the story addresses some serious concerns about American social attitudes and allegiances. During the course of "The Princess," the narrator is involved with three women: Jo Gates, a divorcée who shares his values; and two other women who both represent "something new" to him socially as well as sexually—Anna Lenihan, a young working woman from Brooklyn, the daughter of Ukrainian immigrants; and Imogen Loomis, the wife of an affluent Hecate County advertising salesman. The latter two love affairs can be considered as the narrator's own attempts to escape from what he describes, at the end of the story, as "the prison of the social compartments" (MHC, 239).

Raised in the "compartment" of a solid but rather dull segment of the middle classes—his father is a "management engineer" for a

---

15. Malcolm Cowley summarized the conclusion of the *Memoirs* very well when he commented, paraphrasing Eliot's *Waste Land*, that "nothing seems to change." Although "there is always lightning on the horizon and thunder rumbling overhead . . . the storm never breaks and [Wilson's characters] are all left wandering in Limbo-by-the-Sea" ("Limbo-by-the-Sea," *New Republic*, March 25, 1946, p. 419).

16. Wilson, *Letters*, 439.

huge Detroit corporation called General Tires—the narrator was
trained to be an economist. After reacting against his university's
economics department, "where the professors were mainly apolo-
gists for the bankers," and inheriting a small income, he became a
scholar specializing in the "connection between painting and its
social-economic roots" (102). His love affair with Anna can be seen
as an additional reaction against his family's values, since by loving
her, he is able to establish a human, emotional relationship with
one of the workers who often were treated so callously by large
corporations in the 1930s. Through her, he says, he could encounter the immigrant working classes, "that new Europe of the East
Side and Brooklyn," that "life of the people which had before been
but prices and wages [to me]" (238). Seeing her neighborhood, the
narrator even has a fantasy that he might make a "bold readjust-
ment" in his personal life by going "to live near Anna in Brooklyn." By doing this, he could write his books "immersed in the life
of the people . . . a simple and delightful world of people who
worked and had little to spend," but enjoyed their holiday "fun" at
Brighton Beach and Coney Island (174).

   With Imogen Loomis, however, the narrator is able to escape
from the economic limitations of his career as a scholar. "It may be
that there is nothing more demoralizing than a small but adequate
income," he complains at one point in the story; and with Imogen
he enters—temporarily or vicariously—a nouveau riche world of
luxury, travel, and conspicuous consumption. Imogen lives in a
"mock-Elizabethan," half-timbered house, she and her husband
serve exotic foods at their parties, and she dresses in gowns and
fashions that make her appear to be "some swan princess . . . out of
a Russian or Scandinavian story." Before they become lovers, the
narrator and Imogen talk about their fantasies of running away to
travel together in India or Switzerland, or living together in a
"castle in the south of Ireland" in an "idyl of gay Irish hunting and
rosy-cheeked old Irish servants" (138).

   Both of these love affairs, as Kazin and Sherman Paul have pointed
out, have their ideological connotations. Anna and Imogen can be
interpreted as representing, in ideological terms, the nation's pro-

ductive workers and its consumers during the 1930s. When his romance with Anna is going well, the narrator can conduct (at a safe
distance) his "experiment in misery" and imagine himself a "man
of the left" who has nothing but contempt for middle-class values.[17]
At those moments, he despises the Loomises because Imogen uses
her husband's money to buy "domestic settings and panoramas of
travel abroad that made it possible for her" to ignore the "dis-
graceful economic reality" of the depression (158). But when he is
dissatisfied with Anna and in pursuit of Imogen, the narrator wants
nothing more than the opportunity to become a part of her upper-
middle-class way of life. At one point he even thinks that if Imogen
will marry him, he will "resort to [his] father and go to work for
General Tires, . . . to finance her divorce" (206)—presumably so she
can enjoy the "domestic settings and panoramas of travel" he considered so contemptible earlier in the story.

The romances of Wilson's narrator in *I Thought of Daisy* also
had their social significances. In that novel, when the narrator
stopped loving the poet Rita Cavanagh and spent his day with
Daisy at Coney Island, the change indicated that he had rejected
Cavanagh's Greenwich Village aestheticism and was in the process
of discovering a new "point of view" or "state of mind" with Daisy.
He had "at last, for the moment, made connections with the common life." In contrast, the way that the narrator of the *Memoirs* al-
ternates between Anna and Imogen—and then returns to "my old
girl, Jo Gates" at the end of the story—suggests that he was never
willing or able to make any definite changes in his social point of
view or allegiances. Whether he was imagining that he was going
to join the "life of the people" with Anna in Brooklyn or to work
for General Tries to finance Imogen's divorce, he was—like Imogen—essentially a tourist seeking the sensation rather than the
spirit of a genuinely new state of mind.[18]

17. Kazin, "Le Misanthrope," 377–78; Paul, *Edmund Wilson,* 158.
18. Wilson developed the theme of tourism as a superficial way of encountering
reality most fully in "Glimpses of Wilbur Flick," when Flick escapes from the mis-
eries of his banal existence, not only by becoming addicted to alcohol and drugs, but
also by madly "dashing about . . . to some distant place such as Majorca or Mexico
City and then spend[ing] only a single night" (69). Wilson's narrator is more intelli-

Throughout "The Princess," Wilson characterizes the narrator as being unaware that his values and allegiances contradict one another and that his interest in Anna and Imogen is selfish. Instead, he has sentimental illusions that he has involved himself with both women because he wants to improve their lives. Anna is poor, and the narrator gives her money and helps her to get medical treatment. Imogen believes, probably due to a neurosis, that she has a spinal injury and must wear a brace, and the narrator thinks that he can help her overcome the "humiliation" of this "cruel cage" by becoming her lover. Despite his good intentions, however, he is not able to change either woman's life for the better in any permanent way; and he feels guilty about ending his affair with Anna, because he had wanted "somehow [to] change the shape of her life" (MHC, 229).

But when his "old girl," Jo Gates, comes back from California, the narrator is quite willing to return to his old Hecate County way of life with its banal suburban parties. At the end of the story he does not feel any compassion for either Anna, who is still living in poverty, or for Imogen, who is still trapped in her neurosis. Instead, the narrator feels only self-pity as he realizes that by failing to love Anna enough, he too had failed to change his own life, that his escape from "the prison of the social compartments" had only been temporary. The story ends with his lament, "I was felled by a sudden glumness as I knew, and found it bitter to know, that I was back now in Hecate County and we should never make love again" (239).

By the end of "The Princess with the Golden Hair"—it and "The Milhollands and Their Damned Soul" are the fourth and fifth stories in the Memoirs—Wilson has created a very bleak vision of American life and society. The nation's general culture is being debased by hacks like the Milhollands, and a "superior individual," such as the book's narrator, may possess enough integrity to avoid some of the decadence around him, but he is too selfish and ego-

---

gent than Flick is, but his travels to Brooklyn and Hecate County, in pursuit of Anna and Imogen, can be considered an analogous, social form of tourism. In fact, he refers to the immigrant neighborhoods of Brooklyn and the East Side as "that new Europe . . . for which there was provided no guidebook" (238).

tistical to change his own life, much less anyone else's, for the better. "Mr. and Mrs. Blackburn at Home," the sixth and final story, seems to begin with a sense of revived hope, however. In this story, the narrator's involvement is, implicitly, with America itself, and the "something new" he discovers is in the American landscape. Even in suburban Hecate County, he claims, there was still "something about the American landscape which made you feel that it had just been discovered. . . . America: it suggests to us even now a landscape unfamiliar and wild . . . the mysterious solitude, the inexhaustible recesses and shadows, of a land where we were still frontiersmen" (298–99). Even in Hecate County, in other words, it is still possible to see what Fitzgerald described at the end of Gatsby as the "fresh, green breast of the new world" and to believe in the myth of a virgin America—stated so succinctly by Twain in Huck Finn—where we can still "light out for the Territory" and discover new frontiers. But in the remainder of the story, Wilson's narrator has an encounter that demolishes his illusions of America as a pristine nation.

In I Thought of Daisy the narrator's faith in America is restored not only by Daisy but also by his meeting with a wise old man, Professor Grosbeake, who shows him how it is possible to appreciate American culture in a sophisticated way. This motif is repeated in the Memoirs, but in that book the wise man is a much less benign figure. The Blackburn story is set in the mid-1930s when well-to-do refugees from Europe had begun to arrive in Hecate County. One of these emigrés is a mysterious character named Ed Blackburn who lives in a vast, ugly mansion, gives lavish parties, and resembles the publisher Henry Luce. He even has a wife who is about to run for the Senate, just as Clare Boothe Luce ran for Congress in Connecticut in 1943. This implies that Wilson wanted to suggest that Blackburn has control over the media and has political power as well.[19] But he also emphasized that Blackburn was an ex-

19. In his savage comments on Henry Luce in 1943, Wilson ranked him with Hollywood as a corrupting influence on American culture—one of the "two great enemies of literary talent in our time" who had "reduced [writers] to a condition where they appeared to have been subjected to druggings and secret operations" ("Thoughts on Being Bibliographed," The Portable Edmund Wilson, ed. Lewis Dabney [New York, 1983], 112–13).

tremely cosmopolitan individual of indeterminate age and nationality who was called, respectively, Malatesta, Chernokhvostov, and Swarzkopf by Italians, Russians, and Germans; when he was with Americans, "the name he went by was Blackburn" (301). Besides these sinister names—Malatesta, for example, means "headache" or, literally, "bad head"—Blackburn also has a Rappaccini's garden full of grotesque flowers, so it is not surprising when he implies to the narrator that he is the devil. However, Blackburn does not tempt the narrator with some Faustian offer. Instead, he predicts the atrocities of Hitler's and Stalin's regimes and then expounds, in eighteenth-century French, upon his plans for America.[20]

During this monologue, there is a revealing anachronism when Blackburn says that he "had entertained Jacques Maritain, Aldous Huxley, and Monsignor Darcy" (315). The three men were in the United States during the mid-1940s, and part of Wilson's inspiration for the narrator's meeting with the devil may have been a speech entitled "Of America and the Future," which Maritain gave at the French-American Club in New York in March, 1945. At that time, Wilson was finishing the *Memoirs* and writing "Mr. and Mrs. Blackburn at Home." In this speech, which was printed in the *Commonweal* in April, Maritain claimed that the great difference "from the point of view of moral and psychological experience" between Europe and the United States was that "Europe did not believe in the Devil: [but] for four years Europe has seen the Devil. Here people do not believe in the Devil, and they have not seen his face," and therefore "they hardly believe in the reality of evil." He

20. Two other ominous aspects of the Blackburn story are its setting and Wilson's references to Oswald Spengler's *Decline of the West*. In *Daisy*, Wilson's selecting Coney Island as the book's final, representative American place expressed his populist feelings in the late 1920s. In its heyday, the amusement park was a kind of capitalist paradise where working- and middle-class New Yorkers could enjoy themselves in a "classless society." But Blackburn's mansion at the end of the *Memoirs* is the type of house Wilson described in a 1939 autobiographical essay as a symbol of American oligarchy in its crassest and most aggressive phase: "the spirit that acquires and consumes," the "instinct" to achieve "the lethal concentration of power," and the desire to maximize "the social differences between human beings" ("At Laurelwood," *Wilson's Night Thoughts* [New York, 1964], 177). Also in *Daisy*, the references to Spengler's *Decline of the West* are meant to be a joke. Daisy says that the phrase "the downfall of western civilization" is "just something I picked up in the Ritz Bar in Paris!" (309). In the *Memoirs*, there are allusions to Spengler and the *Decline*, but there are no indications that they are meant ironically (279, 332).

then implied that the devil would soon arrive in the form of a "moral epidemic" that would force Americans to confront "evil's reality," but they would struggle against it through a "renewal . . . of faith and of spirituality."[21] Blackburn expounds several ideas that are similar to Maritain's—particularly that people do not believe in the devil anymore and that a religious "renewal" should take place—but he presents them from a satanic, rather than a religious, viewpoint.

According to Blackburn, the devil has become an insignificant force in human events. He claims indignantly that *"le Malin"* is not responsible for the horrors that will occur during the late 1930s and the 1940s, because people started ignoring him in the eighteenth century; and during this century they have become the perpetrators of their own monstrous crimes. Now people believe in neither God nor the devil. Blackburn has decided to remedy this neglect by emigrating to the United States, where he expects to find converts. As he tells the narrator, "[T]he Puritan sense of sin, the respect for my Distinguished Opponent and . . . a certain fear of myself is still pervasive in American society" (317). As for the revival of religion, Blackburn plans to encourage it. Now he realizes that belief in the devil was strongest in the Middle Ages, when organized religion was powerful and had a Manichaean morality obsessed with the struggle between good and evil. That was another reason he emigrated—America's tradition of obsessive morality dates back to the seventeenth and eighteenth centuries. "Vous avez fait de si belles choses, n'est-ce pas, en fait de forte moralité," he comments with suave irony. "The Mathers and Jonathan Edwards . . . c'étaient de vrais titans" (316).

Although Wilson's narrator does not articulate them, Blackburn's speech has several important implications. First, the immoral and decadent behavior of Hecate County's inhabitants, which was

21. "Maritain Honored at Luncheon Here," New York *Times*, March 16, 1945, p. 4; Jacques Maritain, "Of America and the Future," *Commonweal*, April 13, 1945, p. 644. Wilson planned to make the devil an inhabitant of the county as early as 1941 when he was first planning the *Memoirs* (*Letters*, 433). Maritain's speech could have given him several important ideas for the contents of Blackburn's speech and, what was equally important, made him decide to have Blackburn give this speech in French.

chronicled earlier in the book, becomes more explicable if the devil—in the guise of Blackburn—has made himself "at home" there. Moreover, in the context of Maritain's remark that Americans had not yet seen the devil's face, Blackburn's appearance in Hecate County means that the difference between Europe and the United States has ended. His speech can be interpreted as Wilson's version of a theme that David Noble has described as "the end of American history"—the awareness that the United States is no longer an especially virtuous nation whose history is meant to be an "exception" to the sinful, tragic history of the rest of the human race.[22]

Finally, in terms of Wilson's cultural nationalism, one of the significant features of Blackburn's speech is that it is in French. Instead of "breaking into that new accent" that Wilson had hoped for in *I Thought of Daisy*, America has now become so decadent that its future development can be described in a foreign language. Instead of providing Europe with some new "sensible ideas about society and life," as Wilson had hoped America would do in 1928, the United States has become so corrupted that by the 1940s it will only be another variation upon European history and experience.

The narrator's conscious reaction to Blackburn's speech is relatively mild: "I found that it annoyed and disturbed me to hear him talk about American history in French and from that point of view" (*MHC*, 317). Subconsciously, however, the narrator reacts very strongly by getting drunk and undergoing a kaleidoscopic series of attitude and identity changes during the Blackburns' dinner party. That is, America's loss of its historical and cultural identity seems to make the narrator's own personal identity waver and nearly collapse. In *I Thought of Daisy*, there was a brief and harmless blurring of the narrator's identity when he saw his reflection in a Coney Island mirror and imagined he was "a figure from the funny papers: Mr. Suburban American." The narrator of the *Memoirs*, however, has a more psychologically disturbing loss of identity as he tempo-

22. See David Noble, *The End of American History: Democracy, capitalism, and the metaphor of two worlds* (Minneapolis, 1984), 141–46. Noble's analysis is directed toward American historians, particularly Beard and Hofstadter, but it also applies to Wilson.

rarily succumbs to the mediocrity and the decadence of Hecate County, which he had satirized or described with "Flaubertian irony" in other stories. Earlier in the book, for example, he had despised the Milhollands because they were so corrupt, but at the Blackburns' party he brazenly asks a Hollywood writer to help him get a job at a movie studio. The idea is so out of character that the writer is shocked, and the narrator himself admits, "I was startled by what I heard myself saying" (326). His personal identity becomes so confused that he starts thinking he is the party's host, not one of the guests. He describes himself as becoming "occupied with saying good-by to the guests" (328). His sexual identity also is threatened. In "The Princess with the Golden Hair" he had been a moderately considerate and gentle lover (though often a selfish and jealous one) with Anna and Imogen. As he imagines he is the party's host he starts to make love to Jo Gates in a brutal way to humiliate her. He flees drunkenly from the Blackburns' mansion and returns to his own "buried stone house," where he feels that his "old solitary self, the self for which I really lived and which kept up its austere virtue" will be safe. There he is visited by the poet Si Banks, who makes homosexual overtures to him, and the narrator responds to Banks in an ambiguous way: "[M]y tenderness seemed overflowing in an emotion [that was] uncontrollable, demoralizing, yet too quickly becoming welcome" (336).

Fortunately for the narrator's peace of mind, he is awakened by the singing of ovenbirds and discovers that he has been sleeping beside Jo Gates in his own bed. He assumes that his experiences of the past evening were drunken dreams or reveries, and it is implied that his sexual and personal identity is still intact. After he has gone out to chase away the birds, he makes love to Jo. But the ovenbird has certain symbolic associations. In Robert Frost's poem, entitled "The Oven Bird," it represents decay and change: "a midsummer and a mid-wood bird" that "says that leaves are old . . . / And comes that other fall we name the fall. / He says the highway dust is over all. . . . . The question that he frames in all but words / Is what to make of a diminished thing." Some of these associations may have been in Wilson's mind, since he suddenly returns to the theme of the virgin American landscape when Jo invites the narrator to spend a vacation with her on a New Mexico ranch. "A few weeks on a ranch . . . would rescue me from Hecate County and put me in touch with that heroic America, the America I had sniffed from our inlets and brushed through in the tangled grove," the narrator believes. This hope that he and Jo can "light out for the Territory" turns out to be only another illusion as the story and the *Memoirs* end with his lament for America as a fallen nation that has become, like Europe, an "old country":

> So still we turned West, as our fathers had done, for the new life we could still hope to find—so we sought to regain that new world which seemed still to be just at hand, with its fresh waters and unbroken woods, but from which we now found ourselves divided by a pane of invisible glass. It was not really the new country any more; it was the old country; we had passed it in history. (*MHC*, 338)

Hecate County is everywhere, from the mountains of New Mexico to the suburbs of Connecticut. It is within middle-class Americans, such as Jo and the narrator, who cannot escape from it. The county has become their own and their nation's "history," their society and civilization.

The conclusion of the *Memoirs* is, as several reviewers and critics have commented, a dead end for Wilson's narrator and his Hecate County neighbors. For Wilson himself, however, the book seems to have acted as a signal for some significant new departures. Like the *confession d'un enfant du siècle* he had recommended to Bogan in 1933, the *Memoirs* may have enabled him to get certain experiences "out of [his] system in a . . . literary form," so he could "thumb [his] nose at the world." Or, more precisely, after using the *Memoirs* to criticize and satirize America's mainstream, middle-class national civilization—as purveyed and corrupted by the magazines, book clubs, television, and other mass media— Wilson was able to lose interest in that civilization. "When . . . I look through *Life* magazine," he wrote in 1956, "I feel that I do not belong to the country depicted there, that I do not even live in that country." Indeed, *Life* was crammed with advertisements, cold war propaganda, and hymns to the Eisenhower administration; however, an additional reason Wilson might have felt estranged from that magazine's America was that, by the 1950s, it had become a pretentious parody of his own earlier cultural idealism and nationalism. In *I Thought of Daisy*, for example, the narrator had cheerfully imagined that "literature was as amiable as writing ballads, as necessary as making tables." By 1954, diva Helen Traubel, photographed in full Wagnerian regalia, was appearing in *Life* to explain to its millions of readers that once there had been

a day when the artist—the painter, the singer, the poet, the sculptor—expected people to climb his ivory tower if they wanted to know more about him. Only occasionally did he descend to their level.

Not many artists hold with that today. . . . I like to sing in the same way that I like to cook, or to fish, or watch a ball game, or go to our wonderful St. Louis zoo—or read an issue of LIFE magazine.[23]

After writing the *Memoirs*, however, Wilson was able to ignore this kind of banal, national culture and direct his attention to subjects that were on the periphery—historically, culturally, or geographically—of North American civilization: the Zuni and Haitians of *Red, Black, Blond and Olive*, Judaism and the Dead Sea Scrolls, the Iroquois, Canadian literature and culture, his Talcottville neighbors in *Upstate*, and the Civil War writers he described in *Patriotic Gore*. Fascinated by these subjects, and able to communicate that fascination in his books, Wilson achieved his own personal renaissance as a writer after losing his faith in the national cultural renaissance he had hoped would occur when he was writing *Axel's Castle* and *I Thought of Daisy*.

In this context, perhaps the most significant of his later books was *Apologies to the Iroquois*, in which he was able to discover a green tradition that was even older than the Emersonian. He wrote about it so sympathetically that even the Iroquois approved. The *Apologies* ends, symbolically, with Wilson's detailed description of the Little Water song sequence, a ritual recitation of a death-and-rebirth legend, which he was invited to hear. Listening to these songs, sung by a Seneca medicine society, he interpreted the ceremony as a "builder of morale," an "affirmation of the will of the Iroquois people, of their vitality, their force to persist" in an alien,

23. Wilson, "The Author at Sixty," *The Portable Edmund Wilson*, 44–45; Traubel advertisement, *Life*, February 1, 1954, p. 85.

white society. "I have come to believe that there are many white Americans who now have something important in common with these recalcitrant Indians," Wilson decided. Experiencing the Little Water ceremony must have affirmed his own opposition to a mainstream American culture that he had once tried to improve and then had come to oppose. Like the Iroquois, he had possessed the "force to persist," and perhaps the Indians had recognized this— they allowed him to attend one of their most sacred ceremonies. Indeed, one of the Iroquois—Bette Crouse Mele, a member of the Seneca Hawk clan—was so pleased by the *Apologies* that she offered to adopt Wilson into her clan. He declined, because he felt "he had not done enough to deserve the honor," and Mele respected his wishes. Later she named one of her sons Antonio Edmund Wilson Mele, so that his name would be on the Seneca rolls. It was, symbolically speaking, a kind of citizenship in an America that was a long way from Hecate County; according to Mele, Wilson "was obviously pleased by the honor."[24]

24. Wilson, *Apologies to the Iroquois* (1959; rpr. New York, 1978), 286, 310; Bette Crouse Mele, "Edmund Wilson and the Iroquois," in John Wain (ed.), *Edmund Wilson: The Man and His Work* (New York, 1978), 39.

III / An Age of Enormity: Postwar and
Postmodern

DAVID MARC

The Last Laugh

Begin anywhere. It will unravel.
　　　　　— *The Lost America of Love*

Among the horrors that the postmodern world holds for those faithful to the traditions of Western culture, none (save perhaps the nuclear holocaust) seems quite so catastrophic as the continuing contraction of attention span. Many teachers of literature—including, no doubt, those who themselves have been unable to pass basic literacy "skills tests"—blame the refusal of their students to love books on television, a Pandora's box of intellectually arid, commercially segmented narratives that mocks true art, whose gold-leaf portfolio one learns to respect in graduate school. Although sitcoms, copshows, gameshows, and soap operas usually attract the brunt of more-cultured-than-thou intellectual outrage, the news is probably the genre of mass entertainment that single-handedly has done the most to transform novels into instruments of academic torture. Children who have not yet learned to read have taken the camera tour of Auschwitz, watched The Bomb drop on Hiroshima (shown endlessly on the Cable News Network each year on the anniversary of the event), and listened to daily accounts of murders, rapes, and suicides since the dawn of their consciousnesses. Is it surprising that they are not exactly bowled over by a good old-fashioned cosmic whaling adventure?

Although more culture than ever is intended for millions of people, "mass culture," a special culture for the unwashed that dirties everyone, is in many ways a hopelessly outmoded phrase. It implies that hidden behind the flashing neon façade of the entertainment-industrial complex remains *Kultur*, "the best which has been thought and said," separate, uncorruptible, truthful, and beautiful. If this was once so, it no longer is. Culture has become too large and diversified a business to be identified by any one of its market constituencies. The "consciousness industry," as Hans Magnus Enzensberger calls it, has a high end, a low end, and a ponderous sagging middle, to be sure. But this is the same marketing configuration that challenges automobile manufacturers, shoe companies, soft-drink makers, and any other industry doing large-scale business in an advanced capitalist society.[1]

The legacy of "mass culture" persists, however, as a peculiarly American dream. A vast population composed of functional robots survives the hours between work and sleep sprawled out across Naughahyde couches, its glazed eyes fixed on reruns of *The Love Boat* and *Fantasy Island*. Meanwhile, back in the city, a few crazed bohemians and diligent bookworms, mostly recruited from a barely visible class of surviving WASP gentlefolk and refugees from Nazi Europe, keep the flame of *Kultur* lit with tortured readings of Kafka and Pound. This is a transcendental dream that serves those who see the shoddiness of the twentieth century as its greatest evil. It is a nightmare, however, for those who might hold out any hope for a future or for a role for democracy in it.

In 1924, just when promotion was beginning to surpass production as the central problem of industry, Waldo Frank observed that, to the European sensibility, "America is Dada."[2] This comment may be helpful in explaining Marcel Duchamp's emigration to this country; it is essential to an appreciation of Jerry Lewis' promotion to the rank of Commander of Arts and Letters by the French Minis-

1. See Hans Magnus Enzensberger, *The Consciousness Industry* (New York, 1974).
2. Waldo Frank, "Seriousness and Dada," in Frank, *In the American Jungle: 1925–1936* (New York, 1937), 129. The essay originally appeared in *1924*, III (1924).

try of Culture sixty years later. Little has happened since the 1920s to contradict Frank's contention. With neither a genetic aristocracy nor a socialist bureaucracy to assert balancing prerogatives, entrepreneurship has flourished relatively unfettered by questions of taste or propriety. An environment shaped by mass production and mass distribution technologies has evolved in the service of corporate visions of mass consumption. This has yielded a unique form of cultural democracy that aspires to the ideal of every citizen having the right to buy anything that he or she believes will bring happiness—or at least some measure of relief from the pain of existence. Those with enough money can actually have the thing; those without sufficient credit can have a schlock imitation of it. In a short while, the haves may tire of the item, and the have-nots are likely to find theirs broken. But what better conditions could be imagined for the introduction of new products? Madison Avenue has waged a relentless campaign to portray even the most bizarre and ethereal whims and notions as essential human culture in a struggle against nature. Every trait, inclination, and odor has been improved upon at a reasonable price. Hollywood has offered an emphatically realistic art whose model is precisely this consumer utopia.

Looking out at the hamburger strip from behind the windshield, in mounting traffic, a carefully targeted hit dictating the rhythm, it is difficult to ignore the parody of traditional European *Kultur* that throbs beneath the debris of day-to-day life in what Edmund Wilson called "'the real, the live America' of motor traffic."[3] McDonald's is, after all, a restaurant. A motel is a kind of hotel. An evening at a drive-in movie cannot fully escape the heritage of an evening at the theater. A shopping mall, though resplendent in ample parking, can trace its lineage to the downtown commercial district that was the center of community life during the urban era. Even a mobile-home park, easily accessible from the Interstate, with its laundromat, 7-Eleven, and pay phone, owes a debt to the idea of a city. What happened to these nineteenth-century middle-class cultural institutions that caused them to mutate in

3. Sherman Paul, *Edmund Wilson: A Study of Literary Vocation in Our Time* (Urbana, 1965), 59.

such bizarre fashion in twentieth-century America? Is the physical environment spawned by a new technology always driven to mock the culture of the technology that preceded it? Is there an inherent disjunction in the evolution of cultural form that automatically turns the new into a crazed imitation of the familiar?

At the dawn of the Industrial Revolution in eighteenth-century Britain, several writers, notably Alexander Pope and Jonathan Swift, were among the first to realize that the age-old balance of cultural power that had isolated most people from literate expression was threatened by a radical shift in the technological environment.[4] The new economic order of mercantile capitalism demanded a broad-based clerking class in possession of the skills required to process contracts and keep the books. But while this made it necessary to train increasing numbers of people to read and write in order to conduct business, there was neither economic need nor sufficient social inclination to teach the newly literate to read Homer, Saint Thomas Aquinas, the Elizabethan poets, or any of the writers whose works were considered essential to a gentleman's education. Denied access to the classical canon, the aesthetic energies unleashed by newly acquired literacy shopped elsewhere for satisfaction. The "penny press" that grew up around London's Grub Street became, in effect, the first Hollywood—a primitive commercial community devoted entirely to the production of inexpensive, mechanically reproducible appeals to the emotional and imaginative urges of any and all who would pay for the product.[5]

The old literati watched in horror as advances in printing technology turned the written word from a rarefied treasure of the court elite into a marketplace commodity. Not surprisingly, "serious" writers (those educated in and loyal to Western literary traditions) responded to the "scribblers" with the weapons at hand, producing wild satires of the new literature. Pope, a translator of Greek classics and an editor of Shakespeare, was merciless in his

4. See Dwight Macdonald, "A Theory of Mass Culture," *Diogenes,* III (1953), 1–17, reprinted in Bernard Rosenberg and David Manning White (eds.), *Mass Culture: The Popular Arts in America* (New York, 1957), 59–73.
5. For detailed historical and critical accounts of this phenomenon, see Marshall McLuhan, *The Gutenberg Galaxy* (Toronto, 1962); or Ian Watt, *The Rise of the Novel: Studies in Defoe, Richardson and Fielding* (Berkeley, 1957).

attacks on the "babbling blockheads" of Grub Street.[6] In *The Dunciad* (that is, "The epic of the dunce"), the poet imagines the fate of the life of the mind during the millennial rule of the goddess Dullness (a personification of what, in the twentieth century, would be called Mass Culture):

Beneath her foot-stool, *Science* groans in Chains,
And *Wit* dreads Exile, Penalties and Pains.
There foam'd rebellious *Logic*, gagg'd and bound,
There, script, fair *Rhet'ric* languish'd on the ground.[7]

In *Gulliver's Travels*, Swift parodies a burgeoning pop literature that prefigures modern American supermarket tabloids such as the *National Enquirer* and the *Star*, publications whose readers are no strangers to encounters with midgets, giants, talking animals, and aliens. Voyaging to Birnibiari, a nation populated exclusively by scientists, Gulliver visits the exalted seat of higher learning, the Academy of Projectors in Lagado. The Laputians, who maintain their country on a cloud suspended above the earth so as not to get contaminated by germs, are busily engaged in research aimed at scientifically processing human feces into reusable food. The relationship between economy and taste implied by the scientists' experiments in high-tech nutrition anticipates the dilemma of the modern consumer reading the ingredients on the products for sale in a gleaming state-of-the-art supermarket.

Those twentieth-century intellectuals who are still able to prescribe distinctions between culture and consumption are as defensive on the subject of evolving communications technologies as were Pope and Swift. Throughout the nineteenth century, a culture of subsistence literacy proliferated as basic reading extended across class lines. The realistic prose novel displaced the verse epic, carrying the reading of imaginative fiction outside the walls of the palace. This phenomenon reached what can be seen as its popular apogee with the publication of Dickens' novels as mass-circulation newspaper serials in the 1880s. In the realm of nonfiction, daily

6. Alexander Pope, "Epistle to Dr. Arbuthnot" (1735), l. 304, in *Poetry and Prose of Alexander Pope*, ed. Aubrey Williams (Boston, 1969), 207.
7. Pope, *The Dunciad* (1728), IV, ll. 20–24, *ibid.*, 356.

newspapers and popular magazines created a rhetoric for the mass discussion of politics, history, and culture.

In the twentieth century, however, even as the number of leisure hours was increasing, the nonvocational usage of literacy went into decline. The narrative motion picture relieved the novel of the lion's share of popular storytelling duties, and radio gradually established itself as the clearinghouse of public information (*i.e.,* rhetoric). Since the end of World War II, television has synthesized both of these functions into a single medium. While Pope, Swift, Henry Fielding, and Laurence Sterne were provoked to their eighteenth-century satires by the "bad reading" made possible by the historical marriage of inexpensive printing and cheap literacy, the worst-case scenario for contemporary intellectuals is not so much "bad reading" as the prospect of no reading at all. Peter Conrad expresses the tone of highbrow response to this problem in his book *Television: The Medium and Its Manners*:

In the Oxford college to which I belong, a television set has been supplied for the delectation of the brain-weary dons. It's hidden away in a musty chamber, bottling up the fug of defunct cigars, called the smoking room. In a corner of that room, it stands, masquerading as a Gothic cocktail cabinet, concealed behind panels of fretted wood which have to be opened out like an altar diptych to disclose the screen. People sometimes scuttle across the quad after dark to watch it, conscious (in their furtiveness) that in doing so they're neglecting their pedagogic chores, and the set they watch is as ashamed as they are.[8]

As the cultural primacy of reading continues to diminish, the literary priest class of professors and critics, sensing the disintegration of its constituency, begins to dote on the very form of the printed word. Daniel Defoe's *Robinson Crusoe*, the melodramatic South Seas adventure that inspired Swift to the barbed parody of *Gulliver's Travels*, is now itself piously enshrined in the curriculum as a "classic"; after all, it is centuries old and its *adventure* qualities might capture the interest of nonmajors. Although an occasional movie or even TV program of quality may be discovered—usually a revelation stumbled upon by accident—the chief effect attributed to the electronic nonprint media is theft of the cultural limelight

8. Peter Conrad, *Television: The Medium and Its Manners* (Boston, 1982), 1.

from books. As punishment for constituting this barbaric threat to civilization and tenure, the popular arts are categorically exiled from the continuity of cultural history to the sociological twilight zone of "mass culture." Intellectuals of strikingly diverse political orientations—from Dwight Macdonald to Herbert Marcuse on the Left, from T. S. Eliot to José Ortega y Gasset on the Right—have assured the twentieth century that mass culture stands outside the continuity of the history of human expression. They have portrayed it as a kind of evil anti-culture, a monolithic hypnotist whose purpose is to homogenize our taste (Macdonald), rob us of our traditions (Eliot), lobotomize our erotic impulses (Marcuse), and steal prerogative from the worthy (Ortega). This perception of "culture" and "the mass media" as separate adversarial entities dueling for the attention spans and the souls of the audience is widely held among intellectuals and educators. Utterly obsolete, it has only served to increase the intimacy of the relationship most Americans enjoy with their sets.

Barbara Tuchman spoke for many modern intellectuals when she related in the New York *Times*, with great mortification, a story concerning an English teacher at an "affluent suburban" high school who devoted a week of class time to the study of television. "This," wrote the outraged Tuchman, "in the literature of Shakespeare to Mark Twain, Jane Austen to J. D. Salinger!"[9] One wonders if Tuchman is aware that Twain and indeed American literature itself were dismissed as "pop culture" and kept out of most American college curricula until well into the twentieth century. Would she have sided against the radicals who founded the Modern Language Association in the 1880s?

Tuchman's position is at the heart of the refusal of most university humanities departments to undertake the critical study of the American electronic arts, despite the fact that these arts have become the major vessels of the language. The life, death, or revised meaning of a word, phrase, construction, or inflection is today largely determined by its usage in mass communications. This is especially true of English, a language that has never been under the

9. Tuchman's letter, as cited in J. Hoberman, "Love and Death in the American Supermarketplace," *Voice Literary Supplement* (November, 1982), 12.

formal direction of an official academy, but has instead depended
upon the evolving conventions of common parlance for its grammar. An English department that limits the definition of the language to the sum of the language's (well-) written documents is
clinging to an honorific title; it could more honestly—and
proudly—call itself a Great Literature Department.

In *Media and the American Mind*, Daniel Czitrom describes the
reaction of American intellectuals to new communications technologies in terms of a ritual. A new invention—the wireless telegraph,
the movie camera, television—is patented. At first, intellectuals
welcome it as a panacea for ignorance and indifference, a means to
universalize the distribution of information, bringing democracy, at
long last, to full blossom. Entrepreneurs, however, soon get hold of
the marvel and commercialize it for the sale of popular fantasies.
The common denominator prevails. Millions are seduced; none are
uplifted. Angered and frustrated, the intellectuals get revenge by
refusing to confer the status of art upon the burgeoning form. Instead, they relegate it to the humanistic scrap heap as a "communications technology" whose "messages" are best left for study to
psychologists and sociologists who specialize in the analysis of the
"mass mind." The medium is finally saved from this fate, however,
when a new invention spawns a new medium that is even more
contemptible than the one it is about to replace as the central narrative instrument of the culture.[10] Social scientists whose only text
is "the masses" move on to explore the "effects" of the new medium. As public interest in the old medium decreases, however, a
suspicion grows among certain partisans of the humanities that
there may be an aesthetic dimension to it after all. The grandest example is the elevation of the movies to the status of a respectable art
form in America—a development that took place in direct corre-
lation to the rise and proliferation of television during the 1950s.

Throughout the country's history, many American writers—
Henry James, Henry Adams, Ezra Pound, and T. S. Eliot among
them—have voiced their disdain in no uncertain terms for both the
substance and the symbols of the mindless, semiliterate mass so-

10. Daniel J. Czitrom, *Media and the American Mind* (Chapel Hill, 1982), esp.
Chaps. 4–6.

ciety to which they believe America had lost its cultural possibilities. Finding none of the joy in heterogeneity that led Walt Whitman to exclaim, "The United States themselves are essentially the greatest poem," such writers turned their hearts and souls away from the formlessness of the New World and dedicated themselves to the cultivation of Old World attitudes and the critical recovery of Western civilization. T. S. Eliot, the Missouri-born poet who repatriated himself to the United Kingdom in the 1920s, wrote a manifesto for this point of view in his 1948 essay, "Notes Toward the Definition of Culture." Culture, Eliot concludes, can only thrive where there is cosmic tribal consensus based on national religious unity and a serene social order built upon universal respect for class hierarchy.[11] America, a nation founded with the energies of religious eccentricities, and built upon an economic system institutionally dependent on universal dissatisfaction with personal status, is structurally doomed under these circumstances to become a grotesque cultural monster.

Other writers, however, while mindful of its dangers, have displayed a more bemused ambiguity toward American culture. There is an inkling of this in so conservative a novel as *The Great Gatsby*. F. Scott Fitzgerald's narrator, Nick Carraway, is a recent Yale graduate, from an old Minnesota family. When confronted with modern culture in the form of a wild party in Harlem, he comments, "I was within and without, simultaneously enchanted and repulsed by the inexhaustible varieties of life."[12] Although Fitzgerald paints a picture of emerging twentieth-century mass society that is almost as bleak as Eliot's wasteland, Nick's ambiguity is a significant departure from Eliot's ineluctably tragic vision of modern life. Beneath alienation and denial, there is at least the possibility of celebration.[13] Since 1945, many of the best American novels, while dutifully painting a frightening-enough picture of modern life, betray a

11. Walt Whitman, Preface to *Leaves of Grass 1855*, ed. Malcolm Cowley (New York, 1959), 5; T. S. Eliot, "Notes Toward the Definition of Culture" (1948), in *Christianity and Culture* (New York, 1968).

12. F. Scott Fitzgerald, *The Great Gatsby* (New York, 1925), 24.

13. For a penetrating discussion of simultaneous urges toward celebration and despair in the American hero, see Ihab Hassan, "The Character of Post-War Fiction in America," in Joseph J. Waldmeir (ed.), *Recent American Fiction* (Boston, 1961), 215–30.

profound appreciation of the culture's absurd charms: "To any other type of tourist accommodation," sighs Vladimir Nabokov's Humbert Humbert, "I soon grew to prefer the Functional Motel— clean, neat, safe nooks, ideal places for sleep, argument, reconciliation, insatiable illicit love." As is the case with Lolita herself, America's disjunction from *Kultur* is as seductive as it is exasperating. In *On the Road*, Jack Kerouac's Dean Moriarty does not forfeit his individuality to mass society but instead becomes an avatar of the erotic possibilities of the machine age. The automobile, in addition to destroying the city, the land, and the respiratory system, becomes both the way and the place to get laid. Among recent American writers perhaps no one has shown as much contempt for mass culture or as much taste for what it has to offer as has Norman Mailer. His biographies of Marilyn Monroe and Gary Gilmore are nothing less than epic sagas of redneck America's life in the electronic theme park of mass communiculture. In the final chapter of *An American Dream*, Mailer's Stephen Rojack—a Harvard graduate, a former congressman, a professor of existential psychology at New York University, and a TV talk-show host—takes a cancerous trip "out West, driving through the landscape of Super-America . . . freeways, motor lodges, winged motel inns, the heated pools." On the outskirts of Las Vegas, the very mecca of modern schlock, however, Rojack pauses at the heart of ambiguity, seeing before him "a jeweled city on the horizon, spires rising in the night, but the jewels were diadems of electric and the spires were the neon of signs ten stories high."[14]

The capacity to experience, even for a moment, the comic beauty of America as "a jeweled city," before falling prey to the tragedy of the poison gasses lurking beneath the surface, is what allows Rojack to keep his sanity. Although the end of the novel finds him planning to leave techno-America in search of the unspoiled root of the New World in the jungles of the Yucatán and Guatemala, Rojack, like Humbert and Dean, has the strength to claim some measure of personal/erotic satisfaction and thus survive the deadly inanities of the machine-made society.

14. Vladimir Nabokov, *Lolita* (Greenwich, Conn., 1958), 133; Norman Mailer, *An American Dream* (New York, 1963), 248, 251.

For these would-be survivors of the twentieth century, America becomes, simultaneously, a dehumanized, cultural concentration camp and a fecund surrealistic junkyard—two prismatically related possibilities fighting for control of consciousness. When the barren, lonely vision of the former dominates, it is some comfort to remember that each continent has had its share of both, but America has managed the greater reputation for junkyards while Europe has shown a genius for the camps. At the same time, if the gorgeousness of the automobile stereo giving good bass at seventy miles per hour gets out of hand, one can always switch on The News.

Earlier discoveries of the world by Western imaginations may have required the excitement of the epic to order their exhilarations, or the reversals and recognitions of tragedy to give meaning to their anxieties. The latest discoveries, however, have been so completely depressing, so utterly baffling to any remnant of optimism that may still reassert itself in youth like some vestigial second heart, that laughter has become the mark of courage. The News makes itself available twenty-four hours a day by radio, by television, by newspaper, and by everyone who listens to, watches, and reads it. Logic compellingly dictates how this mammoth narrative must climax. With such a vast stockpile of weapons poised to do the job, gravity itself is likely to depress the button if no one beats it to the punch. Son marries mother? Prince fails to avenge father? What are these things to those of us facing the day after?

The freak-show atmosphere that emerges beneath the nuclear sword of Damocles while cruising down superhighways through crumbling cities, or listening to descriptions of the day's murders to pass the time in traffic jams, or hopelessly scanning the cable channels by remote control is, like any carnival, at once insulting to the learned traditions of Western sensibility and a release from the deathwatch that modern life has become. The choice between tragedy and comedy is underlined by this problem of selective perception. If tragedy has been trivialized by mere reportage, the joke's the thing that puts despair in the service of endurance. Threatened with anonymous, ignominious death, the audience cannot help but make use of its capacity to imagine a happy ending. Slapstick, the "lowest" of comic arts, may be the most appropriate response of all to this insult to the human spirit. The specter of death deserves, at the very least, a pie in the face, a banana peel, or a spritz of ice-cold seltzer.

It is perhaps in this spirit that Dr. Derrick de Kerckhove, Director of the Marshall McLuhan Program in Culture and Technology at the University of Toronto, has characterized thermonuclear weaponry as "the ultimate information medium." Indeed, the message of this hottest of media is straight to the point and easily decodable without the aid of semioticians. The capacity for murder not only has survived the current level of technology but has found in it a realistic scenario for the delivery of a *pièce de résistance*. All that is familiar sits squarely in the sights of a loaded gun. Culture and nature, estranged since the exile of Adam, are ironically reunited as mutual victims of this common threat. In 1945, only several months after the atomic attacks on Japan, the editors of *Reader's Digest* perceptively observed that all of humanity had become "fused unbreakably in the diabolical heat of those explosions."[15]

With civilization at the other end of a burning fuse, the burden of individual mortality can no longer be mitigated by a sense of participation in a grand, permanently accreting cultural history. Religion, which suffered during much of the Industrial Revolution as an antagonist of both unbridled technological expansion and the pursuit of leisure-time sex, is enjoying a comeback among human generations that know they are capable of the ultimate sin. Nineteenth-century humanists, such as Matthew Arnold, held out the hope that culture might act as a fortress to protect what is beautiful and noble from the brutal storms of history. But what fortress is likely to withstand the firestorm? The creatures frequenting the libraries left standing on a nuclear winter's day may be more disposed to eat the books than read them. "You can't do what you want with the bomb," notes de Kerckhove. "The bomb does what it wants to you."[16]

15. De Kerckhove quoted in "A Good Bomb?" New York *Times*, September 30, 1984, p. 41; as cited in Paul Boyer, "The Cloud Over the Culture," *New Republic*, August 12–19, 1985, p. 28.
16. De Kerckhove quoted in "A Good Bomb?" New York *Times*, September 30, 1984, p. 41.

The value of comedy ascends in the face of a plausible end to history. Religions offering their subscribers the "good news" of Heaven have surely benefited from this introduction of a permanent state of man-made crisis concerning a future for the Earth. Secular humanists, on the other hand, have defined themselves by their preference for art over religion. But is the imagination capable of finding a force short of an omnipotent, omniscient being that can save humanity from committing suicide? "Hollywood is the good dream," observed Isaac Rosenfeld, "Buchenwald, the bad."[17]

The Bomb, as those of us who live at its disposal so familiarly call it, stands guard over civilization. Humor—and not tragic empathy—offers would-be survivors the possibility of catharsis. What will it be while waiting for the end? Faithful contemplation of the hereafter? A nihilistic rediscovery of the satisfactions of personal violence? The pursuit of amnesia? Or the laugh that the victim reserves for the tormentor? All of these strategies have their advocates.

Ironically, as television mutates farther and farther away from the traditional dramatic arts that spawned it, even the stodgiest of English teachers, given a future, may one day remember the era of network television with some fondness. At least people watched whole shows in those days; at least Aristotle's prescription for "a beginning, a middle, and an end" was respected, even if, to the tutored eye, ineptly. The ancient TV shows, media historians might someday remind us, actually made use of such time-honored devices as setting, characterization, conflict, and climax.

But those days are rapidly passing. The eight or ten hours it takes to read most novels gave way to the two or so hours it takes to see most movies gave way to the thirty to sixty minutes it takes to watch most TV shows gives way to the three to five minutes it takes to witness a music video gives way to the three to ten seconds it takes to absorb an image, tire of it, and hit the remote control button for another. PBS penguins perform mating rituals in the Antarctic. Kill cockroaches with sonic waves for $29.95. A Soviet

17. Isaac Rosenfeld, "The Meaning of Terror," *An Age of Enormity: Life and Writing in the Forties and Fifties*, ed. Theodore Solotaroff (Cleveland, 1962), 204.

Harry Callahan, "Providence 1967"
Copyright: Harry Callahan   Courtesy Pace-MacGill Gallery, New York

ballerina is defecting. Receding hairline? Fred Flintstone is yelling
for Wilma. *The Maltese Falcon*—in color. A rerun of a college bas-
ketball game. Gold chains for below manufacturer's price on the
Consumer Value Network. Lucy goes to the eye doctor and gets a
glaucoma test that impairs her vision just before her big chance to
perform a jitterbug number down at the club. The House is holding
hearings. Anyone for tennis?

Modern dramatists such as Samuel Beckett, Eugene Ionesco, and
Luigi Pirandello understood that the visceral friction of disparate
images had become more satisfying than a logical picture of order
in a world where reason offers us nothing but bad news. Television,
whether by chance or design, takes this as an article of faith, supplying its audience with endless comic diversion. Why not? Who

would prefer a cogent picture of humanity despoiling its nest with toxic wastes? Who would choose to be reminded of the level of confidence inspired by the men who have the power to wreck everyone's life and possibly life itself? Television is depressing not because it is so bad or so mediocre or because it fails so miserably to produce its share of well-wrought urns. Television is depressing because it is something people need as a hedge against objective conditions. It is the box in which The News is contained; when even that is too much, the channel can be changed.

Staring into the void of the concentration camps in 1949 to describe the meaning of terror, Rosenfeld wrote, "A culture is dead when the experience of men has no place in it." Television challenges the critic's survival skills. What is green, fertile, or fecund in the steelly technological monolith? What seeds will grow in this toxic earth? What mutations will shock the sensibility? Is this new world a willing world, a world propitious to a self? Who will feel the struggle for joy in the numbing chill of a drama committed to rude unreconstructed materialism and gluttony? Rosenfeld offered this warning to those who would dare retain literate sensibilities after the demonstrations of World War II: "We are the guides through the museum of dead culture—or if we, too, have lost our humanity, we are at least the nimble goats who can pick their way among the ruins."[18]

18. Ibid., 206, 208.

LISA PATER FARANDA

"to get the rituals straight":
The Poetics of Charles Olson's
The Maximus Poems

We need only cite such touchstones of the revolt
against formalism as Justice Holmes' "The life of the
law hasn't been logic but experience" to remind ourselves that Olson's argument belongs to a central philosophical tradition—one, moreover, contemporary
with a poetics that opposes, as his does, image to symbol and enactment to description and representation.
—*Olson's Push*

If the early twentieth century has come to be known as the Pound
era, the period since 1950 is Olson's.[1] He stands forth as the Bard
and the Pedagogue for poets whose task it has been to move beyond
their predecessors, the great moderns. The publication in 1950 of
Olson's "kick off piece," as he called his essay "Projective Verse," is
a benchmark in the development of contemporary poetry. In it
Olson recognizes his debt to earlier poets, particularly Pound and
Williams, but he calls for a new advance: "It is time we picked the
fruits of the experiments of Cummings, Pound, Williams. . . . It is
now only a matter of the recognition of the conventions of com-

1. Donald Allen and Warren Tallman, *The Poetics of the New American Poetry*
(New York, 1973), ix.

position by field for us to bring into being an open verse as formal as the closed, with all its traditional advantages."[2]

The advance Olson heralds moves poetry to its proprioceptive, physiological ground, which shifts attention to the poet's physical reality: "I take it that PROJECTIVE VERSE teaches, is, this lesson, that that verse will only do in which a poet manages to register both the acquisitions of his ear *and* the pressures of his breath."[3] Olson proposes a new view of reality, one in which poetry offers a new opportunity to participate in the world. Projective verse is a poetry of presentation rather than representation, participation rather than observation.[4] It presumes a new humanism, one implicit in Whiteheadian process reality as well as primitive (non- or pre-Western) culture. Ultimately, Olson believed in the power of poetry to enable his participation in the world. The implications of this view for the practice of verse warrant a poetics based upon the dynamic, kinetic, and ideographic capacities of language and form. Nonetheless, it is no simple matter to recognize the "conventions of composition by field."

Despite Olson's pedagogical stance in "Projective Verse" and later essays, he is not teaching a new prosody for "an open verse as formal as the closed." Exhortations such as "USE USE USE the process at all points, on any given poem always, always one perception must must must MOVE, INSTANTER, ON ANOTHER" teach more about the way one must live in the world and the "stance toward reality that brings such verse into being" than they do about how a poet may use the language to articulate that stance.[5] This is, however, precisely the point, because the poem, for Olson, becomes a naturally occurring event in a life lived "this instant, in

2. Charles Olson, *Selected Writings*, ed. Robert Creeley (New York, 1966), 22.
3. *Ibid.*, 17.
4. Sherman Paul writes: "What is new, or made so by the way Olson appropriates and stresses it, is, in the words of 'Human Universe,' the insistence on repossessing man's dynamic. Projective verse is not only a poetics of presentation but a poetics of present experience, of enactment. It replaces spectatorism with participation, and brings the whole self—the single intelligence: body, mind, soul—to the activity of creation" (Sherman Paul, *Olson's Push: Origin, Black Mountain, and Recent American Poetry* [Baton Rouge, 1978], 39).
5. Olson, *Selected Writings*, 17, 15.

action," making any question of poetics a concern about how one lives in order to write poems.

For readers, then, an encounter with a poem becomes an event, a reader's stance bears in on a poem's meaning, and a discussion of form is never more than a discussion of content, to adapt Robert Creeley's famous remark.[6] Throughout the poem, words gather and disperse continuously as the poem enlarges, word by word, silence by silence, punctuation mark by punctuation mark. Meaning exfoliates as all elements of the poem reflect, deflect, and change what had been (and remains) a word, or space, or mark before.[7] The questions of how to write and read projective verse are not merely persistent concerns for Olson; they are inextricably bound up with his essential project, appearing in his last work, *The Maximus Poems*, as clearly as they do in "Projective Verse."

In fact, Maximus, the persona Olson creates as an aspect of himself, "emerges as a teacher . . . to tell us to front reality . . . in obedience not in opposition to the 'present dance' of reality."[8] Maximus grapples with many of the same issues which sent Olson off to the Yucatán and led to his seminal essay. Thoroughly interwoven among the personal and public themes of *The Maximus Poems* is the concern for discovering the language strategies necessary to enact his stance. In "A Later Note on / Letter #15," for example, Maximus reasserts that the reality he seeks to demonstrate is "a situation" demanding a new poetics.[9] That situation is free of the Cartesian distinction between subject and object, between a poet and the world: "In English the poetics became meubles—furniture— / thereafter (after 1630 / & Descartes was the value." His is a Whiteheadian universe: "no event / is not penetrated, in intersection or

6. Creeley said that "form is never more than an extension of content," a statement Olson adopted in his essay.

7. I am not suggesting that only projective poems, or only those since 1950, have these qualities. As Olson and many of his contemporaries have pointed out, poetry centuries old can be read projectively or affect us with immediate force. Many twentieth-century poets—Pound, Zukofsky, Niedecker, and Olson—have cited the seventh-century poem "A Westryn Wynde" as one example.

8. Paul, *Olson's Push*, 121.

9. Charles Olson, *The Maximus Poems*, ed. George F. Butterick (Berkeley, 1983), 249. Hereafter, all page references to this work will appear in parentheses, and will be identified by *M*.

collision with, an eternal / event." A situation in which no thing is privileged and the instant has cosmic consequences cannot be encompassed by a poetics based upon a descriptive or discursive use of language: "that the objective . . . / or any form of record on the spot / —live television or what—is a lie." In this early Maximus poem, the speaker concludes, "The poetics of such a situation / are yet to be found out" (M, 249).

The project of The Maximus Poems may be seen as the discovery and demonstration of a poetics equal to the public and private task of establishing the self and thereby fostering "polis." From Ernest Fenollosa's "The Chinese Written Character as a Medium for Poetry," Olson developed his ideas about language (and the poem) as "energy transferred" and the potency of the ideograph to recharge language by its concrete, metaphoric rather than symbolic, components. Thinking about the poetics of his situation, and about the nature of time and history, impelled Olson to return to origins. Behind history (in "The Gate and The Center," Olson pushes back to Sumer, before 1200 B.C.) time is spatialized, "with all-history-there-at-once, the fullness of time."[10]

Unlike the primitivist, however, who "recreates an original space, below time," Olson is a projectivist seeking to "restore the original relation among objects in this space above time." In Sumer's time, he says, "a city was a coherence which, for the first time since the ice, gave man the chance to join knowledge to culture and, with this weapon, shape dignities of economics and value sufficient to make daily life itself a dignity and a sufficiency." This is Olson's "polis." Maximus of Gloucester must find the space to fill in which he can make "traceries sufficient to / other's needs." The push back to a primitive world view and the mythology so prominent in the series, like the move out beyond the present, led Olson to ritual—not only as the methodology of "stance" but as the foundation for the poetic strategies that will ultimately mean "the initiation / of another kind of nation" (M, 633).[11]

10. Martin L. Pops, "On Charles Olson," in Robert Boyers (ed.), Contemporary Poetry in America: Essays and Interviews (New York, 1973), 192; Paul, Olson's Push, 71.

11. Pops, "On Charles Olson," in Boyers (ed.), Contemporary Poetry in America, 200; Charles Olson, Human Universe and Other Essays, ed. Donald Allen (New

The late Maximus poem "[to get the rituals straight" may be seen as an answer to the implicit query in "A Later Note on / Letter #15." It opens with a restatement of purpose, as it takes up again the issues of poetic method and the means of whatever success Maximus (and/or the poet) can claim:

[to get the rituals straight I have
been a tireless Intichiuma eater & crawler of my own
ground until . . .
        topi animated until
   even the Earth 7,500,000 years off us
   is my
   gravel (M, 556–57)

He has repossessed the earth as a place in which to live.

By this time in *The Maximus Poems*, the pedagogue has become the shaman, imaged here as a participant in a totemic Australian fertility ritual, which Olson learned of from Jane Harrison's major work, *Themis*. Olson, "eater & crawler of [his] own / ground," has come to "know order" based not upon the distinction between self and others but upon the "Participation mystique." It is characterized by a way of thinking that is other than the scientific. "It joins not only man and man, but man and all living things, all material things possessed by it, is the link between the whole and its severed part. Things can affect each other not by analogy, because like affects like, but by that deeper thing participation, in a common life that serves for link."[12] The participation mystique also answers Olson's need for a way of seeing one's self in a human universe established upon an "actual earth of value."

This view makes not only ritual but Olson's poetry efficacious. Through the dynamics of ritual as both social activity and personal

---

York, 1967), 19; Paul, *Olson's Push*, 117 (citing *Origin*, 1st ser., I [Spring, 1951]), 53.
   12. Although there is no traditional narrative line in *The Maximus Poems*, this three-volume serial poem creates a story within which we can locate particular significant moments. See Paul, who, when discussing the nature and structure of the massive work, says that "though this his-story tells a story, there is no narrative line" (Paul, *Olson's Push*, 129). Jane Harrison, *Themis: A Study of the Social Origins of Greek Religion* (Cambridge, England, 1927), 84.

experience, Olson and "all those poets" he celebrates in this poem, "whose mental level does permit them to / know order," have recognized the "conventions of composition by field." The very nature of ritual, as Harrison explains it, provides the organic model for the ways the poet may successfully weave his poem to make his themes manifest:

The Greek word for a *rite* as already noted is *dromenon*, "a thing done"— and the word is full of instruction. The Greeks had realized that to perform a rite you must *do* something, that is, you must not only feel something but express it in action, or, to put it psychologically, you must not only receive an impulse, you must react to it. The word for rite, *dromenon*, "thing done," arose, of course, not from any psychological analysis, but from the simple fact that rites among the primitive Greeks were *things done*, mimetic dances and the like. It is a fact of cardinal importance that their word for theatrical representation, *drama*, is own cousin to their word for rite, *dromenon*: drama also means "thing done." Greek linguistic instinct pointed plainly to the fact that art and ritual are near relations.[13]

In a letter to Ann Charters, Olson cites this passage as his "original experience of the word [*dromenon*]." No doubt, Harrison's definition of ritual as *logomenon* and *dromenon*, "what is spoken and what is done," inspired his decision to identify "Fact #2" in *Call me Ishmael* as "dromenon." As Martin Pops says, Olson adopted the twofold nature of ritual as a model for his work so "that as nearly as literature can come, *Call Me Ishmael* is the performance of a rite." Furthermore, according to Harrison, mythology (*muthologos*, originally the equivalent of *logos*) is the spoken corollary of the action performed in ritual, which enacts what is said. This conception of mythology is appropriate to Olson's work, for he claims, "If there is any legitimacy to the world that we call mythology it is literally the activeness, the possible activeness and personalness of experiencing it [Earth] as such [as what Olson calls 'Orb']."[14]

Olson's attempt to "get the rituals straight" brings him to origin,

13. Jane Harrison, *Ancient Art and Ritual* (New York, 1951), 35.
14. Ann Charters, *Olson/Melville: A Study in Affinity* (New York, 1968), 56–57; Harrison, *Themis*, 328–31; Charles Olson, *Call Me Ishmael* (San Francisco, 1947), 76; Pops, "On Charles Olson," in Boyers (ed.), *Contemporary Poetry in America*, 194; Charles Olson, *Causal Mythology* (San Francisco, 1969), 9.

gives him "Earth [as far back as] 7,500,000 years off us." The ritual that he performs in any given situation is determined by his purpose, and Maximus tells us that all has been done toward the "initiation of another kind of nation" (633). He seeks to originate "polis" through a return to the origins of civilization and the human self: "This town / works at / dawn because / fishermen do— it makes therefore a / very different / City . . . / when men / are washed as gods in the Basin of Morning" (*M*, 558). The poetry must not only speak of the return but must enact it; *The Maximus Poems* must be at once the words spoken *and* the deed performed.

As a social enterprise, ritual is a particularly appropriate model for Olson's poetics because it assumes an organic relationship between form and function and because it provides the context in which the poet, "this instant in action," engages the distant past as it is immediately present. Ritual "desires to recreate an emotion, not to reproduce an object,"[15] and Olson's poetics, like ritual, reconcile the present moment with the Eternal and the person with the "image of personality." If he is successful (that is, if he gets the rituals straight), they will make the past present so as to ensure the future:

Sunday
night June 19th with some hope my own daughter
as well as 3 year old Ella may
live in a World on an Earth like this one we
few American poets have
    carved out of Nature and of God   (*M*, 556–57)

Ritual is also an apt paradigm for Olson's poetics because it becomes the nexus for his threefold concern for self, community, and their incarnation through his words. Ritual, according to Harrison, is that human construct that bridges art and life. Furthermore, ritual resolves a philosophical predicament of projective verse. For some readers, such lines as those just quoted express only wishful thinking because the "Big False Humanism / Now on" (*M*, 379) has turned myth into a mere shadow, only a copy of what no longer holds their truth. "It is this downward path, this sinking of making

15. Harrison, *Ancient Art and Ritual*, 27.

Lynn Swigart, "Dog Bar Breakwater," September, 1976
Courtesy Lynn Swigart

to mimicry, that makes us now-a-days think of ritual as a dull and formal thing" and, for some, *The Maximus Poems* as a naïve work.[16]

However, as mythologer Bronislaw Malinowski reminds us, "mythology in its living, primitive form is not merely a story told but a reality lived." In these terms, Olson's verse becomes compellingly real, and the difference between being realistic and being real lies in the way in which "ritual is a frequent and perhaps universal transition stage between actual life and that peculiar con-

16. *Ibid.*, 28, 27.

templation of emotion towards life which we call art."[17] That is, for Olson, the *The Maximus Poems* does not represent an individual or describe a society but, like ritual, creates a transference of energy, generating collectivity and intense emotion that are only available through/in/during the performance of a rite. In the saying and the doing, the ritual performer makes himself known and discovers his world; as a methodology for poetics, ritual connects the personal and public aims to the very *nature* of Olson's art.

In "Maximus to Gloucester, Letter 27 (Withheld)" the poet, in characterizing his poem making, insists on its break from a tradition of abstraction and commits himself to the concrete, the event itself:

> This, is no bare incoming
> novel abstract form, this
>
> is no welter or the forms
> of those events, this
>
> Greeks is the stopping
> of the battle
>   It is the imposing
> of all those antecedent predecessions, the precessions
> of me, the generation of those facts
> which are my words . . .
>   Plus this—plus this:
> that forever the geography
> which leans in
> on me I compell
> backwards I compell Gloucester
> to yield, to
> change
>   Polis
> is this   (*M*, 185)

Here the return to origins is something powerfully willed by the speaker. The poem does not describe events or conceptualize or idealize the world; instead, it is itself an event, "the stopping / of the battle." This recalls the ancient power of the bards, who could literally interrupt a war and, like the officiant of a ritual, could

17. Bronislaw Malinowski, *Magic, Science and Religion and Other Essays* (Boston, 1948), 78; Harrison, *Ancient Art and Ritual*, 205.

magically make the words potent, make them the "very facts themselves."[18]

Mircea Eliade, a mythologer with whose work Olson was familiar, speaks of the power of reciting the origin of a thing: "Reciting its origin myth compels the rice to come up as fine and vigorous and thick as it was when it appeared for the first time. The officiant does not remind it of how it was created in order to 'instruct' it, to teach it how it should behave. He *magically compels it to go back to the beginning* that is, to repeat its exemplary creation." This is the task Olson has set for himself and for his nation. Because he has taken it upon himself to be "of words the speaker and of deeds the doer,"[19] he is actively making, not passively reading, "a mappemunde. It is to include my being" (*M*, 257).

Olson begins with the particular event to find its intersection with the eternal. As in any ritual, the officiant must push the present moment of experience back until it includes the past and becomes the Dream Time of Australian aborigines, or Primordial Time in Robert Duncan's terms, or Aquarian Time in Olson's. What is involved is "not a commemoration of mythical events but a reiteration of them. This also implies that one is no longer living in chronological time, but in the primordial Time, the Time when the event first took place."[20]

In a concluding Maximus poem, Olson achieves just such a transformation of the present and of his sense of being. He begins on the earth: "I live underneath / the light of day." And he becomes

18. The notion of the poet as shaman is ancient and frequently mentioned by mythologers. Robert Graves, in particular in *The White Goddess,* discusses the spiritual power and authority of the ancient Celtic poets, mentioning that the traveling poet could stop an ongoing battle. Also, this role is prominent in the Emersonian tradition and surfaces again in postwar poetry, as Jerome Rothenberg notes in *The Technicians of the Sacred,* a book that seeks to establish the parallels between primitive, oral forms and contemporary poetry. In a set of analogies, he notes that one important intersection of the poetry of the present with primitive poetry is "the poet as Shaman, or primitive Shaman as poet and seer . . . an open 'visionary' situation prior to all system making ('Priesthood') in which the man creates thru dream (image) and word (song)" (Rothenberg, *The Technicians of the Sacred* [Garden City, N.Y., 1968], xxiv).

19. Mircea Eliade, *Myth and Reality* (New York, 1963), 15–16; Harrison, *Themis,* 328.

20. Eliade, *Myth and Reality,* 10.

of the earth with "I am a stone." Then, because "the stones they're
made up of / are from the bottom such Ice-age megaliths," he is
transported:

> that one suddenly is walking
> in Tartarian-Erojan, Geaan-Ouranian
> time and life love space
> time & exact
> analogy   time & intellect   time & mind   time & time
> spirit

Only at this moment is it possible to effect "the initiation / of another kind of nation" (M, 633).

At this late point in *The Maximus Poems*, Olson's assertions,
such as "I am a stone," have the force and power of the poetic experiments that have preceded them. The move from now and here
to "Tartarian-Erojan, Geaan-Ouranian / time" is easy to imagine
and propose; however, the poetic task of the earlier poems has been
to do it, to make his words "those facts."

This involves distorting the present and diminishing the reader's
awareness of chronological distinctions. One way to do so is to
present the past, giving life to its events and beings so that they
live in the present moment of the poem. Olson begins a process of
historiography with "Letter 23" and decides to "find out for himself, the evidence of what is said." The first three books of *The
Maximus Poems* are generally concerned with the actual present
and the recorded history of Gloucester, Massachusetts, but Olson
as historiographer will select and present the history that is of consequence to the present. He does not intervene in the presentation,
so the facts speak for themselves.

Such facts often speak so clearly that Gloucester comes alive. In
an early poem "THE PICTURE," the poet relates history, then
presents it. The last portion of the poem becomes a chart of the
dates "1623, 1624, 1625, 1626 & 1627," with each date containing,
simply stated, the significant events of that year (M, 120). "THE
PICTURE" is not drawn with adjectives, nor does it actually describe anything, but the accumulation of data composes the past
and makes it present. The penultimate line of the poem, "END,

scene shifts to Salem," moves the initial retelling, using the past tense, to the immediacy of the present tense.

Similarly, Olson uses marine soundings to depict the "depths of the channel more interesting as from Eastern / Pt. and the compass rose thus" (*M*, 156). There follows a representation of those soundings as on an actual map, resulting in a manifold distortion of the reader's sense of chronological boundaries. First, Olson effectively shortens the distance in time between himself and the reader by speaking directly to her and making available what is, no doubt, before the poet as he writes. Second, the soundings visually make incarnate the geographical reality of Gloucester and simultaneously evoke the image of a fish and of the arc of the sky. Perhaps we are also to recall the Egyptian sky-goddess Nut, who could be seen arched over Earth at a time when, with mythological vision, one could detect the natural forces from which the human world derives: "Nut is in the world" (*M*, 320).

As Olson pushes back to origins of place and person, *The Maximus Poems* and Gloucester accrue multiple dimensions in the present. Volume II does not discard the historical data but forces them back to include their elemental sources, their mythological beginnings. " '[A]t the boundary of the mighty world' " (*M*, 330) is a rich example of the way the poetry enacts that push backward even while speaking it. The poem deals with the contingency of the present and the concrete upon the eternal and the abstract. It locates the poet on Gravel Hill and makes of him the creator god Ptah, speaking out the world. As the voice enlarges, the present explodes. Olson begins by quoting Hesiod, then himself assumes the stature of the ancient speaker of cosmologies (the poet knows the past of this location): "Gravelly hill was 'the source and end (or boundary' of."

When Earth finally speaks, the voice of what had been called Gravelly hill "Now called Gravel Hill" is heard using the present tense, and the intricate tense shifting is one device by which the poet compels the past to speak in the present. The opening lines announce the present name of what is " 'at the boundary of the mighty world,' " and the substitution of the current name for the particular geographical site enacts the name change in the poem.

Olson employs the past tense to recall the specific past wit-
nessed by this physical location, and the distinction between the
speaker in the present and in the past is at first clear-cut. When the
poet's life is connected to the geographical location, the tenses
move gradually to subtler chronological distinctions: "but I *have
had* lunch in this 'pasture'" (*M*, 330; emphasis added). Temporal
distinctions become clouded as the poet's lifetime now constitutes
the present. By comparison to the immensity of the Hesiodic and
historic past that includes "B. Ellery to / George Girdler Smith /
'gentlemen' / 1799," the temporal distinctions within the poet's
life seem minuscule, if not ridiculous. However, these give way as
the poet becomes "like the Memphite Lord of / all Creation." He
gains a larger view, one "overlooking the town." For the "Lord of /
all Creation" reality is whole, not chopped up into little pieces; "It
is not bad."

With this shift to the continually present and the present tense,
Gravel Hill speaks, and her eternal presence overtakes the poem
and its clock-watching speaker.[21] The accomplishment of this shift
is heightened by the reversal it enacts. At the opening of the poem
the Earth, Gravel Hill, is referred to as a repository of the past. It
was described, not presented: "Gravelly Hill . . . , how the hill was,
not the modern usableness" (*M*, 330). She was known in a mythological past as a "garden." However, the speaker rejects naming
this "nostalgia" by bringing us to the present, physical reality: "if
this is nostalgia / let you take a breath of April showers." The
present tense at this point still locates the speaker, but now includes the sweet-smelling "garden," which was "this pasture,"
which is "Now called Gravel Hill." When Gravel Hill begins to
speak in her own voice ("leave me be, I am contingent, the end of
the world"), the history she relates is her own and is as alive as she

21. Using the feminine pronoun in referring to Gravel Hill may seem surprising.
However, I believe it appropriate for several reasons. First, Olson has developed the
mythic conception of Earth as "The Great Mother" throughout *The Maximus
Poems*. Second, in this poem he specifically manipulates images of the "garden,"
traditionally a symbol of the nurturing Mother Earth or Mother Nature. Even in trying to push backward from this conventional and almost vacant representation of
the ancient Goddess, Olson clearly means to incarnate her. He gives her voice, and
as the whole point of this poem is to push the historical past to an eternal and
mythically potent reality, Gravel Hill may be viewed as the Earth Mother.

is. The poet has told us that Dogtown is the mighty world and Gravel Hill its boundary, and the shift in voice and tense enacts this. The poet not only tells us that the present and particular are bounded by the eternal, he makes it so within the poem.

While this poem makes the present disappear, other poems seem to operate conversely, charging the present with immediacy for the reader. Olson includes in the present the moment of writing the poem, seeming to freeze it in time. There are instances of this strategy in Volume III, and one of these explores the present act of writing:

Glow dying by 5 : 20
　　　　　PM
40 minutes after sunset
light in house now almost
reduced so I cannot see
to write　(M, 485)

As the speaker, engaged in writing, carefully attends the passing moments, he discovers a law of nature: "Evening then is / at the most 40 minutes long." What we delineate as "evening" lasts a mere forty minutes, and the poet experiences the brevity of this portion of the day as light in the house fades, making his writing difficult.

However, two poems later, on "Feb. 3rd, 1966," the poet uses a similar technique to discover the eternal present (M, 490). The time is "7 : 35 AM," the beginning, not the end, of day. This poem starts with an enthusiastic command to the reader and to the poet himself: "Look at Ten Pound Island all white." By 7 : 55, Shag Rock "is floating off by itself from the Island like an Eskimo Pie." A fanciful simile shows the poet's lightening mood, which gives way to a sense of the miraculous: "And WOW now the next morning it's a WHITE SHIP all floating by itself like / a cake of ice." Similes give way to identities—no longer "like an Eskimo Pie," Shag Rock is "a WHITE SHIP," an actual "cake of ice." His attention to the physical world rewards him with a new natural law: things can "float," and each day brings morning.

When we compartmentalize time and space with language, we shut out the universe, but attention to the particulars of life "gets the universe back in" (*M*, 249). This poem rejects the Cartesian world view and the poetics based on representation instead of presentation. A fundamental concern for Olson becomes how to reinvigorate language. As labels for things, language plays false with him; he wants to present the universe in all its immediacy.

Again, ritual provides a context for understanding Olson's poetry. Successfully incarnating the gods and restoring the creative era through ritual depends upon a belief in the metaphorical power of language. The participants in the ritual must use language that means or, rather, is what it says and that does not refer just to the idea or thought of what is said.[22] Olson knows that his poetry, his goal, depends upon such a metaphorically charged language:

an actual earth of value to
construct one, *from rhythm to*
image, and image is knowing, and
knowing, Confucius says, brings one
to the goal: nothing is possible without
doing it. It is where the test lies, malgre
all the thought and all the pell-mell of
proposing it. Or thinking it out or loving it
ahead of time.   (*M*, 584; emphasis added)

Throughout *The Maximus Poems*, Olson violates the conventions of syntax, grammar, and usage. For example, he mixes phrases from foreign languages in both translated and untranslated forms. Although familiar, this device as used here elicits a fresh response to language. In the following passage, we can see how he brings alive what otherwise seem hackneyed images of mythological figures:

I believe in God
as fully physical
thus the Outer Předmost
of the World on which we 'hang'

22. This notion of "metaphorical" languages derives from many sources. Certainly, Ernest Fenollosa, Benjamin Whorf, and Charles Olson have contributed to my understanding of it. Also, for the sense of a period of civilization in which language was not merely referential but evocative, see the work of Giambattista Vico and of Ernst Cassirer. Vico's *New Science* offers a theory of language developing through three stages, the first of which is based on metaphor. Such a language, if it existed, was the verbal equivalent of hieroglyphics.

as though it were wood and our own bodies are
hanging on it   (*M*, 381)

Here we have Odin and Christ made to coalesce. The freshness of
the image complements Olson's innovation upon the conventional
view of God. Olson makes him "fully physical" and has us identify
with God not through religious beliefs but through "our own
bodies."

Many of the poems express Olson's belief in the physical reality
of gods. Mythology, after all, is a necessary component of ritual.
However, just as he has had to discover his own origins, he has also
had to recover and even recreate the gods and heroes whose stories
are part of his own cultural experience:

No Greek will be able
to discriminate my body
          An American
a complex of occasions,
themselves a geometry
of spatial nature.   (*M*, 184)

While Olson's push back in time brings him face to face with
primordial energies ("the Salt, the minerals, of the Earth return—
Enyalion / arises" [*M*, 571], for example), the poet's own presence in
the world is the vehicle for syncretization. Although the migration
theory and the discovery of the continental drift explain the simi-
larities among the gods of various cultures, the way they are alive
in his own culture is nonetheless part of "the dream restored, the
dream being self action."

All night long
I was a Eumolpidae
as I slept
putting things together
which had not previously
fit   (*M*, 327)

Lest this seem too much like traditionally understood mysticism,
it is wise to remember what Olson says in *Causal Mythology*:
"[O]ne of the reasons why I'm trying to even beat the old dead
word mythology into meaning is that I think that it holds more of

a Poet's experience than any meaning the word mysticism holds. The principle would seem to be that the only interest of a spiritual exercise is production."[23]

Unlike the mystic, Olson is concerned with the world. He has returned to origins in order to effect the return of universal creative powers. He moves down and back in order to move on and, in his spiritual ascent, fears he will leave the world behind:

> Praise the mystery
> of creation, that in matter alone, the soul said,
> you shall not walk about in the heaven of intelligence,
> I don't care how much you have felt free in
> the heavens of composite natures, of
> discriminated natures, and of myself,
> said the soul, now you shall not walk
> around the heaven beyond me, "That is no way for thee"   (M, 494)

He must return to the Earth and "build out of sound the walls of the city" (600). This is the product; Olson's ultimate goal is "polis." For this reason, he sees mythology as the only spiritual alternative to a "muse-sick Gloucester." Mythology becomes, through the deeds of his poems, a "reality lived" by the poet and one equally available to the reader. Olson's poetry has its personal dimension, but his purpose is a public one: "[T]he assumption of social action [is] a necessary aspect of Olson's conception of the self."[24] And in any ritual of initiation, the purpose is to bring each individual into harmony with a collective reality. Olson knows that "polis" depends on it: "My problem is how to make you believe / these persons, who lived here then, and from these roads / went off to fish." He makes us believe by traveling "these roads" himself:

> I walk you paths of lives I'd share with
> you simply to make evident the world
> is an eternal event and this epoch solely
> the decline of fishes (M, 208)

These lines belong to a poem dedicated to "Robert Duncan, / who understands / what's going on" (M, 207). They provide but one ex-

---

23. Olson, Causal Mythology, 12.
24. Paul, Olson's Push, 118.

ample of the "Love made known" with which Olson generously seeks to reclaim his world, not merely for himself but for the reader as well. He "finds out for himself, the evidence of what is said" and makes this evidence part of the public record so that it may be shared. Olson's intense desire to be heard, as well as his devotion to poets such as Duncan, who share his faith in poetry and are "the careful ones [he] cares for," derives from the fundamental requirement of ritual—it must be shared: "A meal digested alone is certainly no rite; a meal eaten in common, under the influence of common emotion, may and often does, tend to become a rite."[25] In *The Maximus Poems*, Olson traces the paths of civilization gone wrong in order to summon the energies to "make it new," just as Pound advised. Olson discovers the place to begin; we must only try "to get the rituals straight."

25. Harrison, *Ancient Art and Ritual*, 36.

BRUCE WHEATON

Bound To Be Present: Memory and Imagined Space in the Work of Robert Duncan

Has anyone since Whitman done as much as Duncan
to further Emerson's aesthetics of liberation?
— *The Lost America of Love*

I wish to use memory as a foothold—or, in Thoreau's vocabulary,
as a *"point d'appui"*—from which to begin again a consideration of
the instantaneous and the sequential in the works of Robert Duncan. I mean to take seriously the ancient proposition that Mnemosyne is the mother of the Muses and would have you believe
that memory is one name we give to the impulse toward a spacious
accommodation of the contradictory demands of poetic composition. That memory is at once the generative urge of this body of
poetry and a name for the field of recollection in which the re-
ceiver remembers the verbal action as a spacious, simultaneous
whole. That memory is the *material* of poetic composition—that
the "roots and branches" of poetry come from the same dynamic
mother stuff that their gathered limbs define.

Throughout what follows, I will maintain that memory is an action—"a kind of accomplishment," as Williams calls it [1]—and not a

1. William Carlos Williams, *Paterson* (New York, 1963), 77. The poem is known
separately as "The Descent."

static abstract faculty. I will maintain that memory, as its etymology suggests, is an act of present "mind-fullness"—"a sort of renewal" of the past—and that this renewal is also, simply, new, since the present moment from which memory springs must serve as an "initiation" or, to work from Duncan, as a "passage" from moment to moment. I will maintain that memory is the action by which mindfulness turns time into enfolding space.

Ralph Waldo Emerson honored mother memory by emphasizing, "A seneschal of Parnassus is Mnemosyne."[2] I'll use Emerson's thoughts on memory as a threshold to a consideration of recent poetry because—all disclaimers to the contrary—he is a significant father of the work. An acknowledged progenitor in the case of Duncan, a displaced ancestor recovered through Whitman and Melville by Williams and Olson, respectively. Emerson's essay "Memory" begins: "Memory is a primary and fundamental faculty, without which none other can work; the cement, the bitumen, the matrix in which the other faculties are embedded; or it is the thread on which the beads of man are strung, making the personal identity which is necessary to moral action" (90).

I've added emphasis to the connective "or" because this disjunction balances two contradictory characterizations of memory. Is it a "matrix" or a "thread"?

Emerson located this paradox in the mental images themselves—tacitly affirming his faith in the accommodating aspect of genius. From *Nature*: "A man conversing in earnest, if he watch his intellectual processes, will find that a material image more or less luminous, arises in his mind, contemporaneous with every thought . . . the imagery is spontaneous. It is the blending of nature with the present action of the mind."[3]

---

2. Ralph Waldo Emerson, "Memory," in his *Natural History of Intellect* (Boston, 1921), 95. References to this work will appear parenthetically in the text and will be identified as "Mem" when necessary.
3. Ralph Waldo Emerson, *Nature*, in Stephen E. Whicher (ed.), *Selections from Ralph Waldo Emerson* (Boston, 1957), 34.

Certainly, for Emerson, memory is a significant aspect of the "present action of the mind." It is "not a pocket but a living instructor" ("Mem," 92). Still, memory is a dynamic faculty proposed to us as both a "thread" and a "matrix." An action compounded of both the linear and the circular, both the serialized and the enfolding. There is great similarity between Emerson's thread and Frances Yates's provocative treatment of the sequential array of the classical memorists' *loci*; between Emerson's "matrix" and these memorists' mnemonic houses.[4]

Emerson—rather explicitly, I think—sees memory as the action that arcs sequential time into hospitable imagined space. The emphasis in the quotation is mine. "Memory performs the impossible for man by the strength of its divine arms; holding together past and present, beholding both, existing in both, abides in the flowing and gives continuity and dignity to human life. It holds us to our family, to our friends. *Hereby a home is possible*" ("Mem," 91).

Emerson continues, "Hereby only a new fact has value." This revaluation—in the memory—of empirical data anticipates Bachelard and Williams, and recalls the initiatory memory of the preclassical Greeks noted by Jane Harrison—"Mnemosyne renewed consciousness is new life." Emerson: "The poor short lone fact dies at the birth; memory catches it up into her heaven and bathes it in immortal water. Then a thousand times over it lives and acts again" ("Mem," 103).

Emerson's figuration of the spatialized eternal present as memory's "heaven" should remind us of the hierarchic idealization inherent in his vision—a disposition foreign to Williams, Olson, and Duncan. But this difference should not obscure the fact that his continuing emphasis on the redemption of discrete experiential data in the ever-present makes him much more an ally than an antagonist of the three later poets.

4. Frances Yates, *The Art of Memory* (Chicago, 1966). The whole work is relevant because Yates addresses in turn the rhetorical and philosophic relationships between memory and space.

In the passage quoted earlier, we see that, for Emerson, the "poor . . . lone fact" is rehabilitated not simply by being recalled but by being reconstellated with its mates in the communal "bath of birth." In Emerson's unapologetically Romantic view, it is the domain of the memory to shape the arrayed images of past experience for present use as well as to store them. Wholesome selectivity provides the shape—gracefully bending the linear toward one of the circular forms of which "the eye is the first." Bowing the thread until it—like the rounded outline of the horizon—becomes a matrix.[5]

Emerson names the selector: "The memory is as the affection. Sampson Reed says, 'The true way to store the memory is to develop the affections.' A souvenir is a token of love. *Remember me* means, Do not cease to love me" ("Mem," 104).

The field of memory, like the lost topography recoverable in the Latin *campus*, bends up and inward at its edges. Becomes a "meadow," a place of nourishment, comfort, and delight, when animated by desire and love. Becomes an expansive home when the urge to see and know affectively keeps pace with the widening horizon of experience.

Emerson once more:

"There must be a proportion between the power of memory and the amount of knowables; and since the Universe opens to us, the reach of memory must be as large" ("Mem," 110).

Robert Duncan initiates *The Opening of the Field* with these lines:

Often I am permitted to return
to a meadow

5. The phrase "bath of birth" comes from Walt Whitman, "I Sing the Body Electric," in *Leaves of Grass* [1855], ed. Malcolm Cowley (New York, 1976), 119. Emerson so describes the eye in "Circles," in Whicher (ed.), *Selections from Emerson,* 168.

as if it were a scene made up by the mind,
that is not mine, but is a made place

that is mine, it is so near to the heart,
an eternal pasture, folded in all thought
so that there is a hall therein

that is a made place, created by light
wherefrom the shadows that are forms fall.

Wherefrom fall all architectures I am
I say are likenesses of the First Beloved
whose flowers are flames lit to the Lady

She it is Queen Under the Hill
whose hosts are a disturbance of words within words
that is a field folded.[6]

And now we are talking poetry, and now the ground would appear
to shift. From philosophic speculation on the function of memory,
to critical commentary on re-membrance in writing; from imagined space proposed in the mind, to imagined space composed on
the page. In general, the ground seems to shift from a consideration
of spacious memory as a condition of present mindfulness, to
present mindfulness as a condition of spacious poetry.

This shift is actual, yet only seeming, since poetry stitches the
poet to the world. In the body of poetry I address, the correspondence—the rime—between mind and poem, physique and poem, is
as direct as eyesight, earshot, measured syntax, and provocative
lexicon can weave the matter.

Duncan articulates his extended sense of rime: "This structure of
rime means the poet is not only to depend upon his ear but (may
have in mind) *What he is doing.* (today, I would amend this to:
what is happening, 'taking place,' in what he is doing.)"[7]

A consideration of the workings of the mind—the workings of
the mind in the body—whether the vocabulary is drawn from psy-

6. Robert Duncan, *The Opening of the Field* (1960; New York, 1973), 7.
7. Duncan, "Notes on the Structure of Rime," *Maps,* No. 6 (1974), 43.

choanalysis, mythology, cosmology, or philosophy—is not only
an appropriate prologue to this family of work, it is one of its most
insistent topics.

In Duncan's comment on rime, the parenthetical "rethinkings" and
emphases are his own. Note, in particular, that he has set "taking
place" in quotes, marking it as one of his many instructive puns.
To "take place" or "to happen" is also to create and to occupy an
imagined locale.

From *The Truth and Life of Myth*: "Yet our lives and works are not
simply what they are but are passively or actively, unconsciously
or consciously, creative of what they are. The universe strives to be
what it truly is to be. The poem that moves me when I write is an
active presence in which I work."[8]

"An active presence in which I work." The preposition underscores
the spatial nature of Duncan's present. Also, in this selection, radical juxtaposition: the universe—the *uni-versus*, the single turn en-
wrapping—and the poem—the "made place" in which the poet
works to enfold and exfoliate himself. The universe and poem—
each a field of associations—each striving collaterally to fill the
other. Each striving serially—without end—to come to itself.

Striving to be known as itself in
full simultaneity

Striving to be known as itself, formally

The drama of our time is the coming of all men into one fate, "the
dream of everyone everywhere."
The fate or dream is the fate of
more than mankind. Our secret
Adam is written now in the script
of the primal cell. We have gone

For those of us who search
out the widest imagination
of our manhood—our piety
must seem as appalling to
the Christians as the
Christian's piety is to the
Jews—God strives in all

8. Robert Duncan, *The Truth and Life of Myth* (Freemont, Mich., 1968), 23.

beyond the reality of the incomparable species, in which identity might hold and defend its boundaries against alien territory. All things have come now into their comparisons.

If as Pound began to see in *The Spirit of Romance*, "All ages are contemporaneous," our time has always been, & the statement that the great drama of our time is the coming of all men into one fate, is the statement of a crisis we may see as ever-present in Man wherever and whenever a man has been awakened to the desire for a wholeness in being. *"The continuous present,"* Gertrude Stein called this sense of time and history, & she saw the great drama as man's engagement in a composition of the contemporary. (Duncan, "Rites of Participation")[9]

creation to come to Himself. The Gods men know are realizations of God. But what I speak of here in the terms of a theology, is a poetic. Back of each poet's concept of the poem, is his concept of the meaning of form itself; and his concept of the meaning of form, in turn where it is serious at all, arises from his concept of the nature of the universe, its lifetime or form or even, for some, its lifelessness or formlessness. A mystic cosmogony gives rise to the little world the poet as creator makes. (Duncan, *The Truth and Life of Myth*)[10]

Stein makes manifest the circular form of her object lesson in the syntactic composition of the contemporary:

RO

A   SE

IS   IS

ES   A

OR

9. Robert Duncan, "Rites of Participation," *Caterpillar*, No. 1 (1967), 6–8.
10. Duncan, *The Truth and Life of Myth*, 25.

She has—as Olson does in "For Gerhardt There Among Europe's Things"—"given us a present." An orthographic rose that, despite critical pawing, will not become obsolete. A rose newly risen from itself; a thread of words bent roundly to itself. A rose "is at an end / of roses." Eros. "The Inbinding."[11]

Eros is both an active, informing principle and a principal actor in "A Poëm Beginning with a Line by Pindar"—a title that not only literally describes the opening of the poem but also, as Duncan reports it, describes the generation of the compositional process that results in the poem; the poem grows from his musings over a line from Pindar.[12] It is, among other things, a conflation of the story of Eros and Psyche drawn from Apuleius, with Goya's *Cupid and Psyche.* Duncan recalls the impulse:

When in the inception of a "A Poem Beginning with a Line by Pindar," reading late at night the third line of the first Pythian Ode in the translation by Wade-Gery and Bowra, my mind lost hold of Pindar's sense and was faced with certain puns in that the words *light, foot, hears, you, brightness, begins* moved in a world beyond my reading; these were no longer words alone but powers in a theogony, having resonances in Hesiodic and Orphic cosmogonies where the foot that moves in the dance of the poem appears as the pulse of measures in first things. Immediately, sight of Goya's great canvas, once seen in the Marquis de Cambo's collection in Barcelona, came to me like a wave carrying the vision—out of the evocation of the fragment from Pindar and out of Goya's pictorial evocation, to add to the masterly powers of my own—the living vision, Cupid and Psyche were there; then the power of a third master, not a master of poetry or of picture, but of storytelling, the power of Lucius Apuleius was there too. . . . [T]he living genius of these three stood as my masters, and I stood in the very presence of the story of Cupid and Psyche.[13]

---

11. Gertrude Stein, *The World is Round: Pictures by Clement Hurd* (New York, 1939), n.p.; Charles Olson, "For Gerhardt There Among Europe's Things," in his *Archeologist of Morning* (London, 1970), n.p.; Williams, "The Rose is Obsolete," in *Spring and All,* in *Imaginations,* ed. Webster Schott (New York, 1970), 107. For additional commentary on Stein's puns, see Stan Brakhage, "Poetry and Film," *Credences,* No. 5/6 (1978), 108, 109.

12. Duncan, "A Poem Beginning with a Line by Pindar," in *The Opening of the Field,* 62. Subsequent references to the "Pindar Poem" will occur parenthetically in the text and will be identified by "PP" as necessary.

13. Duncan, *The Truth and Life of Myth,* 25.

We might distinguish, lightly, between "the very presence of the story of Cupid and Psyche" and the story narrated in *The Golden Ass*. For Duncan, the first is an almost palpable immediacy, while the second is a contributing agent to the imagined substance. The "very presence" is a theurgic whole compounded of Goya's painting and Apuleius' rendition of the story in the alembic of Duncan's imagination as it is fired by the line from Pindar. Notice, too, that memory is the salient "bitumen" of the compound. Goya and Apuleius rise from recollection, just as they are bound to the compositional present by the poet's memory.

The dominant action of the tale marks the introduction of the primal, fundamentally unknowable Eros into the human sphere. The pivot of the story, then, is Psyche's stolen firsthand knowledge of him. "Holding the carving knife in a murderous grip, she uncovered the lamp and let its light shine on the bed."[14] For the first time, she sees her husband. Overcome by passion, she throws herself on him but, in her haste, spills a drop of oil from her lamp onto his shoulder. He flies. The rest of the story traces her growth— through a series of trials imposed by Venus—toward a stature that will allow her to be reunited with her lover.

Goya's painting does not portray the narrative's turning point. Instead, it shows Psyche reclining in bed while Cupid leans over her. The canvas marks, then, a variant on the story (a possibility I would not disallow) or it presents the final reconciliation of the couple. In either case, the recalled picture lends to Duncan's imagination a pair of softly defined attractive bodies along with a diffuse, unearthly ambience.

The dominant action of Duncan's poem marks the introduction of Eros into the sphere of his composition. An admission that gives shape to the theogonic urgings generated by Pindar's lines as the

14. Apuleius, *The Golden Ass*, trans. Robert Graves (New York, 1951), 117.

writing proves itself worthy to accommodate both the creative impulse and the in-forming principle.[15]

While the poem does not move toward a static, definitive conclusion—the myth too should be read as a process to be recapitulated rather than as an accomplished fact—it does move from creative diffusion toward a realization of the present act of writing. From:

The light foot hears you and the brightness begins
god-step at the margins of thought,
      quick adulterous tread at the heart.
Who is it that goes there?   ("PP," 62)

To:
            A line of Pindar
moves from the area of my lamp
      toward morning.   ("PP," 69)

Equally, the poem moves from the lightly felt dance at the "margins of thought" to fully imagined intertwining of children: "clockwise and counter-clockwise turning."

As the lovers are introduced into the poem they come from the otherworldly realm of Goya's painting—"waves of visual pleasure," "a bronze of yearning." They are visible "But they are not in a landscape. / They exist in an obscurity." Just as Eros was married to Psyche well in advance of her knowledge of him, so the paired lovers are joined to the poem without taking their rightful place in its field. But even this "wrongness" serves the poem, is "part of the process."

Part II opens with Duncan's assessment that "It is a passionate dispersion." Exhibiting the faith that "Psyche is preserved," the composition nonetheless creates a world wavering on the edge of chaos. Psyche's world after Eros abandons her corresponds to Duncan's world of the late 1950s, in which only the exemplary courage of an

15. For Duncan's elaboration on this myth, see "Two Chapters from H.D.," *Tri-Quarterly*, No. 12 (1968), 67–98.

old man sustains him. The man is William Carlos Williams—one of the "old poets" who even after "A stroke. These little strokes" did not "recoil" but persisted in yearning for Beautiful Thing. Characteristically, Duncan puns on *stroke*, linking Williams' trauma and his sustaining ability to trace coherence on the page. But what if poetic courage should fail? What if linguistic ability should fail? What if the mind is stricken or the poet's strokes on the page become "in-jerred"? The phonetics create the fear and so underwrite the comparison between linguistic and cultural coherence.

damerging a nuv. A nerb
        The present dented of the U
nighted stayed. States. The heavy clod?
        Cloud. Invades the brain.   ("PP," 63)

Duncan now assesses his cultural setting. Just as Ginsberg measured the distance between his circumstances and Whitman's vision and found himself in "the lost America of love," so Duncan shows the anxiety.[16] "What if lilacs last in *this* dooryard bloomed?" An America without Eros. A composition from which Eros has flown—a dry catalog of names. America without love—a catalog of political failures.

Duncan, circuitously working his way back to Lincoln, knows, much as Williams does at the end of *In the American Grain*, that continuity must be made from discontinuity.[17] "There is no continuity then. Only a few / posts of the good remain" ("PP," 64). But Psyche is in love and will persevere. The mythic action rimes with the composed action. Duncan brings Whitman to mind again and recovers the yearning for Eros: "'The theme is creative and has vista.'"

16. Allen Ginsberg, "A Supermarket in California," in *Howl* (San Francisco, 1956), 23.
17. William Carlos Williams, *In the American Grain* (New York, 1956), closes the concluding essay—on Lincoln—with: "It was the end of THAT period" (234). This seems to mark a terrible discontinuity. However, the book, as a whole, seeks to find lines of coherence.

Part III lays out the poet's tasks in his quest for Eros in precisely the same terms in which Psyche's chores are set. The collage of seeds spread at the outset tells, too, the seeds Venus throws down for Psyche. The poet's job is the same as hers. Sort the disarrayed particulars into riming piles. The search for Eros is—in large measure—a search for form. "The Inbinding." Olson, to whom the section is dedicated, equates Eros and form in *The Special View of History*, and writes in the opening poem of *Maximus I*, "Love is form." Williams emphasizes the offspring of Eros and Psyche: "Rigor of beauty is the quest."[18]

The other tasks: Psyche must catch out some "gold wool from the cannibal sheep." Must bring back to Venus the embodied light of the sun without scalding herself. The poet, too, must travel to the peripheries of his imagination to bring back traceries of illumination to weave with the dark.

Also, Psyche must descend to Hell to seek a measure of beauty from Proserpina. So must the poet. But as Duncan says:

These are the old tasks
You've heard them before.

Kora in Hell.[19]

In each of her tasks, Psyche despairs and is "brought to" an instructor. Duncan, too, finds counsel. Another old poet comes to mind. Pound—desperate, there among Europe's things—figures himself as "a lone ant from a broken ant-hill."[20] Even in personal crisis, amid a wrecked civilization—as Duncan recalls it—Pound hangs on. "A lizard upheld me." Duncan remembers Pound's hopeful ad-

18. Charles Olson, "I Maximus of Gloucester to You," in *The Maximus Poems* (New York, 1960), 1; Williams, *Paterson*, 3.
19. William Carlos Williams, *Kora in Hell*, in *Imaginations*, 6–82. Duncan doesn't mention Williams' improvisations by name; they are another instance of a writer undertaking the tasks of descent and subsequent renewal.
20. Ezra Pound, "Canto LXXVI," *Pisan Cantos*, 36 (paginated separately) in *The Cantos: 1–95* (New York, 1956). Thanks to Mark Isham for his help with these lines from Pound.

mission, "the wind is part of the process."[21] Just as the ants helped Psyche arrange the seeds, the old man's composing helps Duncan "draw the sorts."

Then follows an elaboration of Psyche's search for golden light.

Light, which was an agent of Psyche's loss, now becomes one of the conditions of her recovery. To trace the "many movements," Duncan fabricates a composite myth, one of whose characters is Odysseus. The occidental man "on whom the sun has gone down." Duncan's imagination still clings to *The Pisan Cantos* as he recalls Pound's epithet for the hero whose movement is toward home, westerly.[22] Yet the conglomerate myth contains the opposite: the "hero who struggles east," upstream, against the clock, "widdershins." Jason moves east, into Colchis, hoping, as did Psyche, to bring back the "fleecy sun" ("PP," 66).

These "solitary first riders," now contemporaries in the composition, "advance into legend." Advance into the present legend of Duncan's poem, of Duncan's America.

This land where I stand was all legend
in my grandfather's time: cattle raiders,
animal tribes, priests, gold
It was the west.

Duncan, his poem, and his culture are imagined presences in search of Eros, containing, as did Psyche, the contradictory movements of passion; containing both Odysseus and Jason. The part of Psyche that is naïvely driven to know rimes with clever Odysseus. Rimes with "Scientia / holding the lamp, driven by doubt."

The technology of oil spills. The westward movement. Gold in California—the custodial ram gores those who wrench it out.

21. Pound, "Canto LXXIV," in *Pisan Cantos*, 6, 3 and elsewhere.
22. *Ibid.*, 8.

Psyche, in her countermovement toward recovery, on good advice, waits till dusk to take the fleece as it's given from the branches, just as Jason drew upon Medea's dark powers. The poet, proving himself by his tasks, works at night.

In the imagined world of the poem, in which things "come into their comparisons," the composed action moves toward an accommodation of the whole process by which Eros is lost and recovered. An accommodation that holds not only the action but the two aspects of Psyche. She is the one who can both lose and recover. Similarly, there are two aspects of Eros. He is both a wild, primal being and the beautiful figure with whom Psyche is reunited. As Duncan seeks to accommodate these differences a tally of oxymorons suggests the effort required. "Yes beautiful rare wilderness! / wildness that verifies strength of my tame mind" ("PP," 68).

The imagined dance ultimately works the accommodation. Wild urgings are given a rounded, domestic form. The large movements, west and east, now are not seen in the huge scale of historical flailings across a continent, not in mythical meanderings in the Mediterranean, but in the dance. Forward and back. Strophic. A new instance of Pindar's form. "There the childern turn the ring to the left / There the childern turn the ring to the right."

Duncan's continent—now, with the reinstantiation of Eros, Whitman's continent too—becomes complicit: "the grass moved toward the one sea / blade after blade dancing in waves."

The Atlantic and the Pacific are united in "one sea" as they encircle. The west and east winds—rippling the leaves of grass, gathering the disparate blades into coherent waves—too "are part of the process."

The poem comes to rest in the composed space created and inhabited by the linguistically measured dance. An active place within whose lines we see narrative time conflated with a visual image. A field—a rounded "meadow" to which the poet and reader return—in which we remember the telling and its tale. Temporality and countertemporality wound into imagined space: "clockwise and counter-clockwise turning."

The proposition that Eros comes to the composition in and through the dance can be amplified. Duncan notes that the words of Pindar's line become "puns" for him, generating recollections of "Hesiodic and Orphic cosmogonies." From the chapter "Orphic Cosmogony" in Jane Harrison's *Prolegomena*:

It is the primeval life that Eros not Orpheus, begets within us, that wakes now and again, that feels the rhythm of a poem, the pulse of a pattern and the chime of a dancer's feet.

In the beginning when the sun was lit
    The maze of things was marshalled to a dance
Deep in us lie forgotten strains of it
    Like obsolete, chained sleepers of romance.

And we remember, when on thrilling string
and hollow flutes the heart at midnight burns,
the heritage of splendid moving things
descends on us, and the old power returns.[23]

The immediate experience of measured rhythm—in melody or dance—becomes a remembrance of the "marshaling" powers of Eros. But since Eros is double, his rhythms include both dispersion and collection. Duncan's "Pindar Poem," as I've noted, acknowledges both.

If Mnemosyne is a mother, then Eros is her choreographer. Emerson told us as much, naming love as the selective principle of memory.

The dance resonates throughout Duncan's work. In *The Opening of the Field*, "The Dance" immediately follows the initial poem, "Often I Am Permitted To Return to a Meadow." This direct prox-

23. Jane Harrison, *Prolegomena to the Study of Greek Religion* (New York, 1975), 656, introducing and quoting Lucian's "The Dance."

imity underscores the mutual dependence of the enfolding field and the choreographed action by which it is defined and which it contains. Recall that certain Germanic nouns for "meadow" proceed from the action "desire." Loving action creates a space, just as sequential language animated by desire moves toward wholeness, toward form.

Duncan works consistently to make the actions of (and within) his forms rime—fluidly—with the actions and forms of the universe as he knows it. At the limit toward which Duncan moves, story and formal identity coalesce. "Bardically I keep alive the identity of the Universe, / which is our great tribal story."[24]

At this extreme, story is a fabrication, an articulation of the fittings. A temporal tracing and an atemporal tracing; a marking of "the concords and contrasts in chronological sequence, as in a jigsaw puzzle—not by what comes one after another as we read, but by the resonances in the time of the whole in the reader's mind."[25]

"The time of the whole in the reader's mind."

It is memory that piles up the "grand collage." It is memory and her necessary dancemaster, desire, that erect emblems and passages in an imagined space.

"I mean to force up emblems again into these passages of poetry, passages made conglomerate, the pyramid that dense mountain, immovable; cut ways in it then and trick the wall with images establishing space and time for more than the maker knows he acknowledges in it."[26]

This seems to be a memory of Lascaux, that rounded cave whose walls are adorned with images inscribed by our tribal ancestors.

24. Robert Duncan, "Warp and Woof: Notes from a Talk," in Anne Waldman and Marilyn Webb (eds.), *Talking Poetics from Naropa Institute* (Boulder, 1978), 7.
25. Robert Duncan, *Bending the Bow* (New York, 1968), ix.
26. *Ibid.*, 19.

"Our great tribal story" is also a gathering of our "tribal memories," a fabric worked "at the loom."[27] The first two poems of the sequence *Passages* mark the emphasis, get to "the heart of the matter where the / house is held."

The house, as Duncan unfolds it, becomes an expansive household, a maternal domain—nourished by memory.

Mnemosyne, they named her, the
          Mother with the whispering
feathered wings. Memory,
the great speckled bird who broods over the
nest of souls, and her egg
the dream in which all things are living
I return to, leaving my self

I am beside myself with this
    thought of the One in the World-Egg
enclosed   in a shell of murmurings
              rimed round
              sound-chambered child

27. Duncan, "Tribal Memories," in *Bending the Bow,* 9; Duncan, "At the Loom," *ibid.,* 11; the concluding lines are from "Tribal Memories."

JOHN F. CALLAHAN

Becoming a Citizen in the "Country of Language": Storytelling and the Scholarly Voice in *The Book of Daniel*

I recently reread the Port Huron
Statement and was amazed at its
currency, and I was pleased in a recent
letter to be told that the writer,
himself very active in local politics in
the South, senses again, if only a
tremor, the emergence of a similar
spirit.
> —Letter to the author,
> September 13, 1986

In his essays, Ralph Waldo Emerson tells the story of his thought
and, therefore, of his life as a scholar. For him, action and thought
are reciprocal. As a discourse of experience, Emersonian essays
share with fiction an urge to reveal and create personality. Perhaps
because he believed that scholars should be major characters in the
unfolding story of American culture, Emerson made the improvisa-
tory, autobiographical impulse a characteristic of the inquiring
mind and the scholarly essay. He proposed the American scholar as
a leader responsible to act as the conscience of society. But he also
recognized that sometimes, scholarly methods and traditions lead
away from the story of an individual's life and mind toward conformity. In effect, Emerson worried about social and political intimi-

dation, warning that "when the victim of society," a scholar "tends to become a mere thinker, or still worse, the parrot of other men's thinking."[1] In response to feeling themselves victims, intellectuals could choose a cynical position and act as if the search for truth is only a bitter game, but Emerson imagined American scholars advancing the mutual interests of knowledge and citizenship.

Emerson's attempt to overcome the opposition between thought and action is also a preoccupation of the American novel. Novelists compelled by the American democratic theme, from Herman Melville in Emerson's time to E. L. Doctorow in ours, form an uneasy alliance between the critical act of intellectual, scholarly discourse and the creative act of storytelling. In *Moby-Dick*, Melville's democratic spokesman, Ishmael, is a scholar in Emerson's sense of an intellectual unbeholden to institutions. Formerly a country schoolmaster trained for scholarship, he nevertheless satirizes imaginary scholars of his day even as he uses their work to embellish his story and deepen its frame of reference. He mocks the "threadbare" dress of "a late consumptive usher to a grammar school" but endorses his "Etymology." He calls a sub-sub-librarian "this mere painstaking borrower and grubworm."[2] But he then uses page after page of the poor man's "Extracts" to establish the encyclopedic scale and significance of whaling and the whale, before asking us to call him by a name that is also a biblical reference: Ishmael. Once his tale is begun, he interrupts the action with treatises, anatomies, and other forms of highly eclectic scholarly and storytelling discourse. Indeed, Ishmael's citation of many different branches of knowledge makes him the first free-lancing, interdisciplinary scholar to narrate an American novel.

But he is not the last.

In E. L. Doctorow's *Book of Daniel*, narrator Daniel Isaacson Lewin is ostensibly committed to the discourse of scholarship. Although he is a Ph.D. candidate in one of the social sciences at Columbia University, Daniel shares Ishmael's suspicion of scholars

---

1. Ralph Waldo Emerson, "The American Scholar," in Stephen E. Whicher (ed.), *Selections from Ralph Waldo Emerson* (Boston, 1957), 65.
2. Herman Melville, *Moby-Dick*, ed. Charles Feidelson, Jr. (New York, 1964), 4, 7.

and scholarship. Despite his affiliation with an academic discipline and a major institution, he is a radical skeptic hostile to the methodology and, often, the intellectual substance of inquiry. Specifically, he suspects that in the American university of the late 1960s, rational discourse is subject to the agenda and interests of multinational corporations, the Pentagon, and the state.

Daniel, son of parents tried, convicted, and executed in the 1950s for treason as alleged atomic spies, struggles to write his dissertation during a time of personal, social, and national crisis in 1967 and 1968. But his real focus is an obsession with the guilt or innocence of his parents. So he tells his story as part of the passage to identity—an experience that Ralph Ellison, speaking of Daniel's forebears in American literature, calls "*the* American theme."[3] In a discourse of assault, Daniel uses the facts and figures, the dates and places of official history to attack real and imaginary enemies and to protect against any contact intimate enough to penetrate his vulnerable identity. He taunts his readers with the view that scholarly discourse is a limiting and potentially corrupting form of expression, offering history's atrocities and lies as explanation and excuse for his sometimes cruel, perversely detached behavior toward those close to him. But his rationalizations buy time for his secret, slowly developing, inmost identity to solve a puzzle of private and public history. Throughout the narrative, Daniel uses facts and imagination to resolve the conflict between two opposed versions of self and discourse: his arm's length, falsely detached third-person objectivity wherein he reifies his own person as *Daniel,* an outsider; and his sometimes witting, sometimes unwitting shift into a first-person voice whose thoughts, actions, and feelings are often equally culpable but for which he accepts responsibility.

In order to free his imagination, this 1960s apprentice American scholar works his way through an intellectual (and emotional) labyrinth and, as a critical thinker, heeds the facts and clues discovered along the way. But Daniel cannot tell his pressing personal story without using conventional scholarly methods of analysis and dis-

3. Ralph Ellison, *Shadow and Act* (New York, 1964), 177.

course that then must be overcome and revised. In his quest for an American vernacular voice, Daniel falls under the influence of storytelling, particularly the Yiddish invective of his grandmother and the cryptic riffs spoken by Williams, the black janitor. As a novel, *The Book of Daniel* stands or falls on its narrator's ability to meld imaginative and critical discourse into an expression of personal experience and scholarly knowledge.

The problem of narrative identity is couched in the formal, intellectual terms of Daniel Isaacson Lewin's dissertation. Usually a dissertation tests an individual's scholarly mastery of subject and methodology. As an extended treatise backed by an oral defense, the dissertation demonstrates a candidate's readiness to converse with other scholars in his field. But, for Daniel and others who struggle to use scholarship for personal and political ends, the impersonal formal requirements of a dissertation intensify the urge to present one's findings in a unique, individual voice. As if to reinforce the nexus between fiction and scholarly writing, Doctorow, too, confesses to a similar problem of composition and identity because of his initial choice of a too conventional, too detached voice. "I started to write the book in the third person, more or less as a standard past tense, third person novel, very chronologically scrupulous." But the impersonal chronicle voice blunts his purpose: "After one hundred and fifty pages," he continues, "I was terribly bored. That was a moment of great despair in my life because I thought that if I could really destroy a momentous subject like this ["the story of the American left in general and the generally sacrificial role it has played in our history"], then I had no right to be a writer."[4]

Following Emerson's example, Doctorow, like his character, overthrows the safe, sterile confines of an official voice. In despair, he grows "reckless enough to find the voice of the book, which was Daniel."[5] Beginning again, he locates "the historical intersection of social and personal agony" in the novel's unfolding present mo-

4. E. L. Doctorow, *Essays and Conversations*, ed. Richard Trenner (Princeton, 1983), 62, 61, 62.
5. *Ibid.*, 62.

ment, from the chaotic spring of 1967 to the student occupation of Columbia in April, 1968. Now he senses "history moving in Daniel, powering his own pathology—all this had an enormous meaning and interest for me." He brings to his relationship with his character the distinctive combination of personal interest and detachment that characterizes a dissertation advisor from another generation. Above all, Daniel is a liberating figure for Doctorow. And there is a painful identification on his part as he imagines "Daniel's relationship to himself as he sits in that library and does those historical essays and descriptions of himself in the third person, breaking down his own voice and transforming his own being to produce this work."[6] Daniel's desperate craft inspires Doctorow to redefine his novelistic problem: To write a novel that is deeply engaged with history's revelations and secrets, he must overcome conventions of chronology and point of view—the trappings of a novelist's traditional authority.

In his struggle to think and act, Daniel uses the rhetoric and, at times, the methodology of the dissertation to open the circuits of storytelling. He frames his autobiographical narrative with allusions to, and the mannerisms and fragments of, his thesis in progress. In fits and starts, he pursues the personal and historical truth about a time in American life "when all the antagonistic force of a society [was] brought to bear, and focussed on one or possibly two individuals."[7] For Daniel, the discourse of his dissertation conceals and reveals the terror of his private mind. His official work is the dissertation; his and his family's life is organized in support of this task. Nevertheless, the thesis is a sideshow for Daniel. His true preoccupation is the riddle of family history. Yet, when he breaks away from his academic work to try to tell that story, he brings with him an egocentric self-consciousness. His hostility to institutions is that of a 1960s radical whose sensibilities were formed by the American state's single-minded destruction of his parents. He no longer believes in the ethical power of language and, therefore, has trouble finding a comfortable voice. Nevertheless, in order to

6. Tom LeClair and Larry McCaffery (eds.), *Anything Can Happen: Interviews with Contemporary American Novelists* (Urbana, 1983), 98.
7. Doctorow, *Essays and Conversations,* 61.

begin putting his book on paper, he requires the framework of a dissertation for protection and solace.

As he begins to work Daniel adopts the narrative pose of observer. The thing observed is him, his method a narrow recitation of some of the facts about his life on Memorial Day, 1967. But after a few lines, Daniel's mind runs away from his pen. He writes down the wrong word—"and the early morning traffic was wondering." Instead of crossing out the word or throwing away the page and starting again, he copies down the revised passage: "I mean the early morning traffic was light, but not many drivers could pass them without wondering who they were and, where they were going." Daniel's embrace of his mistake leads him to focus suddenly and minutely on the moment of composition. He brings readers into the library where he works, mockingly forcing us to see how divorced from the real world is the closed-off world of his work: "This is a Thinline felt tip marker, black. This is Composition Notebook 79C made in U.S.A. by Long Island Paper Products, Inc. This is Daniel trying one of the dark caves of the Browsing Room. Books for browsing are on the shelves. I sit at a table with a floor lamp at my shoulder."[8] Writing with a primer's exaggerated attention to the trivial detail of the moment enables Daniel, the writer, to liberate the object Daniel from confinement in the mask of the third person. But his narrative liberation is more of a temporary gambit than a turning point. "I feel encouraged to go on" (4), he writes, and resumes his third-person account of Memorial Day, 1967. These shifts from third to first person become the chief formal reflex of Daniel's narrative. His continued change of pronouns signals a confidence game he plays with the reader and himself.

In his profane, self-protective third-person vernacular, Daniel testifies to acts of coldness and sadism. To explore the self buried under alien poses, he presents us through gesture and language with the persona of an ironic exhibitionist. Held in little esteem by society and its masters, Daniel relishes his power over his wife, his "child bride," as he contemptuously calls her. The pathological

8. E. L. Doctorow, *The Book of Daniel* (New York, 1971), 3. References to this volume will be cited parenthetically in the text and will be identified by *BD* when necessary.

metaphor he invents for the inside of her body is "that geology of gland formation, Stalinites and Trotskyites." Nor does his obsession to see the world in terms of Communist factions free him from his demons. More than once he brags of leading her toward "a very cruel come" (*BD*, 6). Like many a self-indulgent graduate student in his generation, he takes for granted his readers' permissiveness. His tendency to substitute invective for dialogue extends to his narrative. The book he writes resembles a succession of cruel climaxes, with the reader filling in for Phyllis as the unbeloved, convenient, half-despised partner. He flaunts his cruel prowess, then recruits the reader for duty as rhetorical confidant: "And if the first glimpse people have of me is this [a deliberately cruel lover], how do I establish sympathy? If I want to show disaster striking at a moment that brings least credit to me, why not begin with the stacks, Daniel roaming through the stacks, searching, too late, for a thesis" (7). Does he really think that sexual cruelty toward his wife (or, later, a violent act toward his infant son) is less damning than delinquency in his search for a dissertation topic? Does he mock his readers? Or is he daring us to declare open season on him and his book from the start?

As a man and a scholar, Daniel is a predator. His phrase "roaming through the stacks" is an essential clue to the form and energy of his narrative. Bits of lore and learning from the Bible, history, politics, science, and music, together with representative anecdotes from the experience of the American Left, become the cement that holds in place the bricks of his and his family's story. Like a conscientious scholar, he writes down the "subjects to be taken up" (16) in his book as if he were compiling index cards for his thesis. In the midst of this, he wonders how others see him and interrupts his list with a riff titled "Silence in the Library." Do others imagine him "going through the shelves like a thief—plundering whatever catches his eye, stumbling back to his place, his arms loaded with Secondary Sources" (17)? Those secondary sources enable Daniel to unseal the primary source of memory and to risk telling his story in the little essays that give *The Book of Daniel* its contemporaneity.

Appropriately, when Daniel evokes the summer of 1967 from his subsequent perspective as writer and character, first- and third-person forms of address merge for him. "But I, Daniel, was grieved," he writes, "and the visions of my head troubled me and," he continues, changing tenses to evoke the moment of composition, "I do not want to keep the matter in my heart" (17). The matter is Daniel's realization of profound convergence between the personal and the political crises of his time. As a self-described "criminal of perception" (75), Daniel characterizes citizenship— "the final existential condition is citizenship"—as treason: "Every man is the enemy of his own country" (72–73). To stir readers out of complacency and goad us to action, he writes his book according to the principle that every narrator is the enemy of his narrative. Why so extreme an inference? Because in the past and present of *The Book of Daniel*, it is only by being an enemy of his country *and* his narrative that Daniel, the citizen-writer, can meet his responsibilities truthfully and become his generation's version of Emerson's American scholar.

Like so much American writing during the 1960s and early 1970s, *The Book of Daniel* chronicles a civil war. A condition of tragic hostility exists between Daniel and his country, between his political inheritance and a potential new politics on the Left, and, not least, between a discourse driven by inflexible, crippling ideology and one responsive to the contingencies and incalculables of lived experience. Thus, when Daniel imagines "the novel as a sequence of analyses" (281), he may seem to hold imagination in fealty to the rational scholarly discourse of cause and effect that he struggles to master in his dissertation. But, in fact, he challenges readers to examine the form of his book. The novel is not a sequence at all in a chronological sense, for chronology is a method at odds with Daniel's mind and its instruments of memory and analysis. Rather, Daniel accepts the mind's unpredictable sequence, and his scholarly work attempts to bring intellectual resources to bear on unofficial and official versions of reality.

Daniel distrusts conventions of scholarly discourse and in his work paradoxically accommodates his mind's chaotic way of perceiving the world inside and outside his personality. His book is a succession of small discrete studies or, rather, a sequence of fragments whose titles falsely imply that they will be neat, self-contained little essays. These ordering gestures allow Daniel to get started, and, once started, he liberates his mind and memory and roams far from the particular subject. Like his entries about various methods of physical torture, many of his autobiographical accounts stir fear in the reader by a stark recitation of facts. Daniel resists having *a* thesis, and he never tells us exactly what he's writing about. But the sources he cites and the disquisitions he composes reveal his subject to be the complicity of the American Left in its own betrayal. And he realizes that discovering, enacting, and telling his sometimes perverse and cruel *individual* story is a necessary prologue to understanding the fate, fiction, and history of the American Left. Daniel's story is both separable and inseparable from the case to be made in a Ph.D. dissertation. Therein lies the authenticity of his (and Doctorow's) narrative form. Mixing the voices, materials, and formal possibilities of fictional and scholarly discourse enables Daniel to face his own pathology of perception and behavior. It also helps him avoid the fraudulence of a narrative intended as either an autobiography or a scholarly treatise, but not both.

When he replaces a third-person chronicle with the multiple angles of Daniel's narrative voice, Doctorow responds to an American crisis of criticism and imagination. And by inventing a narrative uniquely and dangerously his own, Daniel simultaneously becomes a critic of and a participant in the crisis of politics and self common to his generation. In order to define, let alone resolve, the civil war dividing his identities and those of his country, Daniel needs to be able to analyze, experience, imagine, and accept a reality different from his assumptions. He begins to do this in the fourth and last book of the narrative when he goes in search of Selig Mindish, his parents' old friend, whose testimony led to their convictions. At Disneyland, looking for answers from the man who in some sense betrayed his parents, Daniel gets and accepts the old man's kiss of recognition and word of acknowledgment: "'Denny,'" Mindish says simply, tears flowing more freely than words, "'It's Denny'" (*BD*, 293). The scene recalls and answers Daniel's earlier question of his advisor, Professor Sukenick: "Under what circumstances do we suspend criticism?" (192). Now, instead of criticism, Daniel invents a riff ascribing the failure of heart transplants to heart rejection, ejection, and dejection. His deeper subject is his own emotional condition. With a mixture of openness and bitterness, he implies that Mindish has been true, at last, to his heart. Grudgingly, Daniel accepts his old enemy as a brother in grief.

Only after this encounter can Daniel reconstruct from various secondary sources, and imagine in his own heart, the electrocution of his parents. Characteristically, he conceals his pain, loss, and vulnerability beneath a mask of scorn and contempt, directed at the readers who have stayed with him, though at times we, too, have been close to letting him stew in his own bilious juices. "I suppose you think I can't do the electrocution," he sneers. But the sneer is also a desperate reach for human contact and community: "I know there is a you. There has always been a you. YOU: I will show you that I can do the electrocution" (296–97). Daniel's bravado is a peculiar declaration of faith in the possible salutary effects on him and us of the relationship between writer and reader. In discourse as "in electrocution the circuit is closed or completed by the human body" (297). Loyal opposition or not, an audience of readers is necessary for Daniel to descend through the layers of his past. His tone and subsequent taut account remind us that the electrocution of his parents for their allegedly conspiratorial beliefs belongs to our history and, therefore, is our destiny and responsibility, too.

The foregoing is a lesson expressed in a complementary discourse of fiction and scholarship. In its form, Daniel's narrative pays homage to the fragmentary, disparate reality he's lived through, written about, and now experiences differently in the present moment of composition. Even at the end of the novel, he protects his vulnerable identity from the reader's judgment by writing (and including) three endings, numbered consecutively. "The House" evokes his return "to the old neighborhood in the Bronx," where now "the Cross Bronx Expressway runs like a deep trench through what used to be 174th street." He notes that "people still live here," but feeling alien before the black family now in his old house, he lets the moment pass when he could have asked "if I can come in and look around" (299).

However, with readers he drops his narrative guard. He no longer writes in a voice that postures and maneuvers for advantage. Only subtitles and numbers ("1. The House") betray the lingering influence of his research. Likewise, in "2. The Funeral," Daniel re-experiences his parents' funeral during his sister Susan's burial. Freed at last from his mother's bias against Jewish religious practices—"Let our death be his bar mitzvah" (298)—he hires shamuses to pray for Susan. Then, moved by these strange men and their prayers in an unfamiliar tongue, he calls the roll of his dead family, speaking their Hebrew names. His voice testifies to and becomes an instrument of change: "And I think I am going to be able to cry" (302). In "3. The Library," Daniel comments on his process of composition. "For my third ending," he writes, "I had hoped to discuss some of the questions posed by this narrative." But, characteristically for his life and his narrative, the chaos of historical reality forces a change in his plans. "However," he continues, "just a moment ago, while I was sitting here writing the last pages, someone came through announcing that the library is closed" (302). Lest we think what's happening is a fire drill or some other conventional emergency, Daniel recreates his dialogue with an unidentified Paul Revere from the battalion of student revolutionaries:

> "We're doin' it, we're bringing the whole motherfucking university to its knees!"
> "You mean I have to get out?"
> "That's right, man, move your ass, this building is *officially* closed." (302; emphasis added)

To Daniel's "wait"—which of us willingly moves out according to the beat of someone else's drum?—the radical messenger answers, "No wait, man, the time is now." He also gives Daniel a line he'll soon use when he quotes from the biblical Book of Daniel as coda to his book. "Close the book, man," the intruder insists, as if Daniel were an apolitical type hibernating in the dormant world of the library. "What's the matter with you?" he asks. "Don't you know you're liberated?" For once, Daniel allows the irony to stand on its own, and he responds in the voice of a person finally willing to encounter the world with no predisposition for or against what he will find there. "I have to smile," he thinks and writes sometime later. "It has not been unexpected. I will walk out to the sundial and see what's going down" (302).

In the face of someone else's action, Daniel is cautious, measured, and, above all, noncommittal. As narrator too, he once more, and for the last time, surrenders his storytelling voice. In its place, he parodies the headnote that precedes the text of a Ph.D. thesis. "Daniel's Book: A Life Submitted in Partial Fulfillment of the Requirements for the Doctoral Degree in Social Biology, Gross Entomology, Women's Anatomy, Children's Cacophony, Arch Demonology, Eschatology, and Thermal Pollution" (302). Perhaps his dissertation has become his life, for, rhetorically, the work of storytelling now does duty for his thesis. But if so, he tells the news in an ironic form that nonetheless pays a tithe to the graduate college of his university. To the end, then, Daniel plays off against his identity as a graduate student. Maybe his gesture is appropriate homage to the truth because without the paraphernalia of scholarship and the self-absorbed sensibility of the graduate student, it is doubtful that he would have discovered and told his story. The techniques and even the hubris of the apprentice scholar serve him well in his narrative: To face himself, his family, his relationship to the political Left, Daniel needs to place his narrative in proximity to the scholarly tradition he regards as partly responsible for history's atrocities.

Although he has written his book, Daniel does not pretend to have arrived at a decisive point of accomplishment or transformation in his work or his life. He does submit his *life* "in partial fulfillment of the requirements for the doctoral degree." And we the readers—the people—are his examining committee. But the degree is not in any specific or recognized scholarly discipline or field. Instead, Daniel lists a catalogue of subjects whose self-mocking, exaggerated, formal names reinforce the centrifugal quality of his mind and his experience. Moreover, now that he has written his book, he invokes the biblical Book of Daniel in another of the "running changes on voice and character" that Doctorow associates with "the idea of discontinuity and blackouts."[9]

Daniel's abrupt cut from dissertation language to prophetic biblical prose is a joke. But the quotation with which he concludes echoes the radical student's command in the library: "But thou, O Daniel, shut up the words, and seal the book." No liberation is promised, but the biblical injunction declares closure for Daniel's contemporary version of his book. "Go thy way Daniel: for the words are closed up and sealed till the time of the end" (BD, 302, 303). Writing several centuries after the events he describes, Daniel, the Old Testament prophet, closes by asking the angel Michael, "What shall be the end of these things?" And the answer is that words of response are not to be forthcoming and that the prophet's part is to "rest and stand in thy lot at the end of the days."[10] But the excerpts Daniel and Doctorow quote, in conjunction with the words they leave out of the original, make Daniel Isaacson Lewin, unlike the prophet Daniel, an outcast from the promised covenant of righteousness. Clearly, the novel distinguishes Doctorow's Daniel from the wise and righteous, and also plays down the idea of the end except possibly as a doomsday finale of nuclear holocaust. The "time of the end" is vague, yet Daniel, by releasing his contemporary variation of the word, disobeys the biblical command given to the prophet to seal the book. Or has he sealed it by finishing it with an epigraph that restricts the flow of information and stories?

There are no final words in Daniel Isaacson Lewin's book. Moreover, Daniel's editing diminishes the prophetic force of the biblical voice. Although he goes his way, the contemporary Daniel in effect unseals what has been sealed. But he releases his words (and the prophet's) cryptically into the world, because he has been so often tortured by the pain of revelation. In Doctorow's words, "Daniel gives himself to the act of perception and opens himself to it—

9. LeClair and McCaffery (eds.), *Anything Can Happen,* 100.
10. *The Bible: Selections from the King James Version,* ed. Roland Mushat Frye (Boston, 1965), 350.

much as all writers must—and he survives that way, survives by however cold and frightening an embrace with the truth."[11]

Daniel's acts of perception as a writer make it possible for him "to admit everything—all aspects and forms of thought and behavior and feeling, no matter how awful they may be."[12] Thus, it may be fitting that Daniel's last words are his carefully edited excerpts from the Old Testament Daniel. Because the contemporary Daniel, also a victim of society, has risked being devoured by the lions at large in his world and in the den of his mind, he makes the old words new. In the process, he learns to speak for himself and to those around him in a voice of his own for which he is at last prepared to accept responsibility. In the course of the narrative act, Daniel becomes a storyteller faithful in an elliptical way to his experience of private and public discontinuity. Along the way—in the act, as it were—his critical and fictional voices cease to be alienated from one another. In often uneasy but necessary alliance, these two facets of self and voice enable Daniel to overcome his complementary pathologies of identity and discourse. No longer a victim or a predator, Daniel becomes a free man and, therefore, a citizen, on terms of his own making.

As scholar and novelist, Daniel Isaacson Lewin and E. L. Doctorow do not discard so much as reconstruct the relationship between scholarly discourse and fiction. Heeding Emerson's charge to pursue compatibilities between public and private discourse, Daniel responds to crisis "by equating the written word with action."[13] Despite his propensity toward violence and radical distrust, and despite cynicism about intellectual discourse, particularly as it is practiced in contemporary universities, Daniel becomes a scholar, in ways as eccentric and eclectic as those of his narrative brother, Ishmael. In the end, he turns the methods and assumptions of scholarship to personal and social use and, on that basis, performs a vital act of citizenship.

11. LeClair and McCaffery (eds.), *Anything Can Happen*, 105.
12. *Ibid.*
13. Sherman Paul, *Emerson's Angle of Vision: Man and Nature in American Experience* (Cambridge, Mass., 1952), 162.

Like the Framers of the Constitution, whose work Doctorow celebrates, Daniel invents "a country of language."[14] Compelled by politics and personality, he and his mentor Doctorow perform simultaneously for fiction and critical thinking what Ralph Waldo Ellison,[15] another American intellectual in the green (and black) tradition, calls the novelist's duty to his form. "Every serious novel," Ellison wrote in the 1950s, "is, beyond its immediate thematic preoccupations, a discussion of the craft." Like Invisible Man, who goaded Ellison to live up to his creed, Daniel helps Doctorow face the fact that to write honestly about personal or public experience, a writer must traffic openly in unspeakable thoughts. The Book of Daniel revoices the moral outrage from the prophetic books of Hebrew scripture in riffs associated not only with jazz but also with the improvisational comic routines or shticks of Jewish American vernacular culture. Perhaps influenced by the Jewish tradition's gift for and love of prophecy, Doctorow calls the American Constitution "the prophetic text for a true democracy." Its authors' invocation, "We the people of the United States," makes every citizen responsible for the nation's fate. And Doctorow adds "that once this text is in voice, it cannot be said to be realized on earth until all the relations among the American people . . . are made just."[16] In that spirit, The Book of Daniel calls for intellectual and storyteller to abandon their civil war in favor of a community of discourse open to the mutual work of fiction and American criticism. With that in mind, Doctorow challenges his readers to unseal their words and add their amendments to the book of America.

14. E. L. Doctorow, "The People's Text: A Citizen Reads the Constitution," Nation, February 21, 1987, p. 211.
15. Ellison's father named him after Ralph Waldo Emerson. See Ellison's reflections on the significance of names and naming in "Hidden Name and Complex Fate," Shadow and Act, 144–66.
16. Ralph Ellison, Going to the Territory (New York, 1986), 240–41; Doctorow, "The People's Text," 217.

IV / The Emergence of Things:
Poems in the Green Tradition

The Effort

Introduction

"I have seen the first rudiments of the chick as a little cloud in the hen's egg about the fourth or fifth day of incubation, with the shell removed and the egg placed in clear warm water. In the center of the cloud there was a throbbing point of blood, so trifling that it disappeared on contraction and was lost to sight, while on relaxation it appeared again like a red pin-point. Throbbing between existence and non-existence, now visible, now invisible, it was the beginning of life."

Out of Chaos:

> Δίκη δ' ὑπὲρ ὕβριος ἴσχει
> ἐς τέλος ἐξελθοῦσα

So, you will see Justice over Outrage
when you see last things:
> who live in a world without end, who
> can know
> neither first things
> nor last things.
> You will see Justice survive;
> you will see the evening of the scales.

"Since Nature makes nothing in vain"

παθὼν δέ τε νήπιος ᾿έγνω.

now visible, now   ("You who think you will
invisible   get   through   hell in a hurry")

"that theme emerges more and more
clearly" now
that you have discoverd Outrage
is it not an intimation of Justice?

明 this sign
    Bright
or the Moon
as it waxes   as it wanes

Of the Character

The line learnd in the hand
the line learnd in the ear:
like Matisse, blindfolded,
drawing upon the naked door—
"je n'avais pas encore commencé à chanter":
each animal gesture displaying
           intellect
sure   and splendid as the lion
           in his way.

          The line
within which, its muscular variety
           laid bare,
each sound not thought-out
but composed; learnd
           in the touch.
No more difficult than walking
           this leisurely and exact
           talking.   A song
not yet begun.   Yet
           setting the tone.

Notes,
assertions, passages
as if of the song itself,
sections of the needed intensity,
          references
to a completion of still
          another Partial
          gesture.

The line learnd in the hand
like the lions strippd of their skins:
     magnificent when naked,
     each muscle bold with control,
that were, all thru
     what they ought to be.

                    *

Utter devotion to the thing made:
to the stone, cut, polishd.
     "keep a grindin'"
task of course never done;
     the language resisting
one's imperfect counsels but
having within it an endless
     perfectability of forms;
     or
oaths, taxes, impositions:
     the law, too,
demands of the devoted an effort
     obscure;
as if of magic or incarnation
     to the barbarian.

not "the regular everlasting job of making over
     again the absolute content of sensibility
     with which we get on, or with which we
     acknowledge our failure to do so"

     "the old dandy is nothing else but"

not a sublime desperation

but: pleasant to learn

    this sign
    "the rapid and frequent
    motion of wings" a bird
    learning to fly;
    an effort

"of how to enter Heaven?" but Morris Graves
(studying the photograph I see
admirable plain elegance
in leather vest; hierarchic stance)
    is right:
"the cathedral is a diagram."

A diagram of acts displays
personality serious and gay.

A child's absorbd curiosity
in drawing may be a key
to what I mean:
what one admires in Edith Sitwell
transfigured or merely posing
is that invention.   Warm or cold,
excites because it imitates:
the exact and rigorous long nose
or set rigid mouth
sign of a frigidity; wearing
not mere face but conscious
contemplation of pride, pain,
recognizing in experience a test
or proof of the inevitable.

This scar, slashd by a knife,
is witness to the lion's claw:
or tatooed thigh, a design
of endurance that endures.

A bird learning to fly
to realize the flight inherent in its form,
to soar, in learning, into an element
learnd in the bone

or the ear learning greek
touches, touches the weights, estimates
the tones as the throat awakens:
so I listen as if waiting
no language dead: death comes to no tongue:
studying the diagram of speech,
estimating what the eye has known
the hand knows, what the ear
knows the throat has known:
the body of the speech like ones own body
        pleasant to learn

Play: containing a destiny
no more than posing a question
one acknowledges
the rage of the lion, or diagrams
like Satie playing upon a piano
or the immortal Pierrot playing the lover
savoring the moon's changes
of a fortune told;

to play oneself!   this scar
slashd by a knife or
cut by a line is witness
to the violence of the line.

And then: have you seen your true form?
the great vision is . . .
in this city—three generations
because I have loved and lived here
the will for beauty if only in words
the great vision is beyond the eye
which apprehends, awaits—

between the height and the depth beyond
where the city extends to its shore
where the distances shimmer
or where they seem screens, shadows of light,
San Francisco in the far,
Berkeley near, pinpoints of light
where from this height
in the falling away the heart yearns so
obscure to the believer
the beauty of the people is hidden
only when the histories have been exhausted
or when there are no histories, rags
of discomfort and the nude moment
informs, or memory
marks the true thing

there the great vision is . . .
hid in mere gossip, pain, injustice
    if you detect it
obscured in the web of convictions

is there one who is not dubious;
yet dubious, dubious
in the gold light they move

breakfast in the summer glare
friends move as in a clearer air
the company during that war
when we savord the war-bought pleasures
—what pleasures in those times unmixed—
wrath and red wine
and the sublime talk after the table
(Milton then for his richness)
these poets were not English to us
but spoke in that language
partaking of what has yet to come
already contained in their moment.

How many times have I seen her
as she was then, that very morning
and then tho her hair shows grey
    in the rich black
of no quality of age but of living
as if coming to life

the great vision is. . . .
more than the wrath and the red wine

a city transformd because there
these young men sing
once more in words as if they had seen her
of what do I dream?   personal disappointments
futilities   but there is a height of dream
falling away from which
all gleams, washd in the day

and the air between us alive with color
and the near geranium that glows
    more than afire
may be no more than her flower
    for she arranged there
    in the almost dark room
such cheap abundancies of orange
    magenta, deep red
my Beatrice?
    and the near blue shivers
    the far lies in pink haze
    or violet shines to the eyes the far shore
        shows
    as Tommy has shownit;
where vision lies
    drawn outward, drawn
    as if from the great height of years

disappointments, futilities
    drifts of smoke

where signs but where there was smoke
    there is fire

consuming all things:

    is:

like the line, shifts, holding all shapes
    immanent

    about to be.

every moment is not so ecstatic,
    but I remember
Pound in the hospital garden
a sun visor shading his eyes
no father-figure for the Freudians
    but there

in the mind eternal— of what
do I dream? at so young an age?   of

    disappointments then,
    failures of destiny?

    drifts of smoke
mere signs but there come then fires
wherein all things pass away

        no more than vision
        in the center of the cloud
        it disappeard
          appeard
              so trifling
        throbbing

Is there not
a harmony of all things?

inexhaustible.

Who wld choose a lesser knowledge
of one part

against another
    who seeks
the process underlying these things.

      "Let me stoop low.
      Be free
      of all my old compunction."

      "I am listening to something."

The Poem of Praise

 a sign; of great delight;
moonlight; that which was dark
shown clear.

We do not despair.

"only emotion endures"
the sensual mind asserts
the integrity of the thing made.
    This stone
has been nobly cut; this chisel   BRANCUSI
was here guided
with sincerity.
    This hand
was sure in its craft.

    This artist did not
tremble in his boots
    but stood
with two feet upon the ground.

    This endures.

        Surety.

The mind in its brilliance
is sapphire or diamond; defines;
so that the emotion endures

throbbing . . . trifling

so that it disappears
     appears

controlld; sure.

There comes the moment of joy,
     force
like clear water
     "when it spurts up thru bright sand
     setting everything into motion"
moods of oceanic rapport,
embracings of all things—
as vision embraces all things;
the rightness of cobalt
and vermilion, so related
and in such proportion
that we cry:
he has awakend
Beauty again;   MATISSE
     he has made new
the order of sensual things.

So that out of a dark cloud
the heart leaps,
the blood leaps.

     These women
     these flowers
     these rooms
flood the mind with delight,
stir the eye from old ways—
reveal "a single thread
in their argument."

     With what ease
this depth of feeling flows.
There is an imperishable joy;
there is a knowledge in color
that needs no other knowledge.

Rapt and attentive:
   who has calld forth
   my eye's keeness,
   my eye's devotion and praise;
who has raised my eyes
              out of darkness.

There is the joy of natural things seen
once the eye has been stirrd
to the mysterious blue
           the lavender, the rose
BONNARD   the pale vibrant dance in the air
RENOIR   the rippling fall of light
           that is a woman's hair,
           the lavender of death or
           the shadow of the flesh and the life
           that blooms there, fruit rich
           where the blood and the sun
           flood up into the child's face
           setting everything into motion.

So that there is a throbbing
in the center of the cloud.
A dance.   An imitation.
           These things
we praise.

         *

So related; and in such proportion
but without conclusion
These things have no conclusion.
There are no literary values here.
I forgo sentiment.
I show no
sensibility here.   Have we not had
         enuf of sensibility? no complex
rich personality; but

I am no more than my voice crying
out of the blood's dance;
out of the breathing,
answering sea-roar
or wind-roar or
the sound of other voices.

Raw as Walt Whitman.

I do not understand.
I dream.   I chant.
I discourse.   This is a stream
in which words dance.
        No one will ever love these words
        as I love these words
                singing myself.

The music is never the same;   STRAVINSKY
it never ends.   It is now
without beginning.
        Endless variation;
it is the identical symphony in 3 movements.
It is the identical stream of sound,
        the measurements of time
        in which tones dance.
        It imitates
                in contraction
                in relaxation
        the heart
        the melody
                now invisible
                now visible.
It is profound, for I listen
        from the depths of my being—
that needs no other knowledge.

                She is fair.
                Her hair
                falls across her shoulders.

The light
is not
more light
than her hair.

I change the subject?
break the thread?
you have not been listening.

I am deadly dull?
You have not heard me
at all.

In Praise

2. I mean there are no symbols.
    There are signs.
    There are literal things
    in themselves.

There are no associations,
no "stream of consciousness"
        but in the dance
        the emergence of things:
        the presence, literal
        and exact to the mind.

    The Miracle of Brancusi,
    the white light stone
    slowly revolving, almost
    imperceptibly, lucid . . .
            as if
    cutting, he had found life there,
    the stone, imperceptibly,
            about to speak.

"Psychoanalysis" "interpretation"
will only lead you astray.

Rage/or joy

Is this a foolish
dance of all things?
is this no true vision?
is there a serpent singing
   of old seduction
   in the song?

This is a political vision.
This is an imitation
   of the great harmony.
Harvey remarks the sun,
   heart of the universe.
I do not understand.
I hear.

There is a knowledge in sound
that needs no other knowledge.

   A group of estheticians
      will arrive at a set
      of suitable definitions;
   they will realize immediately
      that if this is a work of art
      its esthetic message
      is a formal experience.
I have never seen
      an esthetician dance. Or
the perceptive philosopher
will notice that there
      are no ideas here.
The lady semanticist notes
      declarative sentences,
      simple exclamations,
      exhortatory expressions:
poetry has no meaning
      unavailable to prose:
      the holy

is equal to the sum of its parts.
        or
the serious critic, who has developd
our moral sensibility, will see
        the modern drama
                        will explain,
        if he is not sickend
        by my pretension,
the flaw, Achilles heel, or mystic
        dweeming personality,
the failure not only of mind
        but of nerve.

If they are honest, they will admit
    I am wasting their time.

    Dance, moralists, dance.

Who swerve from the true center
and from the still ecstatic fool's
    point of view
look like fragments
flying around wildly
the heart of all things,
never touching
but whirling
    about one center.

This isn't worth reading,
but listen, listen:
the rapport, the insupportable
insistence of the sound heard.

3. Yet of Ole Ez
    who is   after all
            the Good Teacher.

I mean now not
no ideas

but the play of ideas—
    more of our time
than Yeats or Eliot
    knew to show.

You
who wld get thru hell
in a hurry.

Few are his good students—
Bunting, Zukofsky

And he askd,   how far . . .
without destroying the feel
    of actual speech.

And you will see that Zukofsky
    recaptures
    the actual speech.

It comes as a moment of joy,
live voice
among deadly voices:
the Eliotizers swollen, sounding
    the church knell,
tolling the solemn bell,
church mice of a wealthy parish;
the high-toned, slightly bizarre
    Trappist
    imprimatur etc.
the feverish eye of the exploiter
    of an old Boston tradition,
speech
right out of Gerard Manley Hopkins
    into the American
    mouth.
Or look around in my own work.
    I have a high-flown
    hermetic

rhapsodic diction,
      poet's delirium.

It isn't easy to learn
      the abrupt,
      or to cut
as Brancusi cuts
      without vagueness.

Or Zukofsky discovering
      the ideogram out of Shakespeare—
Henry James's Figure in the Carpet,
      who saw
      a certain irony there.

You say my talk is confused?
      said Kung, the Teacher,
There is a central thread in my argument.

ROBERT   DUNCAN

A Note on "The Effort"

ROBERT J. BERTHOLF

As early as February, 1949, Dallam Simpson had written to Robert Duncan, asking him to be part of a small anthology of four poets who had "obtained status under the 1948 Cleaners' Manifesto": John Rohen, Peter Russell, Dalan Flynn, and Dallam Simpson. The manifesto had appeared in a November 2, 1948, letter to Duncan: "1. We must understand what is really happening; 2. (If the verse-makers of our time are to improve their immediate precursors, we must be vitally aware of the duration of syllables, of melodic coherence, and of the tone leading of vowels; 3. (The function of poetry is to debunk by lucidity." In March, 1949, Duncan sent the first installment of "The Effort," and by August, the poem's "Introduction" was in the mail, along with Duncan's poem "Homage and Lament for Ezra Pound," which had appeared earlier in the magazine *Ark 1* (1944). Duncan sent the ideograms, which are in the manner of Pound but not taken from *The Cantos*, in October. Even as the contents of the anthology were being set in type, Simpson wrote—on New Year's Day—to Peter Russell, editor of the magazine *Nine*, that Duncan was laboring on a long poem entitled "The Effort," which would appear in "The Second Active Anthology." And again in January, 1950, Simpson wrote to Russell but this time called the projected book "The Cleaners' Anthology of Verse." The anthology never appeared, and the poem was lost—only to reappear among the poet's papers thirty years later.

In 1950, Duncan wrote to Pound that "The Effort" was concerned with "poetry as an intellectual act of discrimination ie certain distinctions, propositions (lucidities—see debunk by lucidity proposition) are positive only through poetic discipline." Just as the Cleaners' Manifesto had come from Pound through Simpson to Duncan, so the poem "The Effort" was directed toward Pound through Simpson. Duncan was not misled by the anti-Semitic and fascist tendencies of Pound's political thought; he was honoring his debt to Pound's poetic vision, which at this point was as significant an influence in his development as the work of Louis Zukofsky and William Carlos Williams. "The Effort," then, as Duncan wrote in the unpublished note called "A Note on the Effort," was to deal with a poetic problem: "the problem, for one thing, lies in the disunity between the language by which I participate daily in speech; and literature." This experiment in coming to terms with the difference between daily speech and poetic speech was written by a man who says in "The Effort": "I have a high-flown / hermetic, rhapsodic diction / poet's delirium." In this poem, Duncan attempts to honor his modern masters as he asserts the validity of his own poetic line.

After Frost

for Sherman Paul

He comes here
by whatever way he can,
not too late,
not too soon.

He sits, waiting.
He doesn't know
why he should
have such a patience.

He sits at a table
on a chair.
He is comfortable,
sitting there.

No one else
in this room,
no others, no expectations,
no sounds.

Had he walked
another way,
would he be here,
like they say.

ROBERT CREELEY

Ode on the Facelifting

of the "statue" of Liberty

America is inconceivable without drugs
and always has been. One of the first acts
was to dump the tea. The drug that furnished
the mansions of Virginia was tobacco,
a drug now in much disrepute.
Sassafras, a cure-all, is what they came for
and they dealt it by the bale altho it
was only a diaphoretic to make you perspire—
people were so simple in those days.
The Civil War saw the isolation of morphine
making amputation a pleasure and making
the block of wood between the teeth,
which was no drug, obsolete. Morphinism
was soon wide spread among doctors *and* patients.
At this date interns, the reports tell us,
are among the premier drug ab/users
of said moralistic nation. "Rock" stars
(who notoriously "have" doctors)
consume drugs by the metric ton
even as they urge teenagers to Say No.
The undercurrent of American history
has been the running aches and pains

of the worn path to the door of the apothecary
to fetch cannabis and cocaine elixirs
by the gallon. It has been all prone
all seeking Florida, Ponce de León
was just the beginning of a statistical curve
whose only satisfaction would be total vertigo.
His eager search for youth has become our
frantic tilt with death and boredom,
in fact we are farming death in Florida
with far greater profit than we are
farming food in Iowa—elixirs are as multiform
as the life-style frauds we implore,
a cultural patchwork fit for a fool
in the only country in the world
with a shop called the Drug Store.

4 July 1986
From "Abhorrences"

EDWARD DORN

Haida Gwai North Coast, Naikoon Beach, Hiellen River Raven Croaks

Twelve ravens squawk, squork, crork
Over the dark tall spruce
  and down to the beach.
Two eagles squabbling, twitter, meeting,
Bumping flying overhead

Amber river waters
Dark from muskeg acids, irons,
Murk the stream of tide-wall eagre coming up
Over the sandspit, through the drumming surf,
Eagles, ravens, seagulls,   over surf,
Salal and cedar at the swelling river,

    wheeling birds make comment:

On grey skies, big swells, storms,
The end of summer, the fall run—
Humpy salmon waiting off the bar
  and when they start upstream—

Comment
On the flot and jet of sea crud
And the downriver wash of inland
Hard-won forest natural trash

From an older wildness, from a climax lowland,
  virgin   system,

Mother
Earth loves to love.
Love hard, playing, fighting,
Rough and rowdy love-rassling
She can take it, she gives it,
Kissed, bruising, laughing—
Up from old growth mossy bottoms
Twa corbies rork and flutter

  the old food
  the new food

Tangled in fall flood streams.

Fall of '86–Summer of '87
For Sherman Paul
from "Mountains and Rivers
without End—"

山 河 無 盡

GARY SNYDER

A Flower Cantata

1
he weaves his flowers into flower words,
a flower song beginning
that will become a flower word song
or will become a root song,
song root flowers at his beckoning
inside a house of flowers,
a flower world,
plumed flowers adrift
on flower drums
the fathers would call delicious flowers

2
she who would walk with pleasure flowers
would shake a flower rattle
in a house where flower copal burned,
where there was flower mist below the gates,
where flower rain fell down,
the sound of flower water
circled among the water flowers,
silent flowers,
beside the serpent flowers,
someone announced a paradise of flowers

3
here is a flower brilliance,
here where the mind forms turquoise flowers,
binds them in flower garlands,
turquoise swan-like flowers,
here where the bellbird flowers cry,
where the parrot flowers light a way for you,
here is a road of pink swan flowers,
a road of green swan water flowers,
the ruined flowers you walk among
in dreams, the lines of dead dry flowers

4
weeping flower tears they hide behind
sad flowers
that are weeping, weeping flowers
they would call flowers of bereavement
in the night, the drizzling flowers
are overwhelmed by flower sighs,
sad flower jewels stuck under their skins,
before the golden flowers have come to life
& hummed like darkness flowers,
the metal warriors of flower death

5
war flowers that draw us into war
awaken the knife death flowers for us
before the flower war deaths start,
we wait here among honeyed flowers
the drunken flowers that surround our hearts
like holy flowers
or the green swan cacao flowers of the fathers,
are there raven flowers there or flower ravens?
eagle & jaguar flowers?
or are there flower eagles, flower jaguars, flower ravens,
   chrome black ice blue flame red flowers?

6
sulfur flowers that turn into eagle flowers
or white lead flowers that turn into chalk & feather flowers
flower banners hanging in a field of sapphire flowers
or flower paintings buzzing like electric flowers
or like knife-like yellow flowers that turn into lightning
    flowers
while the fathers blow flower conch horns that explode like
    sonic flowers
or flower water conch horns that turn into siren flowers
in the sleep of yellow flowers urgent & muted like narcotic
    flowers
flower floods under a bridge of angel flowers
or plume flood flowers that turn into moon & planet flowers

7
my eye watches a world of flower fish
in which fish flowers shimmer,
laughing flowers in water kingdoms,
swimming toward flower pleasures,
these turn into flowers of the sun,
the true creation flowers
that are feather flowers in the daylight,
spirit flowers when the moon comes out
& turns them into flower ghosts
the fathers would call immortal feather flowers

JEROME ROTHENBERG

Sources for most of the flower permutations, etc., are John Dierhorst's
translations of the Aztec *Cantares Mexicanos* and J.R.'s *Poland / 1931*.

after *Shoah*

the twisting road by a storybook forest
the cancer surge of 1943
the contagious memory-clouds
cold wind in the apprehending mind.   *you*
shall not live among us as Jews

waste, faces in shit, muddy goulash of blood and the piss
loosed from the naked women standing in a brown wait
they pump their last râles they're part of the bunkered molecules
of the Zyklon-B surround, they're fish-bloat on the strand, this
is the scattering of the Jewish women

in the small boat within the wardening Polish spring air
the young boy sings to the river-banked garrison of red trees.
small stuff is what the asphyxiating dead become   *you*
shall not live among us.
Clean is Good says the wall

in a sluggish recollection
the dazed mind holds off the spring
towards new clarity of recollection, naked membership
in all inheritance of pain: what
can it afford to save, to enter into?
to feel the wind of gas-breathing?   *you*
shall not live.

now, tomorrow, the cells in that surge reborn,
third millennium C.E.

2

the the cold in a sluggish spring the

Apocrypha: The Wisdom of
Solomon 7:

and when I was born I drew in the common air
and fell upon the earth which is of like nature
and the first voice I uttered
was crying

        and I'm the first voice
that I hear, my body
stutters in this place
and reconstitutes through the gas of the prehensile wind

dream, 9/10/87, 3 a.m.:

volcanic I insist
to my second son LOOK WE'RE ALL LIKE THAT WOULD YOU
    HAVE AN ATTITUDE
TOWARDS TIDAL WAVES

        dispassionately I observe his youthful
        being-filled.
we are talking. it is the flowing course
of our talking of + and − and the healable confusion of being.
I apprehend cold,
        fall.
ALL OF US I write bold
in my transcription.
        the cold of like nature.
common
air. peer into the dream for a blundering into awareness. sit
like a mountain: escape

René Guénon:

the Reign of Quantity—

no talking discloses

ARMAND SCHWERNER

dan peck asked me if i could do a talk piece at vassar
that could serve as a contribution to a volume that several ex-
students of sherman paul were preparing to honor his work as a
critic and scholar and teacher   as he was nearing retirement
and i liked the idea of doing a piece for sherman   who had
written so generously and well of so many contemporary poets
*   myself included   and i had intimations that he was*
feeling a little unnerved   as anyone might who was vigorous
*   and strong and at the height of his powers   who was*
*   approaching the chronological age at which educational*
institutions they had served and brought honor to bid them to
step out or down
*   at the same time i knew this wasnt so serious for*
someone like sherman whose life was not really an institutional
*   life but a life of thought and work that he would continue in the*
same way he had always done   only with a bit more time for
work on his house or his book or whatever he felt like doing
*   still it would be a change and i thought i could talk*
about change and the feeling about change   because i had
recently been thinking about a change
*   i'd just had the possibility*
of a change thrust at me with enough energy so that i had to

consider it   an east coast university had made an inviting
    gesture toward me   and while i had no need of a job i was
comfortable in my old one and maybe for that reason i felt i had
    to consider whether i wanted to consider it   and i did
        however lightly
                        i came back from a skiing trip with a banged-up
knee and flew east to have a couple of conversations with several
intelligent and agreeable people in a wealthy and dismal school
    in the great grey city of my childhood and i felt depressed
        and i had no reason to feel depressed   or no reasonable
reason
                        i had no intention of taking their job and they had
    no intention of giving it to me   they were reasonable people
in a distinguished institution that had no interest in changing
    their impoverished departments of art and were merely going
through the motions of thinking they were thinking about it
    and they had invited me there only to imagine an extreme
possibility in their search for what was probably an ordinary fund
raiser   and i was there merely to enjoy a free trip to the city
and limp around taking dozens of photographs of its once great
and now ruined park and get a look at some of the theater and art
that are the overestimated and only advantages that this dying
    city offers to people like me   so i was doing   what
        i wanted to do   but i was depressed
                        i felt sad for the city of my childhood and its ruined
state   as i always feel sad for it as i see it every year losing bit
    by bit of its neighborhoods its ukrainian and polish and czech
neighborhoods   as it had already lost its jewish neighborhoods
    and would eventually lose its italian and spanish and even its
black ones   and was already losing its artists to a remorseless
    real estate inflation that had filled their places with a rich and
    bland expense account world of stockbrokers and bankers
and art directors and advertising executives and the officers of
multinational corporations
                        but they were not serious and i was not serious
and it was as if only for that reason i had to consider the purely
virtual change in my life that this condition contrary to fact

would have subjected me to   and the idea of coming back
to the city of my childhood and youth as a stranger   because i
knew that it was no longer my city and i used to think of it as my
  city   and now it was their city and i had no use for them or
their city and that's why i felt sad as i rode down in the train from
providence
        where i also had something to do   to new york
        and then back up to poughkeepsie watching the spring trying
  to restore some life to the ravaged eastern landscape while the
search committee was still deliberating
        and the horror of the new beginning that i would never have
  to make pressed itself upon me with a weight completely
  independent of its fictional character and i realized i had
something to say to sherman

the river

coming into a space like this   obviously a very friendly
space in that it has a very warm tone to it   in a way thats
almost disconcerting for a poet   mainly because what youre
used to is the randomness of the road   the notion that youre
going somewhere and you dont know where that is or what its
like   and youre going to go do your talking   poem
talk poem talk   piece   do your piece of talking
which is a piece of talking   because essentially your
talking is an ongoing enterprise at least my talking is   an
ongoing enterprise that i try to relate to my thinking
                                                    because
talking for me is the closest i can come   as a poet   to
thinking   and i had wanted for a long time a kind of poetry of
thinking   not a poetry of thought but a poetry of thinking
since getting so close to the process of thinking was what i
thought the poem was   and theres a sense i have that makes
this kind of curious   a problematic enterprise   because
in one sense when i talk about what it means to go   do
talk poems i have used a conversational model   to explain
what i meant
                         this is a kind of dialogical model   that you go
to places and imagine poetry as some kind of ongoing discourse

with people but of course you dont know the people youre going
to talk to in any real sense
                              you might get to know them later or
you may imagine who they are but you dont really know them
    so its a kind of fantasy for me to believe that every time i
come into a place that im going to tailor a work specifically for the
    properties or necessities of some place that i really have no very
powerful grip on
                    obviously i have to rely on the fact that i have
things on my mind before i get here   like most of you   we
    poets   have an agenda a list   of things we think
about   and i can only hope that the things i think about have
    something in common with the things you have on your lists
though they may not form a perfect overlap   if they formed a
perfect overlap there would be no need for me to talk about them
    and if they formed no overlap at all there would be no way
for me to talk about them   so the imperfect fit is probably the
ideal situation   and thats a good thing because i have to face it
    anyhow   and here we are   and being here   ive been
thinking   about doing yet another piece
                                        and i do them with
regularity   not the regularity of the calendar   i do them
several times a year   anywhere from five to thirteen times a
year i may do talk pieces   more than that gets to be a
    nuisance and less than that i feel rusty   and this makes a
    difference because i will also sit down and write   usually i
will write only on the basis of pieces that i go out into the world to
do   usually i'll record them thats why the tape recorder   i
    wont work on any one of them in advance but often i will go out
and do one and take it back and decide whether i want to make a
    version of that one in print   and of course sometimes its a
piece that changes as it goes onto paper   because whatever
    winds up on paper is never exactly like whats in the air although
what i want to do is bring an image of talking out of the air and
onto the page   to make the claim of speech to make the claim
    of thinking within the frame of the book   that im afraid i
sometimes strain significantly

and i want to make the claim for speech and the claim
for thinking in an environment in which i think the claims for
thinking have become somewhat rigid   and in which speech
has no place into which it nicely fits   because if you go into a
library   and a library is the central place in the institution of
writing   there is no bibliographical category into which
speaking fits   and if you go into a library and try to look it up
you might not be able to find it   ive often thought how funny it
would be to look myself up in the library   but i suppose its no
funnier than looking up john cage   who either winds up in
music   which is not so reasonable as all that   sometimes it
may be reasonable but not for a book like silence   silence it
seems to me should have wound up in the poetry section of the
library but it never does   it could have wound up in the
philosophy section and it doesnt   it invariably winds up in the
music section   and my books   when i go out and look for
them   i dont often go out to look for them   but because
theres a streak of perversity in me sometimes i do   i go to
see if theyre in criticism   theyre not   theyre not in prose
theyre not in the fiction section   though they could be
because theyre not invariably true   or not altogether
true   i dont guarantee that   or at least theyre not always
fact
and i look for my books and i dont know where they should be
anyway because talking has no place in a library

in fact i have a publishing problem with publishers
i used to have difficulty convincing new directions that they
shouldnt list me in the poetry section   i never could convince
them   but i tried to convince them to put me in the prose
section as well   and they didnt believe this   so they
consistently placed me beside all the poets   many of whom are
my friends   but then people pick up my book expecting to find
some kind of verse in it and they dont find it   and not finding
verse in it theyre afraid they havent found poetry which is not so
much of a problem for me   but it is for a publisher if he starts

to get returns because of this
                                 somebody says "this is not poetry
take it back"   it doesnt usually happen like this   a book
   buyer usually suffers for a bit and then sells the cause of his
suffering to a second hand bookshop with maybe a couple of nasty
   comments scribbled in the margins i suspect   but thats all
right   it makes a lively ongoing career for my book

             but if i return to this issue of coming to a place with
things on my mind   one of the things thats often on my mind
      is the question of beginning   but it seems somewhat
   bizarre to put the question of beginning at the beginning of a
   piece   its something you should do later   because if you
   start with the question of beginning you say do i begin here
   what do i do take off my pack and unpack it

             come on in   dont worry   feel comfortable here
sit down im not easily interruptible and i dont worry about it

             i once did a piece   i once did a performance at u.c.
   davis years ago and they scheduled it in the cafeteria at lunch
   time   i guess poetry or my poetry was not very popular there
   and they were hoping to get me an audience   and it was very
funny   there was a lunch counter and a large crowd of students
   at tables   and at one end was a little platform about eight feet
   around and two feet high   and while everybody was sitting
and eating and looking politely i was up on the platform doing my
piece   and i would talk for a while   while walking around
and looking at someone i thought i was addressing because he was
eating his egg salad rather reflectively   and he would suddenly
   get up and leave   so i wasnt sure who i was talking to and
who was eating lunch and whether there was maybe some overlap
   between the two   when at one point a very little kid who
   was there i guess with a lunching or listening mother or father

climbed up onto my two foot high stage and finding herself
somewhat surprised to be there while i was talking began to
wander around looking for a way down   and while i was talking
i was suddenly afraid that this tiny kid was going to walk to the
edge and fall to her death   she was so very small

                    and while i was talking she was getting nearer and
nearer the precipice and i realized it was getting perilous   she
    was   looking was standing at the edge looking interestedly
down   so i picked her up while i was talking and offered her
to the audience   and somebody who had been sitting there
    rose up took the kid and sat down to continue listening or
eating   so it doesnt really matter   if that didnt get me
    nothing else will

                    but once again this question of beginnings   because
every time you start something its easy to give the impression that
    youre really beginning   you can create a kind of dramatic
    frame to suggest that some vast silence had intervened for ages
and now youre going to do the new thing   you set it and the
lights dim   or else they come up   you create an imaginary
drum roll and you settle in and you say   NOW   and of
course theres something preposterous about this something silly
        because what youve been doing has been going on all the time

                            i mean ive been here much of the day   i
arrived by train   which is very good because that lets you not
    feel the kind of separation anxieties airplanes produce   i
    dont even know if you can get here by plane   the hudson is a
place you dont normally come up on a plane   but the thing
    about a train is that youre never completely out of the space you
were in before   because the back of the train is still in the same
    space that you were just in while the front of the train is going
into a space youre not in yet

so you keep watching the hudson slide by you
looking at the deteriorated landscape of new york as it
depopulates itself and its industry slips into the water   and
you watch the history of this countryside that i know fairly well
because i grew up here   im a new yorker as my accent will tell
you   not only did i grow up in new york   i also know its
countryside because at various times ive lived in upstate new
york   and i was interested to go through the countryside again
watching the coming on of the spring   which is the kind of
recurrent thing that makes you feel youre always the same when
youre not   its part of the falsification system of nature   the
recurrence of seasons offers a false security that lets you think
nothing has changed   because the flowers come out on the
trees   you see the shadblow   you see the maples beginning
to flower   and you think that because everything is going on
its going to continue going on and you dont think that youre
dying   you dont think that anything will really be born or
die   though it looks like things are being born   because the
trees repeat their same boring performance year in and year out to
our immense delight   because its all very pretty and delightful
to look at and you keep feeling reassured

i felt like that when i was in new york city this morning
and i felt like it all the time i was coming out of new york city
and then i felt i was in the familiar hudson valley all the
time   the familiar hudson valley   and i know its not
familiar   because i know all the things that used to be here
iron works disappear   mills and ice companies and tile
factories and machine shops   you see them disappearing

coming up here one of the most amazing things was
looking at that toy-like castle   you must know it   its a
kind of toy castle   a ruined toy castle that looked as though
some child had been playing soldiers   some oversized kid
playing with tin soldiers and in a fit of rage reached out with one

hand and knocked over one and a half walls   leaving this little
island without its toy soldiers any more   it strengthened a
feeling that had been building in me since i had come to the city a
    couple of days before   where i had passed a day and a night
with my brother-in-law and sister-in-law
                                        which is odd   why
    should i think of that   i suppose because i was coming from
their apartment   i was staying with them in a sunny apartment
overlooking new yorks central park   and central park is right
now beginning to flower and central park flowering   when it
happens once a year is kind of amazing   it gives you an image
of such seductive falseness as it presents itself and the city in an
    impossibly favorable light out of the past   because it is
suddenly an impressionist city   as everything goes soft and
golden green and slightly out of focus   the leaves on the trees
are too small to be seen as leaves the colors are fainter the bushes
    are flowering forsythia and japanese cherry   and when the
maples flower its for a very short period a precarious moment
        and it convinces you that youre really looking at 1871 which
    you still dont believe   because you know its not 1871 its the
spring of 1987   and you know that parts of the lake are filled
with garbage and the great terrace is ruined and the ramble choked
    with weeds   but this grand english landscape that never was
in central park is still there at this moment

                    and from up where my brother-in-law and sister-in-law
live you can see almost the entire park   which is an accident
because theyre about to leave   theyve been living there a while
and now theyre going somewhere else   and walking the floor of
    the light flooded apartment   in the filtered spring sunlight
    falling on the floor youre standing on   which came from
    idaho   its a golden schist that they had rather startlingly
shipped in from idaho   because it was beautiful   at great
effort   because the idaho schist is different from the manhattan
schist that underlies the whole island   its more golden   it

looks as though it has pyrites in it
                              schist is that kind of peculiar
metamorphic rock that has granitic materials in it   but instead
of having that quartzlike hardness it is flaky and the manhattan
  version has bits of mica glittering in it   and its glamorous and
kind of crappy at the same time   and new york sits on this
    glamorous crappy metamorphic rock   over which the soil
seems to creep in a thin layer from under which this grey rock
crops out as if to let you know that the soil isnt very deep and that
central park is not fertile meadow   it was a kind of swampy
  barren out of which olmsted and vaux created their illusion of
england so that the industrial poor could learn to be citizens of a
free republic
              which was an astonishing idea but they had it or at
    least olmsted had it

          they built this park three miles north of the city or two
  and a half miles north of it   so that the throttled overworked
  and dangerous poor   who choked the city and provided its
economic base could come to find a green place that was closer
than the long trip to the country of staten island   or the estates
and farms of the bronx   where it would be possible to enjoy the
  humanly cultivated charms and fresh air and relative solitude of a
  nature otherwise unavailable to the working poor
                                          and theres
something in this   obviously the working poor were under
great pressures in the city   the long hours the low pay the
miserable tenements and   the filthy streets   and in a way
i suppose that olmsted in 1858 looking at this city was making a
  kind of promise to the city in his proposal   he and vaux
      because they did it together   i know that weve gotten into
the habit of talking about olmsted as if he were a single artist and
as far as the park venture went   both central park and prospect
  park it was a collaborative venture   calvert vaux the architect
designer and frederick law olmsted farmer and writer and practical

administrator   that put the park together when the city knew
that it had to do something
                    because people had to be able to live together under
conditions that were already hardly tolerable   because the
working people were already horribly crowded together down at
the southern end of manhattan island the southern end that was
    already hardly habitable since the city had destroyed the greens
around the battery and most of the other small places where people
could gather together in a leisurely way outside of the saloons that
    every christian feared were the plague of the poor   and they
had paved over the little streams and the canal from which canal
    street had gotten its name
                    they had buried the streams of lower manhattan and
    built over them   at great cost too   because in order to
build there you had to pump out the water to make sure that the
    buildings you built didnt sink into the streams that ran under
lower manhattan   you find out about this every time you build
    a new expensive high rise now and discover that the foundations
are in contention with the water that refuses to go away

                    so the city was teeming and filthy and reeking   and
what you had was a population of white slaves living in southern
manhattan as you had a population of black slaves living south of
    the mason dixon line   white slaves living under a slightly
different form of slavery   which olmsted who was a profoundly
    committed anti-slavery person felt was impossible for citizens of
a republic   and olmsted believed that you needed to do a great
    number of things to turn people from slaves into citizens   it
wouldnt be enough to release them into poverty and indifference
    and dirt to create citizens of a republic   which he imagined
you could do
                    maybe you cant but olmsted imagined you could
        maybe we still dont have citizens and maybe we dont have a
    republic   but in 1858 or 1857 olmsted thought you could
        and there were other people who thought so too or thought

you had to try to do it   for whatever reasons   and they
   olmsted and vaux   created this image   of nature
   an artifice representing a benevolent and subtly civilized
nature   north of the city where they imagined people going to
become free citizens   free and responsible
      and to help them be free and responsible olmsted hired a
large police force that he placed inside the park   realizing that
if he didnt have a police force there he might very soon not have a
park   as the peoples baser instincts might emerge before nature
had its chance to civilize them   and they would have a disaster
  on their hands   which at times weve had in central park
   the police notwithstanding

      and looking at central park   at its images of a kind
of humanly scaled nature that laid claim to being exemplary
     functional and exemplary   looking at it you realize that
its a beautiful and marvelous failure   not at being a park but at
civilizing its citizenry   its a great failure   which was not
  the fault of the park or its designers   because what they
wanted couldnt have worked   not in this way   and though
a park can do a lot of great things it doesnt create citizens   a
wordsworthian enterprise does not create citizens   not by itself

      on the other hand it does a lot and i was surprised to see
in a recent report made by a group of people who were examining
the park and trying to see what use it had   that not only do a
wide variety of people from all over the city make use of the park
     but that something like 68% of the people who come to the
  park   which they know by whatever method they tag and
count those people   turn out to be solitaries who come to the
park to be there alone   so it may not make citizens but it may
make certain ways of being meditatively human more possible
     it may restore a special way of being human for brief intervals
    maybe thats one of the things it can do in its way

                    but the park is always under assault   like the land
in general   like the land of the hudson valley   which has
always been under assault   its been under assasult from the
industries that dump garbage into it willingly or unwillingly i
    know they dont always do it on purpose but only because its
cheaper   and sometimes they dont even know what theyre
doing usually they dont really know what theyre doing and all the
    undesirable things wind up in the river   coming up the river i
was surprised at how much dumping goes on along the edge   i
was surprised at how many ruined cars
                                                its very curious how many
    cars get into strange places fragments of cars   so many car
bodies stripped of almost everything   you wonder how they got
    down there and what was carried off   cars minus axles minus
motors minus interior upholstery lying there like flayed carcasses
    flayed somewhere north of rye
                                        they increase in frequency as
you get between rye and here   and all those dumpings of odd
sorts of things   mattresses mattress springs torn fragments of
    things   strips of hanging things like body bags from the
vietnamese war   black plastic sacks dangling from an
embankment   and you wonder what was in it a corpse or old
clothes   and why this dumping right at the edge of the
hudson   its not as if its always easy to get down there   but
its the anonymous place where the land breaks down

                    its as if somehow the cut that the water makes into the
    land creates a space thats not anybodys   its as if everyone
knows that nobody can take possession of it that uncertain terrain
sometimes soggy and sometimes flooded smelling of rotting weeds
    or debris cast off by the river itself   the cut that the water
makes into the land creates at its edge an unpredictable place that
    is absolutely not ownable   so maybe the carelessness with
which its treated is a sign of some insight into the fact that its not
ownable   because its not surveyable usable or even reliably

navigable   sometimes under water sometimes emerging from it
slippery indeterminable its a no mans land   except in the few
places where they have these little boat basins most of them pretty
     shabby at that   and i passed one of them that was pretty
dilapidated   it must have been an old boat yard and there was
this really run down lopsided old barge with shingle roofing on
     that sported in dirty white lettering on its side the proud sign
HUDSON YACHT CLUB
                         i suppose it was a joke   that the barge
was an old garbage scow that had been beached along the shore and
somebody found some use for it some stupid business use for it of
     no great consequence but decided in a fit of humor to proclaim
itself

               and the other side of the river the western side declared
itself more proudly in giant enterprises   fortresses along the
     rhine   a vast power plant thriving on lethal fuel   a great
     space invaders fortress with impregnable walls looking out on a
     subjugated planet for which the conquerors intend no likely
good   and here was the shabby hudson   a grey cut in the
countryside   and you realize   that the river is in a way the
     beginning   of the land   traveling up the river you have
     a sense of it as the beginning   the way it determines the
geography and ecology of the space   and the flood plain of the
     river is a kind of central place for the region   and that without
the river there would have been very little without this glacial cut
     that it must have been all the way down to the sea there would
     be no hudson valley   and it is a strange beginning for a
place   though nothing ever begins of course
                                             i mean you know
rivers begin in the sea and end in the sea after an interval in the
air   and theres this ongoing cycle you know about   and
you cant cut the beginning loose from the end or tell them apart
     but you realize that your own sense of it is different
     because you always look for an onset in the highlands

you look for the headwaters   of the nile   and you
wonder what dirty spring system polluted by what chemical plant
that makes what kind of toxic thing   or what filthy snow filled
with what poisonous waste lies on the hillsides of the headwaters
of the hudson   you think of alan moorhead writing about the
search for the headwaters of the nile   only now we dont do that
        kind of search in the same way   now we want to find what
dioxin plant sits there on top and is sending its effluents down river
        to greet the shad   and you figure the two will come together
somewhere around here   at poughkeepsie

                but beginnings   seem not to really happen that way
        i know there are places that feel as though they could be
beginnings   and then its too late because the beginning has
        happened already   you look at the countryside of the hudson
and you say its too late   and in a way thats a mistake because
        its always too late   and its always too early   its always too
        early to do anything   about the things that have to be done
                but on the other hand its always too late to do it too   and
everybody can always explain to you why its too late and why its
too early   except that the beginning always has to be somewhere
in the middle
                and if you try to explain it to yourself   as i tried
to explain to myself what i was doing there contemplating the
        idaho schist on the floor of my brother- and sister-in-laws
apartment looking out at the manhattan schist outcrops twenty-
seven floors below   and wondering why they were leaving the
        idaho schist   it seemed to me i was thinking of myself being
displaced from new york   which i always considered my city
        as i wandered off to california

                i wandered out there by accident   though in a sense
everything ive ever done has been by accident   and maybe also
        on purpose   accidental purpose

i wound up in california by
accident   i had no desire to go to california   san diego if
somebody had ever said to me in 1950   you know you may
wind up living in san diego   i would have said go away
indianapolis is more likely   san diego stood to me   as a
new yorker   i was almost going to say as an american   as
an impossibility   the idea of it was preposterous   as if san
diego was a street in the center of which an admiral stood greeting
all arrivals   at least a chief petty officer
it didnt seem to me
that anyone in his right mind would ever want to live in san
diego   except maybe sailors or mexican workers i didnt even
think of them as living in san diego   i thought of it as a
retirement home for shoestore owners from indiana and nebraska
and when i got there in 1968 it turned out that san diego was
the place that indiana and arkansas went to retire or open furniture
stores or restaurants   and they brought all the excellences of
wichita and indianapolis cuisine to san diego   where it
combined with the cuisine of kentucky and virginia   which
added sugar to it   and i thought this was really a very strange
place i hardly knew what to make of it

san diego is like the end   its really very beautiful but
it was beautiful before they got there from kansas and oklahoma
part of it they neglected and thats remained beautiful   but
what they didnt neglect hasnt remained beautiful   because
they decided that san diego was on the mediterranean   they
had a strange sense of geography   they decided they had landed
on the algerian coast   so they put up palm trees date palms
but they also imported korean grass and bougainvillea and
australian sweet gum trees   and after a generation of feeding
these exotic blooms with water from the north they began to
think of them as native flora   and the australian eucalyptus
flourished   they had imported it in the 1880s to provide ties for
the railroad   and its wood was not good enough   but

southern california is a lot like the australian desert so the
eucalyptus flourished anyway   and the farmers thought to use
rows of eucalyptus as windbreaks for their mediterranean orange
trees   which didnt flourish without the provision of lots
and lots of water   because san diego is very much like the
australian desert   in which it rains rarely and heavily   that
is when it rains it often rains heavily but it is a rare occasion
                                                                    from
june to october it almost never rains   hardly a drop of rain
        there is sun and sun and more sun except for an overcast
morning or evening   and there isnt a drop of rain for months
on end   this untroubled place dries and dries and dries   yet
        trees flourish   luxuriant palms and jacaranda and orange
trees and olives   green tentacles extend all over san diego
        supported by water coming down from the north or from the
east   which they send down to grow these strange things that
they exhibit to tourists as the native thing   because now nearly
        nobody remembers what native forms there were except in a few
places spotted irregularly around the county

                        we live on a patch of native growth   three acres of
        chaparral   you let it alone and it grows   we live on three
acres of it it keeps people away because its like a thicket and its
        marvelously fragrant and hospitable for birds coyotes and small
        deer and we like it   but were on the outside and being on the
outside is like being at the beginning
                                                        i got to san diego and i didnt
know i wanted to join it   i suppose i wanted to be there   i
        didnt have to be there and i was there   it was an accident
        somebody said to me how would you like to come teach in san
diego   i thought it was as reasonable to teach in san diego as
        anywhere
                        theres no reason not to teach in san diego   what
should i have said to him   no   i dont want to teach in san
        diego   the question was did i want to teach   i wasnt
        thrilled by the idea but it was intriguing for a moment to think

of teaching   i hadnt done any teachingi had done a lot of other
   things   and now somebody suggested teaching   and i
thought it over and it was a possibility and i was persuaded   to
go out there and teach

              and there wasnt much there   a few concrete
buildings and the remains of an old military camp   which
had been turned into a university with the help of a checkbook
        and there it was   the regents of the university of
    california had taken over some thousand or more acres that had
once belonged to the marines when it was camp matthews and
they joined it to a powerful oceanographic research institute and
    made it into a high powered science university that required a
certain degree of respectability   and i was there to help give
    it that respectability   which i thought was very funny
                                                              they
brought me in to add a certain cultural respectability because you
    cant let scientists all alone by themselves   theres no telling
what they might do   so what you do is bring in people from the
arts and humanities so they might feel ashamed
                                        or they might feel
gratified and flattered and beneficent   so that you would stand
in the corner of their nuclear reactor and they would feel better
        and then they would make gifts to you and you could make
art and art would go on the walls of the nuclear reactor or whatever
else they were constructing   so i thought that was an amusing
    way to live   weve been court jesters before   and i took the
opportunity to go out there and found out it was not really like
that
        in those days there were more scientists   scientists who
    were really scientists not mere number crunchers   now we
    have more technicians than we used to   then there were
    actually many cultivated men and women in the sciences out
    there   the engineers hadnt arrived yet and the numerical
analysts   and lots of the scientists were educated   some
    were from europe and they could even converse and had certainly

read   we dont have many of those left now   the young ones
are not like that at all   theyre completely barbaric and
wonderful its a generation of visigoths and what we need now is a
new wulfilas to write them a testament in their language that will
   reenact st peter cutting off the tax collectors ear in a dramatic
enough way to get some conversions   and then we can start
   working again   but in the meantime a race of brilliant
technicians has replaced the scientists   many of whom have
retired or gone on to other places   and its a sad state of affairs
   that we're dealing with cheerfully   because what else can
we do

            we're certainly rich we're affluent   which is always
nice even in a war type economy   a science university
                                                its nice
to be rich   so we're rich   we're rich and we're dangerous
   and we sit there being rich and dangerous and talk about the
dangers of our richness   and we have a chancellor who is a
wonderfully handsome little man who has white hair and looks
   like a child who sits under a sunlamp every day and is infinitely
   charming to ladies and developers and bankers from whom he
brings in lots and lots of money to build us the ugliest buildings in
all san diego   and he does this out of a prodigious good will
   with which he defaces the landscape of eucalyptus that are not
native but are the only trees the university has got   and he has
   built us prestige after prestige   and gradually destroyed the
environment with these buildings   and he does it with the best
will in the world

            theres nothing you can say to him about this   i know
   because weve tried   and when you explain it to him   that
these buildings are appalling   he says what would you have me
do   if i couldnt build this building now i wouldnt ever be able
   to build it again   and if we say then dont build it ever they
dont seem to be able to hear   one of the science buildings is

just now about to be built on what was until now a very attractive
meadowlike space   and the faculty   much of the faculty
       even some of the science faculty   except for the biology
and chemistry departments   were in a state of rage about them
putting this tall building there and defacing one of the nice green
       areas when they had hundreds of acres they could put it on
elsewhere

              so we said do we have to put it there   why do you have
to put it there   our school prides itself on being a democracy so
this was at an academic senate meeting where almost everything
winds up getting discussed   so we said why do you have to put
       it there   and they answered   "so that the coastal winds
can dissipate the pollution from its stacks"   so you can see its
hard to get anywhere in a rational way   and it always feels like
we're dealing with some kind of crazy beginning there   we're
always starting to fight battles to stand off this continuous eating
away at the place

              recently a number of us tried to present a plan for them
       to treat the land the environment we live in   in a more
respectful way
                     there is a very attractive park in san diego   once
olmsted and vaux created the germinal park of the united states
       which was central park and then prospect park   the park
movement caught on   and nearly every city in the country
had to have its park   and the one they have here is a very pretty
spanish looking park called balboa park naturally after one of the
       conquistadors   and it was built up at the time of the great
columbian exposition at the turn of the century with lots of stucco
       and spanish tile buildings in the style of a new spain colonial
fantasy   and there are several museums down there and a zoo
and lots of green lawns and tall palm trees   and its a very nice
       looking park situated not far from the center of downtown san
diego about twelve miles south of the university   which is up

on a mesa overlooking the pacific ocean and la jolla
                                                    and we tried
to sell them the administration of the university on the hope of
trying to save the university's thousand or so acres by thinking of it
    as a kind of park   and i came up with this term in the hope
they might like it and find comfort in it   and i suggested that
    they try to turn the university of california san diego into an
academic park   whats an academic park   i dont know but
    i had some hope for them liking it   based on an analogy
principle   with an industrial park   which was something
theyd heard of and could approve of   and i guessed they might
    imagine it sounded a little like a science park only a little more
general
              i suppose i could have said a philosophical park but that
would have killed it altogether   but i figured theyd know that
an academy was a good place because thats where you get grants
        so we suggested to them that what we really needed was an
    academic park that would be a model to the community of an
ecologically humane place that would set an example in
    how to build and above all not build when natural conditions
required it   a place that would inspire with its surroundings
    a discourse with nature and graceful ways of living within and
    around it that would let the ravens continue to nest in our
buildings and the hawks and leave the coyotes enough breeding
    space and the little iguana and deer   we have an awful lot
of land   and i thought under that emblem we might be
able to protect it   and we made this suggestion to them
        and while we were working out this suggestion they kept
eating away at the landscape   they said oh its a good idea
    chomp chomp   chomp   and they put up a building here
they knocked down trees there   we said why did you have to
    knock down five hundred and fifty trees to build the student
center   we have so much land and we have so very few big
    groves of trees and we had this beautiful grove of eucalyptus
right across from the only attractive building on the campus
        which was the library   a kind of science fiction looking
building out of concrete and glass shaped like a slide projector

designed for communication with extraterrestrials a lovely
impractical building surrounded in its charming preposterousness
by a splendid grove of eucalyptus trees

       one day we got there at the end of the summer and the
trees were gone   in their place were these amputated stumps
five hundred and fifty stumps of living eucalyptus trees   weird
   looking little tables   and theyd gone through there and put
little red flags up near them to show that this was no accident
     we'd tried to get them to turn this place into an academic
park and theyd turned it into a field of carnage   we'd even
promised to design a lake in a godforsaken eroded spot that would
   draw on the natural drainage system and we'd proposed a variety
of pleasant things that people could deal with

       theres a sculpture program here   a good one called the
stuart collection   thats placed radical sculptural constructions
   all about the campus   we would integrate this with various
walks and groves and circles and knolls   we would work this
all out
      but there was no time   as always it was too late to begin
   or too early   they said were not ready for this yet   so it
was too early   then they said it was too late because the trees
were already destroyed and the plans for the space already made
     so it was also too late   and once again we were between
too early and too late

       and to this day my wife is mad on this subject   shes
on one of the powerful committees that never have any power this
   committee with a very great title   shes a professor here and
shes an artist and people like her   they think shes a marvelous
   lunatic artist   and she goes around pounding on peoples desks
saying how can you let this happen   and they say eleanor youre
   right and it continues to happen   the chancellor likes her and

invites her to breakfast and she says how can you let this happen
    and he says eleanor how could i stop it   and its like
punching a pillow

        we're constantly aware that what we're dealing with is
like being in a chute   its like a chute and we're falling in it
    and maybe its like being in a river and we're being swept out
to sea   but we're not sure whether we're being swept out
to the ocean or sucked into the bottom of some very foul swamp
    because at least if its the ocean you figure   california
will lead america over the cliff and everything will fall in   and
thats one of the reasons for praising california architecture   i
know a lot of people praise california architecture   what they
like about it is its lightness   it looks as if   if you move your
hand quickly you could knock it into the sea
        and theres something
consoling about this lack of permanence   as if its damage is
only temporary and not enduring   and its not built for the ages
because the people have no faith in ages existing   and they
may be right   there may not be ages existing if they continue to
build this way
        now this sense of being swept   of being swept up
and away   it seems to me that it still doesnt make you feel
hopeless   theres a paradox in this   theres a paradox that for
all of this im cheerful   i bring you good news of disaster
    its a disaster i refuse to be depressed about   because what
difference would it make if i was depressed   i know that i was a
very bad leftist as a kid   because i wasnt sufficiently depressed
    the history of the american left had two psychological
forms   one growing out of its sensitivity to the wrongs suffered
by innumerable victims was a profound glumness   the other
which sometimes accompanied this grew out of a humorless sense
of the importance of their mission and their sense of everyone elses
responsibility and seemed to involve a mental construction akin
    to a kinetic sculpture   that it seemed to me almost all their
    writing turned into   something like a single long finger

wagging in strong disapproval   and i suppose i wasnt much
    good at either of these   and as for the american right nobody
can take it seriously   unless you have a kind of kamikazelike
    playfulness and are for the sport of it willing to follow william
buckley over a cliff

        but given our alternatives it seems to me you may as
    well be cheerful even though things are pretty bad   because
things have always been bad   you know i used to believe there
    must have been golden days once   it took me a long time to
get over this belief   but im over it now and i figure there was
always a bad situation that you took on more or less well   and
    if it somehow started out fine you would come to the bad scene
pretty soon bye and bye   and i think of my father-in-law   as
a man for whom things started out fine   so fine he can never
    stop telling you the story of his great beginning   and now his
situation is not so fine but he's ninety years old and he's learned
how to face it with the ongoing charm of a man who's been living
so long he's gotten quite good at it

        now he's ninety years old and we meet to play tennis
    and i suppose thats already a sign of a good situation   or at
least the way that he plays it is a sign of the way that he lives with
it
    im not a very competitive tennis player   because it takes too
    much time and effort if you want to play it that way   so im a
good partner for my father-in-law   who has always been a kind
    of elegant player with easy looking strokes and he likes to keep
    diffidently returning the ball   and if i dont hit it too far
        because he's lost some of his mobility he always gets it back
to me very prettily because he has elegant ground strokes   so i
dont knock myself out and i keep playing with him and i enjoy
the cheerfulness of his game and i enjoy having him instruct me
        being ninety years old he always gives me tennis lessons
    he tells me how i could improve my serve   he tells me

how my backhand could get more top spin on it   and he
interrupts the game any number of times and he does this to
everybody   if there are people on the neighboring court he'll
give them advice too   especially pretty young women and even
   young men   who seem to enjoy hearing quaint tennis lore
from a slender old gentleman with a small pointed beard and
courtly ways   even though it slows up everybodys game
                                                      but
   his idea of the game goes back to borotra and rene lacoste and
   has a strong esthetic component because he's a painter and a poet
living here in san diego   which i suppose is not so strange
      because there are plenty of poets and painters living in san
diego   but peter happens to be a serious ninety year old
hungarian poet and painter living here in san diego   and thats
   where his situation is not so fine   because what good is
   hungarian poetry in san diego and what good is it to be a very
good and idiosyncratic and unfamous painter when youre ninety
years old even if you have shows

                  but once peter was famous   or felt famous   for a
very short time   and it was at the very beginning   and then
   he was famous again   not so famous as before but for a longer
period of time   but what he remembers most and cant ever
   forget is the story of his beginning   a beginning that was so
   blessed it took him completely by surprise   and to this day i
dont think he can quite understand it   which is why i think
   he's told it to me so many times

                  peter   his real name was joszef   joszef barna or
   barna joszef the way they did it in hungarian   was a bright
   young jewish kid from the provinces with a gift for his own
language and some drawing talent   and because his father was a
craftsman   a painter of church interiors with formulaic christs
and angels and lots of gold in the little town of keckemet   and
   because he had an older brother who had a job in a bank in

budapest   and because he'd done well in the gymnasium they
sent him to study architecture in the capital   where he painted
   delicate water colors and wrestled with projective geometry and
read poetry and wrote tortured stories about sexual experiences he
had never had   violent stories about squalid relations between
   a hunchbacked woman and a dwarf in an environment of abject
poverty   about a high school boy going mad on his first trip to a
local whorehouse   stories that peter remembers now because
   they were filled with lurid atmosphere and fantastical events
      and written in a language wild with fear and loathing and
compassion   as surrealistic   but i think might be better
described as expressionist because it was 1914 or 15 and this was
   very much the sense of the time

            and as young barna joszef had written three of these he
   showed them to a friend   who was a student at the university
      and he was so impressed by these fantasies that he showed
   them to his professor   who it turned out was a man named
babich   who peter assured me was after ady and someone else
   whose name i cant remember   the number 3 poet of all
hungary and it just so happened an editor of nyugat
                              and it was with
babich the number 3 poet of all hungary that these stories sat and
sat and sat   till peter   still joszef then   became restless
   and finally persuaded his friend to find out what had become of
his stories

            and then as the often repeated story goes   the editor
of nyugat   the great hungarian magazine founded by ady to face
"west"   which was its name (nyugat means west)   from
   hungarian ground   the chief editor   a man named
Oszat   a distinguished critic and scholar   and not babich
   the number 3 poet who had sat on peters stories all this time and
had now finally passed them onto this man   Oszvat the chief
   editor summoned peter to the journals offices   to warn him

sternly to care for his talent that he most surely could not
understand   and inform him that he was going to print not one
   but all three of the stories in successive issues of the magazine

             now can you imagine what this must have been like
   at the age of eighteen to be picked up by your countrys leading
   literary magazine   it was like being picked up by an eagle
and in the intoxication of his flight barna joszef changed his name
       to moor peter or peter moor
                          now to speakers of english this
   may not sound like very much   we might think of the wistful
songs of thomas moore and "all those endearing young charms" or
the bleak moors of scotland   but for the slender and delicately
   handsome young poet   he was assuming a name that called
to mind the smouldering moor of venice   thats what an eagles
   flight can do

             and he seems to have remained in the air for quite a
   long time   waiting for his story to appear   and soared
even higher after it came out   though it appears that an uncle
   of his who set a lot of store by his own literary sensibility got
angry with him for not revealing to him anything of this great
hidden talent   and under the name of moor   peter rapidly
   made the acquaintance of the small glittering art society of
budapest in which he was celebrated as a kind of golden youth
whose star was rising   and all through the great war   from
   which he was excused because of a condition like asthma   he
remained in budapest and wrote and was widely admired by the
artistic society of cultivated men and lovely sensitive ladies for the
one story he had published in the great literary magazine   so
   much so that he withdrew from the architectural school
       where the mathematics was troubling him anyway   and
prepared to lead the literary life
                          but publication was slow in nyugat
   it was an older magazine   its editors were busy men

there was a war on   the finances were uncertain   and
then the government collapsed and reformed under count carolyi
and the magazine temporarily suspended operations
    meanwhile peter got engaged to an attractive young pianist
and waited for the appearance of his second story   for which he
had already checked the proofs   and then the carolyi regime
collapsed and then reformed briefly as a communist government
under bela kun   oszvat   nyugats chief editor   took an
administrative position in the commune and the magazine
    which had seemed on the point of resuming operations
discontinued them   so peter took a minor job as a censor with
    the new government and waited some more   then came
admiral horthys right wing coup bela kun fled and there was a
general roundup of liberal and left wing intellectuals   and peter
as a minor functionary of the left wing government and a jew got
arrested and thrown into a jail   where he was held for a while
at the local police station   a notorious place where people were
    interrogated and tortured before being sent off to detention or
execution   because the horthy government quickly made itself
known for violence and nastiness   and peter was beaten up and
questioned and he has terrible memories of that jail where people
he knew were tortured in unspeakable ways and sent off to their
death   and he tells the story of standing in a room filled with
other prisoners waiting to be sent off from one detention place to
another and seeing a man that he knew who had been horribly
violated and was now nearly unrecognizable in a state of shock
leaning against a wall   when a dandyish young officer and a
beautiful woman in evening clothes swept into the room   they
had been dancing and they were still slightly drunk and laughing
    and they suddenly stopped   and the officer looked around
and pointed to the exhausted prisoner and said "that man is a
communist"   and the woman went up and stared at him
pulled her cape around her and spat in the mans face
                                              but peter was
lucky because an old school friend an aristocrat wandered into the
    police station spotted him there and used some influence to get

him out
          so peter slipped down the river to vienna where he was
safe   but here his situation was not so fine   he was no
longer a rising star   he was simply another hungarian emigre
whose german was not so good   who had no profession and
    now had a wife   he had married the young pianist and now
they were poor emigres together   she gave piano lessons and he
got a few jobs as an extra in films made by a hungarian director
          and life was pretty miserable for him there in vienna   it
was as if somehow the eagle that had picked him up and flown with
    him toward olympus had suddenly dropped him at the foot of a
    barren mountain slope where he was wandering around trying to
get his bearings   so they emigrated to the united states where
his wife had relatives
                              now he had spoken poor german but he knew
no english and he was still further from the literary world he had
    known in budapest   and he had to start a life as a craftsman
doing lettering and signs for local merchants while his wife taught
    piano high up in the upper heights of northern manhattan
    where he lived for a long time as a quaint emigre with a
charming accent   preparing signs during the day and writing
    at night   in hungarian   long novels that there was no
audience for or a very small audience   because he managed to
find here in manhattan a hungarian emigre community in exile
    hungry for their native language and culture
                                                        so he was
suddenly discovered again by an antifascist hungarian newspaper
and by hungarian radio   and he wrote articles and stories for
    the one and read poems for the other   and he was something
of a star once again   this time in a smaller emigre community
    or maybe it was even the same size   who knows how big
the literary community of budapest was before 1920
                    and he lived by his commercial art during the day and
    wrote during the night and was a lion of new yorks hungarian
    emigre community and his wife left him and he was happy or
    cheerful as he expressed the painful struggles of the citys poor

in the great depression and denounced the rise of the nazis in
brilliantly rhymed folkish ballads that he explained to me were not
so modern as what he had written before but just as good and
maybe better to reach the people   which he had never thought
about before
                and maybe they were   i cant tell   i only know a
    few sentences of hungarian and snatches of verse   peter had
promised to teach me once   but he was a terrible teacher and i
    never had the time   so i cant really tell
                but for the community of hungarian emigres living in
new york they were eloquent and powerful poems   and many
years later a hungarian scholar came over who was researching the
emigre writers and collected peters texts and wrote an article about
    him for a journal published by the magyar academy of sciences
        so i suppose they were eloquent and powerful if traditional
poems
                but after the war the second world war things were different
        all through the thirties and forties you write these poems
    denouncing horthy and fascism   and then horthy and the
fascists are swept away and you suddenly have nothing to do

                        i suppose he was exhausted   i imagine he could have
    gone back to hungary   to budapest and tried to pick up his
career again   if you can call it that   as a hungarian writer

                and he went over there after the war   to see if thats
what he wanted to do   but the hungarians werent interested
    in him   somehow the last issue of nyugat   in which his
    first story was published hadnt been widely distributed and had
gotten lost   the other one that had been set up in proofs had
    disappeared   nobody really knew him or wanted to know
him   he was just another hungarian emigre   and peter wasnt
sure that he wanted to be there anyway   his mother was dead
    his brother was dead   killed by the nazis just before theyd

pulled out   most of his friends were gone   only his sister
marika remained   and peter had been living in the united states
  so long that maybe he was no longer a hungarian writer but an
american hungarian writer   so he turned around and came home
and cheerfully became a painter

          or maybe not so cheerfully and only gradually
                                                            he had
      always painted   slight watercolors   impressionist
landscapes that he painted on trips he took with his hungarian
    friends to the adirondacks or the rockies   and he'd painted
      watercolors in architecture school   so he returned to the
watercolors   and they became more elaborate as he worked
    them over with inks and chalks and the surfaces became
more ambiguous and the images became more fantastical
          underseascapes with exotic fronds twisting roots and
menacing shapes   sunken rock structures vaguely resembling
    monsters or titans   and they became surreal

          among his hungarian friends there were one or two
painters to whom he showed his paintings   and they encouraged
  him to enter them in shows sponsored by watercolor societies or
    associations of american artists   and his paintings were
accepted and exhibited   and he won a few prizes and he was
awarded a medal by a museum in new jersey   and he really was
  cheerful and somewhat surprised to be accepted by this small
world   in which i think he regarded himself at first as something
  of an imposter because he wasnt formally trained and had no
  understanding of anatomy or perspective   because he was
really a poet

          and he continued to write stories and poems at the same
time   but in english now because he had married again   my

mother-in-law   a passionate dark haired little woman of russian
and polish extraction   and she didnt know any hungarian
      only russian and polish and english   so he eventually got
   tired of reading his marvelous sounding hungarian poetry to
her   because it was as unintelligible to her as pushkin was to
   him   but she was a wonderfully appreciative audience for
   his fantastical stories   of paintings that came alive in the
metropolitan museum at night   rubens horsemen riding
   down 5th avenue and up 53rd street to shoot arrows into the
cezannes on the walls of the modern   but even more for his
dreamy and menacing watercolors   that she never got tired of
studying and criticizing and admiring   and as he continued
to make more paintings that they argued about and admired
   together   he began to consider himself more of a painter than
   a poet   and because jeanette was an energetic and gregarious
woman she encouraged him to exhibit his paintings and arranged
   a couple of shows for him in small but respectable new york
galleries   from which he received some friendly reviews in the
   newspapers and art magazines   and he began to regard himself
somewhat more confidently as a painter   and even then in his
fifties he might have made a kind of cheerful career for himself as a
   painter   only he simply had no idea of how to do it
                                                      because he
had this idea of beginnings from his early days back in hungary
      an idea of being picked up by an eagle and soaring   and
making a career as a painter meant even in this little world
      besides making paintings and entering shows   going to
openings and talking to other artists and gallery owners and joining
   associations and going to meetings and generally hanging around
and becoming part of a world   and i made the mistake a
   number of years later when i got to know him and peters
paintings had become even more elaborate and fantastical in style
   as well as subject matter   of introducing him to betty
parsons   who was still running a serious gallery then   and
she came down with her gallery director   who was jock truman
   i think   to their dark apartment off central park and studied

the paintings and looked interested and said little　　but invited
peter to come down and visit the gallery

　　　　　　　which peter never did　　because he was slightly
offended that they hadnt praised his paintings　　and jeanette
was a little resentful that they had declined her cookies and tea
　　and they never went down to the gallery and were a little
irritated with me　　because what they didnt understand was
that peter was supposed to go down to the gallery and see a few
shows　　and bring down new work　　and generally talk to the
gallery people and hang around and give them enough time to get
　　used to the work　　so that they could finally feel comfortable
with it and give peter a show

　　　　　　　but peter knew how to make paintings even if he didnt
know how to make a career　　and he continued to make them as
　long as he could show them to jeanette for her to argue with him
and admire them　　and the paintings got even more bizarre and
　　wonderful when peter and jeanette followed us out to san diego
　　　　where he fell in love with the sunlight and exotic flora and
　　fanciful architecture of southern california　　which he
abstracted in the paintings into evocations of tropical architectures
and cliff structures floating or drowned in luminous atmospheres
　　and he painted so rapidly and well that then in his middle
eighties　　he filled two one man shows in two successive years
in san diego　　with over forty new paintings　　and he would
　still be painting cheerfully now

　　　　　　　but as they both got older jeanettes mind started to fail
her memory went　　and she panicked and grew frightened and
　angry and was no longer a good audience for every new painting
because she couldnt remember what she had seen or said　　and
　she got furious to be reminded of what she forgot　　and she bit

him and kicked him in the shins   and finally had to go into
   an old age home where she could afford to forget that she had
   forgotten   and peter was no longer a painter again
                                        he had
the paintings they were all around him   but he was no longer
painting new ones and he was deeply depressed   for a while
      but then he started to read again   and one day he was
reading a hungarian literary magazine that we'd brought back from
   new york for him   and he came on a long poem by a new
hungarian poet that struck him as so new and so modern that he
   started to translate it
                        which may seem like a strange activity for
this 90 year old hungarian emigre who had never really mastered
   idiomatic english and had to have his own poems and stories
   translated for him   but peters english written english was
   serviceable enough when he was moved by a feeling to write
      not serviceable enough perhaps to translate his own hungarian
stories and poems   because there he was moved too deeply by
   his own hungarian impulses   but serviceable enough to
translate someone elses hungarian impulses   and it was a long
and fractured work about a kind of existential christ   and the
   hungarian was difficult and its vocabulary was technological and
sacramental   but peter worked cheerfully at it for a long time
   and finally finished it   and then he didnt know what to do

            so he sent it to hungary to the hungarian poet by way of
   the magazine   and sent him also some of his own hungarian
poems   the rhyming antifascist poems from his days with the
   emigre magazine   by way of introduction   and then he
waited a very long time for an answer
                              and while he waited he began
to write again   in hungarian   he began composing a novella
   dealing with his childhood   and he got very happy writing
   down memories from those times in keckemet   and he read
   small portions of it to us in fractured translations which always

dissatisfied him   but he kept on writing at it   and finally
the hungarian poet wrote back

        he was clearly flattered that peter had translated his
poem   but pointed out that it had been translated into english
before and told him in what magazine   and he thanked him for
the translation   but of peters own poems he made no mention
    at all   and of course being a modernist poet in budapest in
    nineteen eighty-three or -four   with russia not nazi germany
breathing over his shoulder   what could he have made of those
    rhyming antifascist poems of 1943 or 44

        so now peter has stopped writing again   and he's
stopped but in a way he's still cheerful   and he's reading again
    this time in english   not goethe   but stendhal again
        novels of young men and their desires   and he looks with
desire at attractive young women and with delight at children and
    babies   he strolls about the streets of la jolla taking in with
    pleasure the exotic plantings and the crystalline air   and he
still has his writings and paintings gathered around him   and
    he still takes his slides around to the galleries   where the
    gallery owners often admire them   because the paintings are
admirable   but what can the galleries do with them   theyre
    in business to make money   and peter is a very good and
    unfamous painter who is 90 years old   and a 90 year old painter
    has to be famous   because he cant be promising any more

        so he's gone back to reading stendhal and kurt vonnegut
    who he tells me is very good but too smart to be a very great
    writer   and we talk about them   and he likes to tell me
about goethe   who he thinks is very great but knows i have no
taste for   so we sit in chinese restaurants and yell at each other
    cheerfully because his hearing is not very good about goethe and
    stendhal and sometimes about vonnegut and nabokov   and

sometimes he complains about the hungarians for not valuing his
poems and stories and reminds me of his great beginning how he
was picked up by the eagle and dropped on the way to the mountain

and still he has his paintings and writings gathered around him
and he plays tennis and walks out in the sunlight and he's ninety
years old   and he has his sense of the meaningfulness and
strangeness of his work strangely collected here in san diego
    and when he dies it will probably be no stranger than most
things in this environment at all

DAVID ANTIN

Lynn Swigart, "Sherman Paul at Home in Iowa City," 1974
Courtesy Lynn Swigart

Art Sinsabaugh, "Midwest Landscape #53," 1962
Courtesy Indiana University Art Museum

A Bibliography of Sherman Paul

Because the development of this volume proceeded without the knowledge of its dedicatee, it was not possible to check this bibliography with him for completeness. It is, I believe, reasonably complete through 1987.

H. D. P.

Books

"Emerson's Literary Ethics." Bowdoin Prize Essay. Harvard University, 1950.
Emerson's Angle of Vision: Man and Nature in American Experience. Cambridge, Mass., 1952. Second edition, 1965; third edition, 1969.
The Shores of America: Thoreau's Inward Exploration. Urbana, 1958. Second edition, New York, 1971. Paperback edition, Urbana, 1972.

Louis Sullivan: An Architect in American Thought. Englewood Cliffs, N.J., 1962. German edition, Berlin, 1963; Indian edition, Bombay, 1967.

Edmund Wilson: A Study of Literary Vocation in Our Time. Urbana, 1965. Paperback edition, 1967. For Wilson's detailed response to this work, see *EW Corrections and Comments SP* (Iowa City, 1976).

And Four with Birds. Iowa City, 1968. Poems.

The Music of Survival: A Biography of a Poem by William Carlos Williams. Urbana, 1968.

Hart's Bridge. Urbana, 1972.

Repossessing and Renewing: Essays in the Green American Tradition. Baton Rouge, 1976.

Olson's Push: Origin, Black Mountain, and Recent American Poetry. Baton Rouge, 1978.

The Lost America of Love: Rereading Robert Creeley, Edward Dorn, and Robert Duncan. Baton Rouge, 1981.

In Search of the Primitive: Rereading David Antin, Jerome Rothenberg, and Gary Snyder. Baton Rouge, 1986.

Monographs and Pamphlets

Randolph Bourne. University of Minnesota Pamphlets on American Writers Series, No. 60. Minneapolis, 1966. 48 pp.

So To Speak: Rereading David Antin. London, 1982. 54 pp.

The Onward Way: First Annual Presidential Lecture, The University of Iowa. Iowa City, 1984. 20 pp.

In Love with the Gratuitous: Rereading Armand Schwerner. Grand Forks, N.D., 1986. 68 pp.

Works Edited

Moby-Dick, by Herman Melville. With an Introduction. Everyman's New American Edition, New York, 1950. Reissued, with a new introduction, London, 1954.

Essays by Ralph Waldo Emerson. With an Introduction. Everyman's New American Edition, London, 1955.

Walden and Civil Disobedience, by Henry David Thoreau. With an Introduction and "A Note on the Composition of *Walden.*" Riverside Edition, Boston, 1957.

Masters of American Literature. With Leon Edel, T. H. Johnson, and Claude Simpson. Boston, 1959.

Port of New York: Essays on Fourteen American Moderns, by Paul Rosenfeld. With an Introduction. Urbana, 1961. Paperback edition, 1966.

Thoreau: A Collection of Critical Essays. With an Introduction. Englewood Cliffs, N.J., 1962.

Nature, The Conduct of Life and Other Essays, by Ralph Waldo Emerson. With an Introduction. Everyman's New American Edition, London, 1963.

Six Classic American Writers. With an Introduction. Minneapolis, 1970.

Criticism and Culture: Papers of the Midwest Modern Language Association, number 2. With an Introduction. Iowa City, 1972.

Some Early Poems, by Charles Olson. With an Introduction. Iowa City, 1978.

Olson at Iowa: Highlights of the Charles Olson Festival. With Bruce Wheaton. Iowa City, 1979. Videotape.

Some Others: Contemporary American Poetry. With Preface and Essay. *North Dakota Quarterly,* LV (Fall, 1987).

Contributions to Books

"Resolution at Walden." In the following collections: *Interpretations of American Literature,* ed. Charles Feidelson, Jr., and Paul Brodtkorb (New York, 1959), 161–75; *Critical Approaches to American Literature,* ed. Ray B. Browne and Martin Light (New York, 1965), 164–77; *Walden and Civil Disobedience: Authoritative Texts, Background, Reviews and Essays in Criticism,* ed. Owen Thomas (New York, 1966), 336–48; *American Literature: A Critical Survey,* Vol. I, ed. Thomas D. Young and Ronald E. Fine (New York, 1968), 199–212; *The Merrill Studies in Walden,* comp. Joseph J. Moldenhauer (Columbus, Ohio, 1971), 68–81; and *Accent: An Anthology, 1940–1960,* ed. Daniel Curley, George Scouffas, and Charles Shattuck (Urbana, 1973), 429–41.

"Melville's 'The Town-Ho's Story.'" In *Discussions of Moby Dick,* ed. Milton R. Stern. Boston, 1960, pp. 87–92.

"Ralph Waldo Emerson." In *Encyclopaedia Britannica* (1960), VIII, 391–92.

"Henry David Thoreau." In *Encyclopaedia Britannica* (1961), XXII, 152abc.

"American Letters and Essays." In *The College and Adult Reading List of Books in Literature and the Fine Arts,* prepared by National Council of the Teachers of English. New York, 1962, pp. 191–98.

"The Angle of Vision." In the following collections: *Emerson: A Collection of Critical Essays,* ed. Milton R. Konvitz and Stephen E. Whicher (Englewood Cliffs, N.J., 1962), 158–78; and *Emerson's Nature: Origin, Growth, Meaning,* ed. Merton M. Sealts and Alfred R. Ferguson (New York, 1969), 131–33. Second edition, enlarged, Carbondale, 1979, pp. 131–33.

"Transcendentalism. The New England Transcendentalists." In *Encyclopaedia Britannica,* XXII (1964), 396.

"The Identities of John Jay Chapman." In *Transcendentalism and Its Legacy,* ed. Myron Simon and Thornton H. Parsons. Ann Arbor, 1966, pp. 137–49. Paperback edition, 1969.

"The Photography of Harry Callahan." In *Harry Callahan.* New York, 1967, pp. 6–10. Introductory essay.

"View Points." In *Twentieth Century Interpretations of Walden,* ed. Richard Ruland. Englewood Cliffs, N.J., 1968, pp. 12–14.

"A Sketchbook of the Artist in his Thirty-Fourth Year: William Carlos Williams' *Kora In Hell: Improvisations.*" In *The Shaken Realist: Essays in Modern Literature in Honor of Frederick J. Hoffman,* ed. Melvin J. Friedman and John B. Vickery. Baton Rouge, 1970, pp. 21–44.

"Lyricism and Modernism: The Example of Hart Crane." In *English Symposium Papers,* III (1973), 36–59.

"Edmund Wilson." In *Encyclopedia of American Biography,* ed. John A. Garraty. New York, 1974, pp. 1212–13.

"Randolph Bourne." In *Makers of American Thought: An Introduction to Seven American Writers,* ed. Ralph Ross. Minneapolis, 1974, pp. 120–56.

"A New England Saint." In *Teacher and Critic: Essays by and about Austin Warren,* ed. Myron Simon and Harvey Gross. Los Angeles, 1977, pp. 99–102.

"The Ordeal and the Pilgrimage." In *Van Wyck Brooks: The Critic and His Critics,* ed. William Wasserstrom. Port Washington, N.Y., 1979, pp. 206–10.

"Interview with Lynn Swigart." In *Olson's Gloucester: Photographs by Lynn Swigart.* Baton Rouge, 1980, pp. 1–18.

"John Jay Chapman." In *Twentieth-Century Literary Criticism, VII,* ed. Sharon Hall. Detroit, 1982, pp. 197–98.

"Lyricism and Modernism: The Example of Hart Crane." In *Hart Crane,* ed. Alan Trachtenberg. Englewood Cliffs, N.J., 1982, pp. 163–79.

"Charles Olson." In *Contemporary Literary Criticism, XXIX,* ed. Jean Stine and Daniel Marowski. Detroit, 1984, pp. 329–31.

"Criticism." In *World Book Encyclopaedia* (1985), IV, 912–13.

"The Long Way Home." In *Hart Crane,* ed. Harold Bloom. New York, 1986, pp. 139–53.

"Gripping, Pushing, Moving." In *Robert Creeley's Life and Work,* ed. John Wilson. Ann Arbor, 1987, pp. 40–48.

Contributions to Periodicals

"Melville's 'The Town-Ho's Story.'" *American Literature,* XXI (May, 1949), 212–21.

"Morgan Neville, Melville and the Folk Hero." *Notes and Queries,* CXCIV (June 25, 1949), 278.

"The Wise Silence: Sound as the Agency of Correspondence in Thoreau." *New England Quarterly,* XXII (December, 1949), 511–27. Broadcast by the Voice of America, 1950.

"Hawthorne's Ahab." *Notes and Queries,* CXCVI (June 9, 1951), 255–57.

"Alcott's Search for the Child." *Boston Public Library Quarterly,* IV (April, 1952), 88–96.

"Resolution at Walden." *Accent,* XIII (Spring, 1953), 101–13.

"Hawthorne's America." *Thought* (New Delhi), IV (March 15, 1952), 12–14.

"Sherwood Anderson and the Small Town." *Thought* (New Delhi), VII (May 14, 21, 1955), 12–13, 10–11.

"Thoreau's 'The Landlord': 'Sublimely Trivial for the Good of Men.'" *JEGP,* LIV (October, 1955), 587–90.

"The Folk Basis of American Literature." United States Information Service. Vienna, 1958.

"Major Themes in American Literature." *Moderne Sprachen,* II (1958), 8.

"Persistent Themes in American Literature." United States Information Service. Vienna, 1958.

"Melville's Typee." *Everyman* (London), III (1959), 17–19.

"The Identities of John Jay Chapman." *JEGP,* LIX (April, 1960), 255–62.

"Portrait of Paul Rosenfeld." *Accent,* XX (Spring, 1960), 99–111.

"Sullivan's Treatise on Ornament." *Arts Magazine,* XXXVII (1962), 62–66.

"Randolph Bourne and the Party of Hope." *Southern Review,* n.s., II (July, 1966), 524–41.

"After Concord." *Southern Review,* n.s., III (October, 1967), 1010–19.

"Paul Goodman's Mourning Labor: *The Empire City.*" *Southern Review,* n.s., IV (October, 1968), 894–926.

"An Art of Life: Pasternak's Autobiographies." *Salmagundi,* XIV (Fall, 1970), 17–33.

"From Lookout to Ashram: The Way of Gary Snyder, Part 1." *Iowa Review,* I (Summer, 1970), 76–89.

"From Lookout to Ashram: The Way of Gary Snyder, Part 2." *Iowa Review,* I (Fall, 1970), 70–85.

"Images of a City: Art Sinsabaugh's Chicago Landscapes." *New Letters,* XXXIX (Summer, 1973), 36–59. Also see "Images of the City," in *The Chicago Landscapes of Art Sinsabaugh: Essays by Henry Holmes Smith and Sherman Paul. A History by the Photographer.* Privately printed, Iowa City, 1976, pp. 17–33.

"In and about the Maximus Poems, Part 1." *Iowa Review,* VI (Winter, 1975), 118–30.
"In and about the Maximus Poems, Part 2." *Iowa Review,* VI (Summer-Fall, 1975), 74–96.
"A Letter on Rosenthal's 'Problems of Robert Creeley.'" *boundary 2,* III (Spring, 1975), 747–60.
"*Maximus*: Volume 3 or Books VII and After." *boundary 2,* V (Winter, 1977), 557–71.
"Rereading Creeley." *boundary 2,* VI/VII (Spring/Fall, 1978), 381–418.
"Clinging to the Advance: Some Remarks on 'Projective Verse.'" *North Dakota Quarterly,* XLVII (Spring, 1979), 7–14.
"Open It Up: An Open Discussion with Sherman Paul and Max Westbrook," ed. Robert W. Lewis. *North Dakota Quarterly,* XLVII (Spring, 1979), 50–75.
"Birds, Landscape, Place, Cosmicity." *Iowa Review,* XI (Fall, 1980), 45–61.
"Journals: The Dialogue Between Self and Text." *Iowa English Bulletin,* XXX (Spring, 1981), 5–6.
"Here/Now." *O.ARS,* II (1982), 31–34.
"Open(ing) Criticism." *North Dakota Quarterly,* L (Winter, 1982), 9–18.
"Some Etymologies." *America One,* I (1982), 60–66.
"Thinking With Thoreau." *Thoreau Quarterly,* XIV (Winter, 1982), 18–25.
"From a Summer's Journal." *Lunatack* (1983), 6–10.
"A Letter on Olson and Burke." *All Area* (Spring, 1983), 64–65.
"From Walden Out." *Thoreau Quarterly,* XVI (Winter-Spring, 1984), 74–81.
"The Life of the Mind." *Iowa Review,* XIV (Fall, 1984), 146–51.
"In Love with the Gratuitous: Rereading Armand Schwerner." *North Dakota Quarterly,* LIV (Summer, 1986), Sec. II, 1–68.
"The Husbandry of the Wild." *Iowa Review,* XVII (Spring-Summer, 1987), 1–18.

Reviews and Review-Essays

Melville, by Geoffrey Stone; and *Herman Melville,* by Newton Arvin. *New England Quarterly,* XXIII (September, 1950), 405–407.
A Reading of Moby-Dick, by M. O. Percival. *New England Quarterly,* XXIII (December, 1950), 530–33.
The American Writer and the European Tradition, ed. Margaret Denny and William Gilman. *New England Quarterly,* XXIV (March, 1951), 126–28.
Milton and Melville, by Henry Pommer. *New England Quarterly,* XXIV (December, 1951), 550–52.
Spires Of Form: A Study Of Emerson's Aesthetic Theory, by Vivian Hopkins; and *Thoreau: The Quest and the Classics,* by Ethel Seybold. *New England Quarterly,* XXIV (September, 1951), 399–402.

Melville's Mardi, by Merrel Davis. *New England Quarterly*, XXV (December, 1952), 555–57.
Emerson Handbook, by F. I. Carpenter. *New England Quarterly*, XXVI (December, 1953), 546–48.
"Hawthorne's Ambiguities." *New Mexico Quarterly*, XXIII (Autumn, 1953), 339–42.
"Hemingway's Symbols and Myths." *New Mexico Quarterly*, XXIII (Summer, 1953), 220–25.
The Literary Criticism of "Young America," by John Stafford. *American Literature*, XXV (March, 1953), 103–104.
Moncure Conway, by Mary Burtis. *New England Quarterly*, XXVI (March, 1953), 128–29.
The Spirit above The Dust, by Ronald Mason. *New England Quarterly*, XXVI (September, 1953), 276–77.
Symbolism and American Literature, by Charles Feidelson, Jr. *Accent*, XIII (Summer, 1953), 189–92.
Walt Whitman, by Arthur Briggs. *JEGP*, LII (April, 1953), 278–79.
Emerson as Mythmaker, by J. R. Reaver. *New England Quarterly*, XXVII (December, 1954), 561–62.
Freedom and Fate, by Stephen Whicher. *New England Quarterly*, XXVII (March, 1954), 118–20.
Indian Superstition [a poem by Ralph Waldo Emerson], ed. Kenneth W. Cameron. *New England Quarterly*, XXVII (June, 1954), 282–83.
"Jarrell's Defense of Poetry." *Accent*, XIV (Winter, 1954), 74–76.
The Savages of America, by Roy Harvey Pearce. *JEGP*, LIII (July, 1954), 481–84.
Transitions in American Literary History, ed. Harry H. Clark. *New England Quarterly*, XXVII (December, 1954), 550–53.
The Burning Fountain, by Philip Wheelwright. *Accent*, XV (Spring, 1955), 147–49.
The Individual and the New World, by J. M. Anderson. *New England Quarterly*, XXVIII (September, 1955), 428.
Thoreau: A Century of Criticism, by Walter Harding. *New England Quarterly*, XXVIII (June, 1955), 274–75.
Thoreau, by William Condry. *JEGP*, LIV (April, 1955), 291.
The American Adam, by R. W. B. Lewis. *New England Quarterly*, XXIX (June, 1956), 254–58.
The Cycle of American Literature, by Robert E. Spiller. *JEGP*, LV (July, 1956), 520–21.
Leaves of Grass: One Hundred Years After, by Milton Hindus. *JEGP*, LV (January, 1956), 183–85.
Criticism in America, by J. P. Pritchard. *JEGP*, LVI (April, 1957), 306–309.
The Making of Walden, by J. Lyndon Shanley. *New England Quarterly*, XXX (December, 1957), 556–58.

After Walden, by Leo Stoller. *JEGP,* LVII (October, 1958), 832–33.
"Architect of American Thought." *Nation,* CXCI (October 1, 1960), 212–13.
A Thoreau Handbook, by Walter Harding. *JEGP,* LIX (July, 1960), 586–87.
The Transcendentalist Ministers, by W. R. Hutchinson, *JEGP,* LIX (July, 1960), 587–89.
Alfred Stieglitz, by Dorothy Norman. *JEGP,* LX (July, 1961), 603–604.
"Architect of Society." *Nation,* CXCII (June 17, 1961), 524–26.
The Chicago School of Architecture, by Carl Condit. *American Quarterly,* XVI (Fall, 1964), 507–508.
The Early Lectures of Ralph Waldo Emerson, Vol. II, ed. Stephen Whicher, Robert Spiller, and Wallace Williams. *American Literature,* XXXVII (November, 1965), 327–28.
Emerson on the Soul, by Jonathan Bishop. *New England Quarterly,* XXXVIII (September, 1965), 412–13.
"The Ordeal and the Pilgrimage." *New Leader,* XLVIII (February 15, 1965), 19–20.
"The Test of Form." *New Leader,* XLVIII (September 27, 1965), 26–28.
"For Love of Chicago." *Nation,* CCII (May 30, 1966), 657–59.
"The Mumford-MacNeil Films on the City." *Journal of the American Institute of Planners,* XXXII (1966), 58–59.
"New England Saint." *Nation,* CCIII (December 12, 1966), 647–48.
"Pathology of Underdevelopment." *Nation,* CCII (January 24, 1966), 102–103.
"Seeing Williams with Fresh Eyes." *Nation,* CCIII (October 10, 1966), 356–57.
The Thoreau Centennial, ed. Walter Harding. *New England Quarterly,* XXXIX (June, 1966), 261–63.
"Interior Order." *Nation,* CCIV (January 23, 1967), 121–22.
"The Middle-Age Blues." *Nation,* CCIV (May 15, 1967), 632–34.
"The Politics of Art." *Nation,* CCIV (June 19, 1967), 792–93.
Three Children of the Universe: Emerson's Views of Shakespeare, Bacon, and Milton, by William Wyncoop. *American Literature,* XXXIX (May, 1967), 224–25.
"A Child's Garden of Verses." *Iowa Defender,* XIV (1968), 14.
John Ruskin and Aesthetic Thought in America, by Roger Stein. *Modern Language Quarterly,* XXIX (June, 1968), 234–36.
The Literary Manuscripts of Hart Crane, by Kenneth Lohf. *JEGP,* LXVII (April, 1968), 332.
The Poetry of Hart Crane, by R. W. B. Lewis. *JEGP,* LXVII (April, 1968), 329–32.
"Public Speech." *Nation,* CCVI (May 20, 1968), 676–78.
Hart Crane: An Introduction to the Poetry, by H. A. Leibowitz. *JEGP,* LXVIII (April, 1969), 324–26.

The Magic Circle of Walden, by Charles Anderson. *American Literature*, XLI (May, 1969), 285–87.
"Making It as a Poet." *Nation*, CCVIII (January 6, 1969), 27–28.
"No Loitering!" *Nation*, CCIX (October 27, 1969), 450–51.
"Something for Everybody." *Nation*, CCIX (December 15, 1969), 672–73.
The Hieroglyphics of a New Speech: Cubism, Stieglitz, and the Early Poetry of William Carlos Williams, by Bram Dijkstra. *JEGP*, LXIX (July, 1970), 548–50.
Robber Rocks: Letters and Memoirs of Hart Crane, by Susan Jenkins Brown. *JEGP*, LXIX (October, 1970), 682–84.
Voyager: The Life of Hart Crane, by John Unterecker. *JEGP*, LXIX (April, 1970), 325–31.
Edmund Wilson: A Bibliography, by Richard Ramsey. *Resources for American Literary Study*, I (1971), 128.
The Legacy of Van Wyck Brooks, by William Wasserstrom. *JEGP*, LXX (October, 1971), 699–700.
Edmund Wilson, by Leonard Kriegel. *South Atlantic Quarterly*, LXXI (Summer, 1972), 450–52.
The Imperial Self, by Quentin Anderson. *JEGP*, LXXI (January, 1972), 154–58.
Walden, ed. J. Lyndon Shanley (Princeton edition). *American Literature*, XLIV (March, 1972), 155–56.
William Carlos Williams: The American Background, by Mike Weaver. *JEGP*, LXXI (October, 1972), 555–58.
Endless Experiments, by Todd Lieber. *American Literature*, XLV (November, 1973), 487–88.
Hart Crane: An Annotated Critical Bibliography, by Joseph Schwartz; and *Hart Crane: A Descriptive Bibliography*, by Joseph Schwartz and Robert C. Schweik. *Resources for American Literary Study*, III (1973), 135–37.
The Party of Eros, by Richard King. *JEGP*, LXXII (April, 1973), 252–55.
William Carlos Williams: The Later Poems, by Jerome Mazzaro. *JEGP*, LXXII (October, 1973), 580–81.
"Cowley (Re)collects." *CEA Critic*, XXXVI (January, 1974), 37–38.
Thoreau as Romantic Naturalist, by James McIntosh. *JEGP*, LXXIII (July, 1974), 458–59.
"Intellectual History." *Michigan Quarterly Review*, XIV (Summer, 1975), 216–19.
Letters of Hart Crane and His Family, ed. Thomas S. W. Lewis. *JEGP*, LXXIV (January, 1975), 151.
"Noble and Simple." *Parnassus*, III (Spring-Summer, 1975), 217–25.
The Early Poetry of William Carlos Williams, by Rod Townley. *JEGP*, LXXV (April, 1976), 310–12.

The Embodiment of Knowledge, by William Carlos Williams. *JEGP,* LXXV (April, 1976), 307–10.

William Carlos Williams, by Robert Coles. *JEGP,* LXXV (October, 1976), 617.

William Carlos Williams: Poet from Jersey, by Reed Wittemore. *JEGP,* LXXV (October, 1976), 617–19.

Charles Olson & Ezra Pound: An Encounter at St. Elizabeths, by Charles Olson, ed. Catherine Seelye. *JEGP,* LXXVI (April, 1977), 283–85.

The Adventurous Muse, by William Spengemann. *South Atlantic Quarterly,* LXXVII (Autumn, 1978), 533–35.

"Dancing the Man." *boundary 2,* VI (Winter, 1978), 623–27.

Emerson and the Orphic Poet, by R. A. Yoder; and *Emerson and Literary Change,* by David Porter. *Criticism,* XXI (Spring, 1979), 175–79.

Hart Crane and Yvor Winters, by Thomas Parkinson. *JEGP,* LXXVIII (April, 1979), 284–86.

A Recognizable Image, by Bram Dijkstra; and *William Carlos Williams and the American Scene,* by Dickran Tashjian. *JEGP,* LXXVIII (October, 1979), 576–79.

Robert Creeley's Poetry: A Critical Introduction, by Cynthia D. Edelberg. *JEGP,* LXXVIII (October, 1979), 579–82.

Ralph Waldo Emerson and the Critics, by Jeanetta Boswell. *Resources for American Literary Study,* X (Spring, 1980), 106–107.

"Gripping, Pushing, Moving." *Parnassus,* IX (Fall-Winter, 1981), 269–76.

The Republic of Letters, by Grant Webster. *JEGP,* LXXX (April, 1981), 273–77.

At Last, The Real Distinguished Thing, by Kathleen Woodward. *JEGP,* LXXXI (April, 1982), 282–85.

"Holding." *North Dakota Quarterly,* L (Summer, 1982), 119–26.

"Serial Poems from Canada." *North Dakota Quarterly,* L (Spring, 1982), 108–18.

The Transcendental Constant in American Literature, by Roger Asselineau. *JEGP,* LXXXI (January, 1982), 151–52.

Emerson's Fall, by B. L. Packer. *JEGP,* LXXXII (July, 1983), 466–68.

"Entering." *North Dakota Quarterly,* LI (Spring, 1983), 144–51.

"Minds Like Compost." *North Dakota Quarterly,* LI (Summer, 1983), 142–53.

Psyche Reborn, by Susan Friedman. *JEGP,* LXXXII (January, 1983), 149–52.

Apostle of Culture, by David Robinson. *JEGP,* LXXXIII (January, 1984), 146–48.

"Eros and Logos." *Iowa Review,* XIV (Fall, 1984), 200–204.

Ideogram, by Laszlo Gefin. *JEGP,* LXXXIII (January, 1984), 104–107.

The Poetry of Charles Olson, by Thomas Merrill. *JEGP,* LXXXIII (October, 1984), 585–87.

Thoreau: A Naturalist's Liberty, by John Hildebidle. *JEGP*, LXXXIII (July, 1984), 460–63.

The Visual Text of William Carlos Williams, by Henry Sayre. *JEGP*, LXXXIII (October, 1984), 580–83.

"Ethnopoetics: An 'Other' Tradition." *North Dakota Quarterly*, LIII (Spring, 1985), 37–44.

Gary Snyder's Vision, by Charles Molesworth. *JEGP*, LXXXIV (April, 1985), 294–97.

The Great Circle: American Writers and the Orient, by Beongcheon Yu. *JEGP*, LXXXIV (October, 1985), 586–87.

William Carlos Williams and Romantic Idealism, by Carl Rapp. *JEGP*, LXXXIV (October, 1985), 583–85.

American Poetry and Culture, 1945–1980, by Robert von Hallberg. *JEGP*, LXXXV (October, 1986), 602–605.

"Arriving." *North Dakota Quarterly*, LIV (Winter, 1986), 51–58.

Imagining the Earth, by John Elder. *JEGP*, LXXXVI (January, 1987), 152–54.

New England Literary Culture, by Lawrence Buell. *JEGP*, LXXXVI (October, 1987), 584–87.

Thoreau's Complex Weave, by Linck C. Johnson. *JEGP*, LXXXVI (July, 1987), 466–68.

Henry Thoreau, by Robert D. Richardson, Jr. *JEGP*, LXXXVII (January, 1988), 144–46.

"(The) Going(s) On." *North Dakota Quarterly*, LVI (Winter, 1988), 109–18.

"This to Keep (You) On." *North Dakota Quarterly*, LVI (Spring, 1988), 21–29.

ALFRED KAZIN

Afterword: Sherman Paul and the

Romance with America

I have always felt the deepest fellowship with Sherman Paul's writing. In honoring him, we honor a tradition of which he has been the most faithful custodian and celebrant in the American university, a tradition that he has loved, taught, analyzed, and documented with wonderful effect on his students and encouragement to the many tonic writers in the same tradition who have joined here in acknowledgment of what they owe Sherman Paul.

The "green" tradition, as Sherman Paul calls it with such innate affection for its naturalness and life-enhancement, sprang from an exultant sense of "democratic vistas" in politics and personal religion, in love of nature that soon led to preservation of the natural environment, in pride of the legendary example that America provided to a world forever struggling for freedom. Yet the most obvious thing to say about this tradition just now is that people like Sherman Paul are more alone than they ever imagined possible, that the green tradition is dishonored, overlooked, and even despised nowhere more than in the American university today.

The essence of the tradition: literature and art even in their subtlest and most refined effects come out of some deep instinct for life, the widest and deepest kind of life, made possible by a limitless sense of democracy. The aesthetic sense always exists in relation to democracy's measureless sense of intellectual and spiritual freedom. The enjoyment of the fullest democracy strengthens the power and authority of democracy as *the* inclusive all-central movement of life. This was what Walt Whitman (the central actor in the tradition) celebrated as self-realization in and through a living community, yet all the while reflecting the individual soul's awe and even trembling before the "unfathomable universe": "One's self I sing, a simple separate person, / Yet utter the word Democratic, the word En-Masse."

It was Emerson, the subject of Sherman Paul's first book, who in his opening addresses to the spirit of American "possibility" used his very titles as motif-words—*Nature, The American Scholar, Self-Reliance*—to foster the popular belief that we were fortunate beyond all other nations, that the key to the most glorious future was in the resolute independence of the individual soul and an equivalent passion for the "ordinary": "It is a great stride, is it not? of new vigor, when the extremities are made active, when currents of warm life run into the hands and the feet. I ask not for the great, the remote, the romantic; what is doing in Italy or Arabia. . . . I embrace the common, I explore and sit at the feet of the familiar, the low. Give me insight into today, and you may have the antique and future worlds."

Thoreau movingly said that in Emerson he found "a world where truths existed with the same perfection as the objects he studied in external nature, his ideals real and exact." Thoreau himself—the subject of my favorite of Sherman Paul's many books—tried to live, with a saint's obstinate seeking of perfection, the life Emerson had preached to lecture audiences, audiences he regarded as standing in for the whole American congregation. A lecture audience was a spiritual body that could be born again in the light of all that visible American hope! Thoreau did not live for himself alone. He had so much faith that America could remain the country of his "infant dreams," of the world's dreams at the time. In far-off Massachusetts he condemned slavery as if abolition depended on *his* speaking for it. He read his famous tribute to John Brown, said Emerson's son Edward, "as if it burned him."

Walt Whitman more than anyone else in the American story of the time personified the unity of nature and civilization—nature even in its most "primitive" aspects of self. It was Whitman's all-inclusive, ever-expanding, and mobile lyricism, his feeling for "creation" and the world in the same verse, that made him a hero to Sherman Paul's later heroes—Randolph Bourne, Alfred Stieglitz, Hart Crane, Paul Rosenfeld, Van Wyck Brooks, Charles Olson. All these representative American master spirits, early and late, were united by political faith, by a belief totally natural at the time in what Herbert Croly called "the promise of American life."

In what Sherman Paul likes to honor as "passionate humanism," these writers, critics, not to forget the pioneer architect Louis Sullivan, were not a whit less concerned with art because of their political optimism, incisiveness, and intransigence in favor of a "Little America" over the "Empire" model favored by monopolists in industry and by jingoes like Theodore Roosevelt. Art and social faith were two ends of the same chain. And the force behind it all was not just the rebellious spirit, but a delight in American life, in the freshness and buoyancy of the American temperament, democracy "in the American grain," as William Carlos Williams (another of Sherman Paul's representative geniuses) called it. What seemed "American" to Williams was as indomitable as it was plain. Through all the crises and falterings of the old spirit as America moved onto the world stage, something in art, music, and architecture, said Paul Rosenfeld in the book so fittingly called *Port of New York* that Sherman Paul so fittingly admired, seemed deeply, securely founded on a passion for experiment.

Sherman Paul's recent books celebrating rhapsodic poets of his own generation are further affirmations of the tradition Emerson opened up with his old ministerial gift for *sursum corda,* lifting the heart. Emerson's own rhapsodic gift (like Thoreau's and Whitman's) was founded on the kind of *thinking* that in another age united poets with the universe—an addiction to nothing less than cosmology, universe-thinking, that is now more common among physicists than it is among our leading chic poets. Emerson himself, so inclusive and penetrating, so obviously concerned that we not be all "of one mind" (as the toastmaster said at the dinner honoring him after he had delivered "The American Scholar"), certainly would find the intellectual life of our time in "the degenerative state"—the condition, as he prophesied in his address, that would result from our becoming "the victim of society."

Obviously the green tradition is not in favor with the fashionable literary types just now. Glowing in the example Sherman Paul has given our generation, I nevertheless see that the acerbic and nihilistic Gore Vidal, who describes himself as "America's biographer" because he has published one scornful documentary novel after another about our old leaders, describes history as "the final fiction." He smirkingly adds, "None of our institutions are of any use at all at this point in our history."

A sense of melancholy and alienation, of infinite disappointment with America that is clearly more political than anything else, pervades the literary scene. As the gifted John Cheever put it in two different pieces of fiction, "Why, in this half-finished civilization, in this most prosperous, equitable and accomplished world, should everyone seem so disappointed?"

It is easy enough to offer answers. America-as-Empire has increasingly baffled our old optimism. Specialization has become inevitable in a world shaped by technology and one in which science, not literature, provides the ideal model to intellect. The literary world is full of itself alone, bemused by language as theme as well as instrument. It is so conscious of its separation not only from the world of power but from *intelligence as power* that it calls daily reality "absurd." The writer is thrown back on sensibility and conscience, understandably maddened both by the frightful crimes of our century and by the ever-growing indifference to cries of "J'Accuse!"

Grau, teurer Freund, ist alle Theorie, said Goethe in *Faust*—all theory is gray. It is especially so in literary theory just now. It has become more and more unfashionable to view literature in a public context. The search for a style analyzable in the classroom—for literature reduced to meditation by seminar gurus—has become so exigent that it is now a sort of blasphemy to refer to content, to the surroundingly related, all-dynamic moral, intellectual, and political worlds. Whitman said that in literature "the light comes curiously from elsewhere." For many years now, literature as taught in this country, as approvable by the most influential connoisseurs, has been a light to itself, has had to create its own light. So it was natural for modernism to become the curriculum and to dominate all judgment even of the past; for a poetry to arise increasingly witty and chic in the style of modernism, a kind of travel poetry full of personal echoes but without a sense of tragedy; for a fiction so minimalist that you had to admire the silences in it more than the words; for a literary criticism that convinced docile undergraduates not much given to reading anyway that literature is just performance.

But if "all theory is gray," Goethe added that "the golden tree of actual life springs ever green." The green tradition remains for many of us, still, not just a literary school but the very embodiment of America at its best. This is the America poignantly represented in the literary classics Sherman Paul has so long defended, and for which he remains so resolute and eloquent a spokesman for our time *now.*

The Contributors

DAVID ANTIN's collections of performance poetry include *Talking* (1972), *Talking at the Boundaries* (1976) and *Tuning* (1984). His critical essays on visual art, literature, and culture appear in a wide variety of journals.

JEFFREY BARTLETT, recently a Fulbright lecturer at the Universidad de Deusto in Bilbao, Spain, has completed a study of the Beat generation titled "One Vast Page: Writing, Experience, and History."

ROBERT J. BERTHOLF, Curator of the Poetry/Rare Books Collection, State University of New York at Buffalo, is the author of *Robert Duncan: A Descriptive Bibliography* (1986) and editor (with Ian W. Reid) of *Robert Duncan: Scales of the Marvelous* (1979).

EDWARD BRUNNER's *Splendid Failure: Hart Crane's Making of The Bridge* (1985) won the Modern Language Association's 1986 award for the best book by an independent scholar. A deputy auditor for Johnson County, Iowa, he is completing a study of the poet W. S. Merwin.

JOHN F. CALLAHAN, professor of English at Lewis and Clark College, is the author of *The Illusions of a Nation: Myth and History in the Novels of F. Scott Fitzgerald* (1972) and *In the African-American Grain: The Pursuit of Voice in Twentieth-Century Black Fiction* (1988).

ROBERT CREELEY's recent works include *The Collected Prose* (1988) and *The Collected Poems of Robert Creeley: 1945–1975* (1982). The edition of his correspondence with Charles Olson has reached seven volumes.

HUGH J. DAWSON, professor of English at the University of San Francisco, is a member of the editorial committee preparing an edition of George Santayana's works. He has written on a wide range of eighteenth- and nineteenth-century American authors.

EDWARD DORN's books of poetry include *The Collected Poems: 1956–1974* (1983) and *Slinger* (1975). Among his prose works are *What I See in the Maximus Poems* (1960) and *The Shoshoneans: The People of the Basin-Plateau* (1967).

ROBERT DUNCAN's most recent works are two volumes of poetry, *Ground Work: Before the War* (1984) and *Ground Work II: In the Dark* (1987), and a collection of essays, *Fictive Certainties* (1985). He died on February 3, 1988.

LISA PATER FARANDA, assistant professor of English at Pennsylvania State University, Berks campus, is the editor of *"Between Your House and Mine": The Letters of Lorine Niedecker to Cid Corman, 1960 to 1970* (1986).

JAMES GUIMOND, professor of English at Rider College, is the author of *The Art of William Carlos Williams* (1968) and *Seeing and Healing: A Study of the Poetry of Galway Kinnell* (1986). He is completing a book titled "American Photography and the American Dream."

RICHARD HUTSON, associate professor of English at the University of California, Berkeley, has written essays on topics ranging from colonial American literature to contemporary culture. His current project is a study of 1950s political attitudes as expressed in Hollywood westerns of the period.

ALFRED KAZIN's volumes of autobiography, criticism, and literary history include *A Walker in the City* (1951), *Contemporaries* (1962), *Bright Book of Life* (1973), and *An American Procession* (1984). Presently he is writing a book about the religious imagination in American writers.

VIRGINIA M. KOUIDIS, associate professor and director of graduate studies in English at Auburn University, is the author of *Mina Loy: American Modernist Poet* (1980).

DAVID MARC, assistant professor of American studies at Brandeis University, is the author of *Demographic Vistas: Television in American Culture* (1984) and of the forthcoming *Comic Visions: Television Comedy and American Culture*.

H. DANIEL PECK, professor of English at Vassar College, is the author of *A World by Itself: The Pastoral Moment in Cooper's Fiction* (1977) and editor of the forthcoming American Novel series volume on *The Last of the Mohicans*. He is completing a book titled "Thoreau's Morning Work."

JEROME ROTHENBERG'S recent books of poetry include *That Dada Strain* (1983) and *New Selected Poems, Nineteen Seventy to Nineteen Eighty-Five* (1986). He is editor of a number of assemblages of traditional and contemporary poetry, such as *Technicians of the Sacred* (1968) and *America a Prophecy* (1973).

THOMAS HILL SCHAUB, associate professor of English at the University of Wisconsin, Madison, is the author of *Pynchon: The Voice of Ambiguity* (1980). Presently he is writing a book on politics and American fiction in the years following World War II.

ARMAND SCHWERNER'S most recent book of poems is *Sounds of the River Naranjana & The Tablets I–XXIV* (1983). His other works include *The Domesday Dictionary* (with Donald Kaplan; 1963), *The Tablets I–VIII* (1968), and *The Work, the Joy & the Triumph of the Will* (1977).

GARY SNYDER'S *Turtle Island* (1974) won the 1975 Pulitzer Prize for poetry. His most recent books of poems are *Axe Handles* (1983) and *Left Out in the Rain: New Poems 1947–1985* (1986).

BRUCE WHEATON, a playwright, is artistic director of the Riverside Theatre in Iowa City, Iowa, where his *Outward* was performed in 1987. He is also the head of the University of Iowa Technology Innovation Center.

JEAN FAGAN YELLIN, professor of English at Pace University, is the author of *The Intricate Knot: Black Figures in American Literature, 1776–1863* (1972) and editor of Harriet Jacobs' *Incidents in the Life of a Slave Girl* (1987). She is completing a book titled "Women and Sisters: The Anti-Slavery Feminists in American Culture."

Index

Page numbers in italics refer to photographs.